The Conception of Punishment in Early Indian Literature

The Conception of Punishment in Early Indian Literature

Terence P. Day

Published for the Canadian Corporation for Studies in Religion/
Corporation Canadienne des Sciences Religieuses
by Wilfrid Laurier University Press

Canadian Cataloguing in Publication Data

Day, Terence P. (Terence Patrick), 1930-
The conception of punishment in early Indian literature

(Editions SR ; 2)
Bibliography: p.
Includes index.
ISBN 0-919812-15-5

1. Punishment – Moral and religious aspects – Hinduism. 2. Philosophy, Hindu. I. Title. II. Series.

BL1147.D39 294.5'48 C82-094425-4

82 83 84 85 4 3 2 1

Cover design by Michael Baldwin, MSIAD

Order from:

Wilfrid Laurier University Press
Wilfrid Laurier University
Waterloo, Ontario, Canada N2L 3C5

TABLE OF CONTENTS

PREFACE

"No individual by himself can effect anything considerable, but only he who unites with many at the right time."

These words of Goethe are applicable to any worker in Indian Studies. The vastness and complexity of the field preclude independence of fellow-workers or disregard for the substantial scholarly works of generations of Indic scholars who built upon the foundations laid by pioneer European Indologists. The bibliography of secondary sources in the present work is a kind of acknowledgement of my indebtedness to them, though it does not highlight my indebtedness to the major works of F. Max Müller (1823-1900) and P. V. Kane (1880-1972).

My debt to Müller is evident not simply in numerous citations and quotations from the Sacred Books of the East, but in the works of his co-workers in the series and their successors whose works reflect the utilization of a hermeneutical method which Müller adopted from Franz Bopp and other earlier workers in Sanskrit and made central in his formulation both of the character and the agenda of German Indology.

Even if one were to doubt the primacy of Müller's influence, it would be difficult to challenge the breadth of it. However, it is doubtful whether there is a single major Indological work in German or in English which does not reflect the centrality of the philological approach which Müller demonstrated in his monumental work on the Ṛgveda and made central for Sanskrit studies through his Lectures on the Science of Language (1861-1864), in his Introduction to the Science of Comparative Religion (1863), and through his editorship of the Sacred Books of the East during the 1870's.

Recognition of the brilliant contributions of scholars who skillfully implemented Bopp's method cannot be without perception also of the implications of the severely limited perimeters of their highly specialized investigations and of the need for validating their interpretations in the light of the totality of primary sources from which they made arbitrary selections and contrived particular theories. While drawing attention to misrepresentations of major themes in Hindu ethics, P. V. Kane alerted readers to misinterpretations of the vast regulative literature on Hindu life and society known as Dharmaśāstra which could arise from the sole instrumentation of the linguistic analytical method without recognition of the interpretational significance of contexts which are not amenable to such analysis.

Readers of Herbert V. Guenther's works will have noticed an even more explicit caution in concerns which he expressed in fairly mute tones in Tibetan Buddhism in Western Perspective (Calif.: Dharma Publishing) in 1977, but which he explicitly vocalized through his presidential address to the International Association of Buddhist Studies during the XIVth International Congress of the International Association for the History of Religions in Winnipeg, Canada in August, 1980. He deprecated that "reductionism" which is particularly evident in "the philological analysis of the propositions and words that made up the propositions" inasmuch as "it was not always realized that in the Sanskrit language, substantives (nouns) have a verbal meaning--the dynamic coming-into-being of what seems to be statically given." The method was deficient, in his view, on account of the failure of its users to take into account "the different realms and levels of discourse which determine the usage, and by implication, the meaning of words." The users were wrong, however, in confusing philologically-determined meanings of words with the real or essential philosophical or religious meanings, a mistake which might not have arisen if they had been sufficiently careful to ascertain the inner meanings of words by reference to their literary contexts and to the experience of their authors and the intended readers of these authors' works.

If Guenther can be considered to have made a valid case against the veracity of much, if not all, of the major secondary literature which is at our disposal for introductory studies in ancient Indian literature, it does not follow that his own hermeneutical approach, which relies heavily upon the intuitive perceptions of the researcher, is more valid. For it could be argued that he has merely replaced the narrow subjectivity of arbitrarily selected dictionary definitions and static meanings for words, by the broader subjectivity of empathetic intuitionism which likewise lacks a validating criterion. While the exploration of early Indian literature undoubtedly throws up the matter of contexts and justifies something more than linguistic analysis, one is still faced with the question of how contextual observations and interpretations may be verified.

The contextual criteria which emerge in Guenther's hermeneutical concerns are relevant to the interpretation of dharmaśāstra literature whose abundant availability is due to the considerable degree of British interest in the literature during the British sovereignty in India. That interest was largely confined to the literary sources of Indian politics, economics, and jurisprudence which were dissected in a manner reflecting total disregard for the contextual matrices from which those subjects derived their distinctive character and spirit. The prolific literary products of the British study of Dharmaśāstra were focussed on *naya* in the broad sense of "civil administration" but with specific reference to all regulations to which penal sanctions are attached and which comprise regulations, prescriptions of penalties for their infractions, unwritten conciliar regulations, and those "approved customs" known as *sadācāra* which were deemed to be necessarily followed inasmuch as violations of them are punishable. But by limiting the employment of "professors of śāstra" to a juriconsultative role on a strictly limited range of topics related to sections of the literature on litigation known as *Vyavahāra*, on marriage and succession laws, laws of inheritance, systems of juridical administration, and approved customs, drawn from a limited number of authoritative texts, the British, while prospering the publication of much literature, disseminated a one-sided view which reflected neither the spirit of its original composers nor of the śāstra as a whole. When that interest rapidly declined following the gaining of national independence by India in 1947, the study of Dharmaśāstra in its entirety was kept alive as an antiquarian interest of a few distinguished scholars such as the University of London's Professor of Oriental Law in the School of Oriental and African Studies, J. D. M. Derrett, Ludwik Sternbach of the Collège de France, and the University of Pennsylvania's Professor of Sanskrit in the Department of Oriental Studies, Dr. Ludo Rocher. Other Indologists have embraced Dharmaśāstra interest within their Indological studies, notably the Wales Professor of Sanskrit at Harvard University, Daniel H. H. Ingalls, whose interests in Indian law, in addition to Indian astronomy, drama, poetics, poetry, politics, is richly represented by his substantial essay on "Authority and Law in Ancient India" in a special edition of the Journal of the American Oriental Society (17; [1954], 34-45).

The general lack of interest among Indic scholars in Dharmaśāstra is not for want of accessibility to editions and translations of Dharmaśāstra texts. Not only was there a flood of productivity in this field in British India, but also an abundant amount of historical and exegetical writing by European scholars. The outstanding contributions of P. V. Kane in setting the vast corpus of Dharmaśāstra literature within a fully documented historical framework are readily available. The indispensability of Kane's work for Dharmaśāstra and related studies is aptly stated by Derrett (Religion, Law and the State in India, NY: The Free Press, [1968], 561) in the remark that "no one can afford to ignore the massive work of Mahāmahopādhyāya Dr. P. V. Kane."

Kane's interest in the history and the scope of Dharmaśāstra appear to have been powerfully stimulated by controversies of interpretation arising from the development of the Hindu Code--an authoritative compilation of jurisprudential prescriptions culled from the most widely accepted ancient dharmaśāstra texts to be used in the administration of law in British India. Kane's distinctive contribution to the compilation of a history of Dharmaśāstra stemmed from his professional interests as a practicing lawyer and High Court judge in Bombay and pride in his Indian cultural heritage. His history was to realize an exceptional holistic perspective which integrated religious law, moral law, civil law, and even natural law as treated in Dharmaśāstra inter-relationally in striking contrast to the misinformative piecemeal approach to the literature which served the British interest in the administration of justice in India. The all-too-frequent distortions and misinterpretations which arose when texts were torn out of context made Kane strongly critical of substantial parts of the Hindu code, and he was equally critical of scholarly interpretations of Dharmaśāstra which he perceived as reflecting too narrow or one-sided perspectives. The importance of recognizing contextual "realms and levels of discourse" when one is interpreting dharmaśāstra statements and prescriptions is evidently recognized by Kane in a quite lengthy exposition (History of Dharmaśāstra, III, [1973], 831-855) of implicit motives of smṛti regulations which arise from the complexes of philosophical and religious assumptions which underlie them. His opposition to forcibly contrived scholarly interpretations which appear plausible when references are isolated from their textual contexts and are subjected to a predetermined historical framework is seen in his piercing criticism of Professor Paul Deussen's account of the development of the Karma doctrine which Deussen had contrived from disconnected upanishadic texts, and in his disputation against Vaman Shivram Apte's philologically devised interpretation of the word *vrata* which could not be supported by, but was frequently contradicted by, its Vedic contexts.

The general validity of Kane's criticisms gives pause to any over-ready acceptance of prestigious secondary sources, although there is admittedly much that would never have been known of the history of Indian ideas without the work of European scholars through their brilliant instrumentations in Sanskrit literature of Bopp's original philological method. The caution, however, gives point to Derrett's advice (Religion, Law and the State, 1968, 565) that "when all is said and done, the student does best to start with famous texts and to read them as *continua*, bearing in mind that each verse is influenced by its context and each context by the theme of the sections, and so on."

He would probably admit, however, that an intelligent reading of the sources could well be served by an historical grounding in Dharmaśāstra literature such as Kane has provided, even if, finally, it is only through reading the texts themselves that one can become aware of the pervasive influence of intellectual and religious assumptions and presuppositions upon formulations of moral principles and judicial regulations, and upon representations of retributional themes and topics.

The vastness of the literary field, on the other hand, and the abundance of superficial and hidden data, impose upon the explorer the qualities which belong in Derrett's words to "a curiosity tough enough to wrestle with tedious and multifarious details." Yet even this could hardly be sustained without a self-regenerative confidence that such exploration is worthwhile. In this regard, I am grateful for the strongly positive recognitions which my present work received from experts in the field under the invitation of the Social Sciences and Humanities Research Council of Canada or by invitation from the University of Manitoba, and who also freely provided valuable suggestions which enhanced the present work. Fourteen of my peers in the University of Manitoba representing different disciplines in the Faculty of Arts brought their expertise to bear on the work for my benefit. I was most fortunate moreover in the friendship and helpfulness of my colleague in the University of Manitoba, Professor K. K. Klostermaier, whose advice, informed by an advanced knowledge of Sanskrit, a rich academic background in Indian history and culture, and an extensive personal library, could hardly have been bettered by anyone. My colleagues of the South Asian Studies Committee in the University, in particular Professors "Ed" Moulton, Ram Tiwari, Ian Kerr, and G. N. Ramu, proved particularly supportive of this work at a most difficult stage.

This book has been published with the help of a grant from the Canadian Federation for the Humanities, using funds provided by the Social Sciences and Humanities Research Council of Canada. Preparation of the camera-ready copy of this work for the Wilfrid Laurier University Press was generously funded by the University of Manitoba and Social

Sciences and Humanities Research Council Fund Committee. It owes its accurate and aesthetic appearance to the expertise and patience of the editors of the Wilfrid Laurier University Press and the secretarial skill and professional dedication of Ms. Linda Block. Over the years, however, Meena, my wife, has borne the full brunt of the demands which this exacting work made upon our domestic life, yet never failed in her faith in the worthwhile value of the work. To Meena, therefore, this work is gratefully dedicated through a rendition of P. V. Kane's closing quotation from Browning's poem "The Last Ride Together":

> Look at the end of the work,
> contrast
> The petty done, the vast undone.

TRANSLITERATIONS AND TEXTUAL REFERENCES

1. Quotations of the Upanishads in English are from R. E. Hume (*The Thirteen Principal Upanishads*, London: Oxford University Press, second edition revised, 1931) unless otherwise indicated. Those of the Bhagavadgītā are from W. Douglas P. Hill (*The Bhagavadgītā*, Oxford: The Clarendon Press, [second abridged edition, 1953]) unless otherwise indicated. Quotations in English of other texts are from the *Sacred Books of the East* unless otherwise indicated.

2. Obsolete transliterations of Sanskrit words and letters found in older translations have been made to conform to present-day forms.

3. English translations quoted in this essay have been modified where necessary so that transliterated words are italicized and enclosed in parentheses after their appropriate English equivalents; for example: law (*dharma*), pleasure (*kāma*), wealth (*artha*).

4. To effect uniformity of textual citation, references are given entirely in arabic numerals. Manu VII.11, for example, is reproduced as Manu 7.11.

5. Transliterations of Sanskrit letters conform to present-day forms. Gutturals accordingly are rendered as: k, kh, g, and gh; dentals as t, th, d, and dh; labials as p, ph, b, and bh; palatals as c, ch, j, and jh; and cerebrals as ṭ, ṭh, ḍ, and ḍh.

6. These consonants are pronounced as indicated except that the aspirated letters are lightly "exploded" approximately as in bankhouse, doghouse, bridgehead, hothouse, madhouse, sumphouse, and tubhouse. C is pronounced 'ch' as in chalk and never as 'c' in 'cake'; ch is pronounced 'chh' as in churchhouse. The cerebral letters ṭ, ṭh, ḍ, and ḍh differ in pronunciation from the dentals t, th, d, and dh by sounding harder. However ṭh or th are both aspirated consonants and are pronounced as in hothouse, *never* as in 'their' or in 'theatre.' Likewise ph is pronounced as in sumphouse but never as in 'phone.'

7. Consonants are frequently conjoined with 'soft' or voiced nasals. With gutturals the form is ṅ, with palatals it is ñ, with cerebrals it is ṇ, with dentals it is n, and with labials it is m.

8. Letters tabulated in the grammars as semi-vowels are h, y, r, l, and v. These have the common pronunciations of these letters save that v is sometimes pronounced as w. Other letters referred to as 'spirants' include ḥ, ś, ṣ, and s which have distinctive Sanskrit forms. The letter ḥ (called *visarga*) is generally articulated as a light explosion of breath following a preceding vowel. Ś and ṣ may be pronounced simply as 'sh' as in 'show.' S is the same as in 'sun.'

9. Vowels are long or short. The transliterated sanskrit vowels are a, ā, i, ī, ṛ, ṝ, u, ū; their diphthongs e, ai, o, and au, and the vowel ḷ. Their pronunciations are as in cat, palm, kit, machine, riddle, reflex, put, hoot, late, rhyme, note, and cow, while ḷ is pronounced 'lri' (try pronouncing 'lriddle').

10. A common unvoiced nasal in which there is not a closure of the vocal organs which occurs in sounding other nasals is called *Anusvāra*. Its transliteration is the cause of much confusion. This nasal, the *Anusvāra*, appears as a dot above the sanskrit letter which it follows. It is transliterated as ṃ and may be pronounced as the English letter 'm,' or the following consonant may be nasalized.

11. Wherever the Sanskrit letter 'a' is the first letter of a word, but has been elided, and that elision denoted in European editions of Sanskrit texts by the *avagraha* or 'separator' in the printed form of an italic S, then this has been transliterated simply as an ' as in *te 'pi* (for *te api*) instead of the inverted comma which appears in printed works.

12. Single or double vertical-line marks which indicate in Sanskrit texts the first and second parts of metrical stanzas are transliterated herein as semi-colon and full-stop punctuation marks.

13. To avoid contentious questions relating to the reverse application of the classical rules of euphonic combination (*sandhi*), Sanskrit quotations have been transliterated with the divisions and spacings found in their identified sources.

14. Common Sanskrit words such as Ṛta, Dharma, Karma, and Yoga have not been italicized unless appearing in parentheses or occurring in philological discussions.

15. The word 'Upanishads' is used throughout for the general species of philosophical literature bearing this name. Titles of such works however appear in the normal transliterated form, as in Chāndogya Upaniṣad.

16. The word Brahman occurs solely as a reference to the upanishadic philosophical Absolute.

17. In place of the older and correct transliteration of the word for the priestly-teacher class, brāhmaṇa, the common form of brāhmin is used unitalicized.

18. Quotations from European translations of Sanskrit sources may be disputable for reasons relating to current editions, optional or alternative equivalents of meaning, diverse interpretations, and so on. Quotations from translations presented in support of arguments, or as illustrations of arguments in this essay, do not rule out other translations and interpretations supportive of different or even contrary arguments.

LIST OF ABBREVIATIONS

AV	Atharvaveda
Ait.	Aitareya Upaniṣad
Ait.Ār	Aitareya Āraṇyaka
Ait.Br	Aitareya Brāhmaṇa
Āpast.Dhs	Āpastamba Dharmasūtra
Ang.Nik	Anguttara Nikāya
Baudh.Dhs	Baudhāyana Dharmasūtra
BrhS	Brahmasūtra of Bādarāyana
Bṛhas.Dhs	Bṛhaspati Dharmasūtra
BhG	Bhagavadgītā
BhP	Bhāgavata Purāṇa
Bṛhad	Bṛhadāraṇyaka Upaniṣad
Chānd	Chāndogya Upaniṣad
Gaut.Dhs	Gautama Dharmasūtra
JB	Jaiminīya Brāhmaṇa
Kaṭha	Kaṭha Upaniṣad
Kāty.Dhs	Kātyāyanīya Dharmasmṛti, Kātyāyanasmṛti
Kauṣ	Kauṣitaki Upaniṣad
Kauṣ.Br	Kauṣitaki Brāhmaṇa
Mbh	Mahābhārata
MS	Maitrāyani Saṃhitā
Mahanar	Mahānārāyaṇa Upaniṣad
Mait.Br	Maitrāyaṇi Brāhmaṇa
Māṇḍ	Māṇḍūkya Upaniṣad
Manu	Manusmṛti
Matsya	Matsya Purāṇa
Muṇḍ	Muṇḍaka Upaniṣad
Nār.Dhs	Nārada Smṛti (Nāradīya Dharmaśāstra)
Praśna	Praśna Upaniṣad
RV	Ṛgveda
Rām	Rāmāyaṇa
SV	Sāmaveda
Śat	Śatapatha Brāhmaṇa
Śvet	Śvetāśvatara Upaniṣad
TA	Taittirīya Āraṇyaka
TB	Taittirīya Brāhmaṇa

TS .... Taittirīya Saṃhitā

Tait .... Taittirīya Upaniṣad

VS .... Vajasaneyi Saṃhitā

Vas.Dhs .... Vasiṣṭha Dharmasūtra

Vis.Dhs .... Viṣṇu Dharmasūtra

Yājñ.Dhs .... Yājñavalkyasmṛti

ABORI .... Annals of the Bhandākar Oriental Research Institute, Poona

AIOC .... All India Oriental Conference

AO .... *Acta Orientalia*, Leiden/Copenhagen

BIISMEO .... *Bolletino del istituto Italiano perie studio del medio ed Estremo Oriente*

BORI .... Bhandākar Oriental Research Institute, Poona

BORS .... *Journal of the Bihar and Orissa Research Society*, Patna

BSOAS .... *Bulletin of the School of Oriental and African Studies*, London, England

CR .... *Calcutta Review*

ERE .... *Encyclopedia of Religion and Ethics*

GOS .... *Gaekwad Oriental Series*, Baroda

HOS .... Harvard Oriental Series

IHC .... Indian History Congress

IHQ .... *Indian Historical Quarterly*

IOC .... International Conference of Orientalists

JAOS .... *Journal of the American Oriental Society*

JBRS .... *Journal of the Bihar Research Society*, Patna

JGJRI .... *Journal of the Ganganatha Jha Research Institute*

JRAS .... *Journal of the Royal Asiatic Society*

OH .... *Our Heritage*, Sanskrit College, Calcutta

OT .... *Oriental Thought*, Nasik

PEW .... *Philosophy East and West*, Honolulu

QJMS .... *Quarterly Journal of the Mythic Society*, Bangalore

RMIC .... *Bulletin of the Ramakrishna Mission Institute of Calcutta*

SBE .... Sacred Books of the East

SBOB .... Sacred Books of the Buddhists, London, Oxford University Press

SBH .... Sacred Books of the Hindus, Allahabad, The Panini Office

SP .... Summary of Papers

WZKM .... *Wiener Zeitschrift fuer die Kunde des Morgenlandes*

INTRODUCTION: LITERARY SOURCES OF THE INDIAN CONCEPTION OF PUNISHMENT

Thousands of literary texts house countless statements, references, and allusions which bear on retribution and imply a conception of punishment. Nowhere is this conception formally defined, as if knowledge of its nature and structure had always been assumed; that is, as if the writers and their readers, during more than twenty-five centuries of literary transmissions, had carried in their minds a mental definition of the thing, even distinct from verbal expressions of it in penal prescriptions and other retributional statements. Although the absence of a formal definition renders necessary investigative observation of ideas of punishment and ascertainment of the structure of the conception in the matrix of the manifold literary references, the investigation can show that the connotations of punishment in Indian literature are broader than those attributed to punishment in modern Western penological discussions.[1] Antony Flew's assumption that the meaning of punishment could be derived from "a standard case of punishment" is hardly acceptable without a prior conception of punishment with which to identify a "standard case."[2] Hegel's germinal notion of an "hypothetical model of punishment" (T. M. Knox, Hegel's Philosophy of Right, London: Oxford University Press [1942]) of which thousands of cases of punishment could be more or less perfect examples, seems promising.[3] But it is doubtful that such a model could be contrived without an a priori definition of the conception of punishment or one which is derived from numerous specific cases. On Hegel's behalf it could be said that Indian jurists could sympathize with Hegel's complaint that the theory of punishment "suffers in the positive science of law whenever the concept is lost in the functions which are attributed to it."[4] For, "the essence of the matter depends on the concept" inasmuch as the concept distinguishes quasi-punitive acts from true punishments. The question, therefore, of whether punishments are so because they function in a certain way[5] to express social disapproval or to uphold the laws of the society or to discourage would-be offenders or to reform the characters of criminals,[6] and would be less punitive if they functioned less efficiently,[7] is certainly a critical one. But a prior question must be whether there can be a definition which is precise enough to exclude all quasi-punishments and yet broad enough to embrace all expressions of the idea itself. For it is not apparent that A. C. Ewing's definition (The Morality of Punishment, London: Kegan Paul [1929], 53) embraces all that the Indian authors on Dharmaśāstra perceived it to be. The definition that "Punishment means pain properly inflicted by an external agent as a mark of disapproval for wrong done" does not apparently embrace self-inflicted penances. Nor does it admit reasons other than expressions of disapproval. Hegel's definition of punishment (Knox, Hegel's Philosophy of Right [1942], para. 99) as "the negation of a negation,"[8] is too broad even despite the economy of his words, since it admits negations which might not normally be considered to be punishments nor would warrant such interpretations. Hegel's definition suggests what Punishment does but is comprehensible only through a prior comprehension of what Punishment is. It could also be faulted on account of carrying no implicit or explicit reference to pain in a moral or ethical context as either an essential or as a normal adjunct of punishment.[9] Furthermore, it apparently carries no inference of justice in the sense that the "negation" ought to be deserved, and ought to be neither more nor less sufficient compensation to balance the degree of wrong committed. But here too, the question arises of whether or not justice is an essential reference in punishment or an (albeit desirable) adjunct of it.[10]

The numerous Indian references to punishments imply or recognize: (a) a standard of Right of which any violation warrants punitive retribution; (b) the possibility of its violation which is treatable as a wrongdoing; (c) answerability for the violation which determines the guilt of the transgressor; (d) degrees of guilt as determining the deserts of the transgressor with respect to forms and severities of punishment; and (e) approved or authorized forms in which punishments may properly be administered.

The particular literary tradition, known as Dharmaśāstra, in which the laws and customs of brāhmanical India were articulated and explicated covers at least twenty-five centuries. Contrary to the expectation, however, that the conception of punishment expressed by the many references therein would have undergone progressive sophistication during this long period, one finds remarkably little development. Instead, the literature reflects a persistent conservatism in the transmission from Vedic times down to the modern period of a sophisticated pattern of beliefs, ideas, practices, and institutions whose authoritative forms had been formulated in ancient times. In this light, the use of the word "early" in reference to the sources of the Indian conception of punishment is preferable to such words as "vedic" or "brāhmaṇic" or "sanskrit" for several reasons. It distinguishes the primary sources from medieval and modern writings on law and retribution which did not arise within the brāhmaṇic culture. It does not, on the other hand, exclude early Jain and Buddhist literatures which express ideas and themes bearing on punishment found in brāhmaṇic literature. Nor does it exclude non-Sanskritic writings which are properly included in early brāhmaṇical literary collections.[11] The word "early" does not exclude, but rather permits, consideration of retributional references in later compilative works in which early texts may be partially or entirely embedded. The number of such later sources from which widely known minor dharmasūtras and dharmasmṛtis have been synoptically reconstructed well justifies references to them for the conception of punishment in early Indian literature.

Continuous synoptic composition from early times has made the historian's task most difficult in the matter of assigning certain dates to numerous pieces of early literature which have survived to modern times. The synoptic character of early works in which borrowings and quite arbitrary handling of literary materials have been guided more by utilitarian than by historical considerations, has not only created vexatious historical problems, but has vitiated all modern attempts to fit the history of Indian literature into an evolutionary framework. Even where a general history of Sanskrit literature is attempted, a single linear development would not be tenable for the diverse literary traditions of the different schools (*śākhas*) of arts and sciences in ancient India. For any one of these, one could follow such literary historians as Arthur A. Macdonell (A History of Sanskrit Literature, London, [1925]), F. Max Müller (A History of Ancient Sanskrit Literature, Allahabad, [1926]), and M. Winternitz (A History of Indian Literature, Vols. I, II, Calcutta, [1927, 1933]) in identifying stages of development in each of the literary traditions and one could provide some general indications of the over-lapping time-periods in which different literary traditions emerged.

The earliest stage is that of written composition in which the oral traditions of a school of arts (*karma*) or science (*ĵnāna*) were first put into writing either in a discursive or metrical form sometime between the nineteenth and the ninth centuries B.C. This is followed by the stage of exegetical or commentarial writing which includes the earliest attempts at organizing information into rudimentary and progressively sophisticated systems between the ninth and the sixth centuries. This systematization reached the greatest sophistication in the so-called "*sūtra*-stage" of development between the fifth and the third centuries in which the systems were reduced to summary form in *sūtras* or aphoristic texts. Of these, Pāṇini's fourth-century Treatise on Words (*śabdānuśāsana*) is the most outstanding example and said to be "at once the shortest and fullest grammar in the world" (A. A. MacDonell, A Sanskrit Grammar for Students, 3rd edn. [1927], xi).

Affixing of commentorial appendixes, either by an author of a work or by members of his school, introduced the "stage of commentary" in the development of a literary corpus. The accent on brevity which is the feature of *sūtras* created a need for obscurities to be explained, corrections interpolated, and supplementary rules of interpretation. The commentators, however, were not only interpreters of the works; they also established the canonicity of the authors whose titles they adopted and endorsed. They also reaffirmed that authority for successive generations even in the process of continuously reinterpreting their teachings and adaptating them to contemporary conditions. This means, of course, that there was no period in which commentary-making ended, so that by the modern period authoritative commentaries already numbered many thousands.

The composition of the 'major commentaries' (*mahābhāṣyas*) marks the highpoint in the history of Indian literature even though only general datings can be given for the commentarial stage of that history. For the dating which is allowable as the high point in the commentarial development of the dharmaśāstra literature, which Kane sets between the seventh and the tenth centuries, is much later than the high point of commentarial development of grammatical literature if this is taken as being the date of Patañjali's "Great Commentary" on Pāṇini's treatise composed in the second century B.C. The peak of the commentarial phase of any of the contemporaneous literary traditions in India might have coincided with other literary developments in other disciplines. The major commentaries on the dharmaśāstra literature coincided with a vigorous productivity in specialized works on themes and topics of jurisprudence alongside the production of specialized works on grammar such as Śāntanava's Phiṭ Sūtra (post-second century B.C.). The specialized works were bound, in turn, to provide models and to generate further commentaries in repeated attempts at more readily intelligible or concise or convenient presentations of early major authorities.

On the whole, however, it can be said that: (a) no literary development was simply a linear one, nor did contemporaneous literary traditions develop simultaneously at equal paces; (b) the sūtra-style of composition may not have been the earliest literary form if it emerged as a condensation of earlier lengthier treatises; (c) the major sūtras which scholars agree to have been the earliest extant works would not, accordingly, have been original compositions if, indeed, they are only cryptic versions of lengthier treatises; (d) the earliest commentators were the first to promote the canonical authority of selected works of their dharmaśāstrika schools which they edited and redacted and generally published repeatedly for future generations even to the extent that statements which might have become obsolete or embarrassing were reinterpreted in a manner supportive of the prestige of the primary source or its school of interpretation rather than in a manner which could have discredited them. Finally, (e) the commentarial and exegetical literary tradition thus generated fulfilled a conservative function by rarely introducing new rules to replace old ones, and by recapitulating and contemporizing the ideas, beliefs, and judgements of the ancient authorities.

The highly conservative character of this tradition accounts for the survival of numerous ancient texts either as independent sources or through extensive quotations in commentaries, compendia, and thematic digests. The respect of the commentators for named authorities, particularly of legendary authors, and their seeming indifference to historical dates, make it difficult and even nearly impossible to fix with certainty the date of any early text and thereby the historical order of the major texts. For the order in which citations of such works are made reflects not a sense of historicity but an order of prestige among texts which treat similar subjects. Among the sources of Dharmaśāstra, the Manusmṛti acquired early the leading authority. All other smṛtis on Dharma became authoritative only insofar as they reflected and generally supported the Manusmṛti. The date of composition of the Manusmṛti has vexed Indian historians for so long that it has held in suspense certainty on the dating of other early texts. It is certainly an early work, since so many works agreed to have early datings cite either the Manusmṛti or earlier versions of it, or follow the order of its contents. On the other hand, stylistic, structural, and substantive evidence indicate that the presently extant Manusmṛti may not be original but a compilation of earlier works. Composite origins and character are evident in Manu's attribution of authorship to the sage Bhṛgu (e.g. Manu 1.35; 1.59ff., etc.), in references to the *Manu-saṃhitā*[12] at the end of each section (*adhyāya*) which could be to an earlier work; and an early title of the work as the *Bhṛgu Saṃhitā* which may refer to an original composition. Scholars, however, have disagreed over whether or not an early sūtra existed which was named after Manu and which formed the basis of the extant Manusmṛti. P. V. Kane and other Indian scholars cited by him disputed the thesis of Max Müller--which Georg Bühler (SBE XXV) had defended--that an hypothetical *Mānavadharmasūtra* was the original source of the extant Manusmṛti.[13] No such source has, as yet, been found. The possibility of different compilations of Dharma-teaching even in the same school from which the Manusmṛti originated, which are comparable in subject matter and are attributed to the same author, but are different in approach and treatment, virtually destroy any positive results of attempted dating. Well-known smṛtis whose titles bear such prefixes as *vṛdha*-(ancient?), *bṛhat*-(greater?), or *laghu*-(combined? compiled? or condensed?) do not include evidences conclusive to the question of whether such titles as *Vṛdhamanusmṛti*, *Vṛdhayājñavalkyasmṛti*, and *Bṛhatparāśarasmṛti* belong to earlier or later works than their unprefixed counterparts. One is bound to recognize the point of Kane's remark (*History of the Dharmaśāstra* [1930], 1.107) that "the chronology of all ancient works is somewhat in a nebulous state." The problems have proved too unyielding for more than only the broadest tentative datings for the early dharmasūtras and dharmasmṛtis and their earliest commentaries. Kane (*History of the Dharmaśāstra*, vol. III, [1973], xvii) conjectures for the earliest dharmasūtras a date-range between 600 and 300 B.C. and for the major dharmasmṛtis between 200 B.C. and A.D. 100. His historical order for the sūtras is given as follows: Gautama (600-499 B.C.), Baudhāyana (c.500-200 B.C.), Āpastamba (c.430-350 B.C.), Vasiṣṭha (1st cent. B.C.?), and Viṣṇu (an uncertain early date). The minor dharmasūtras such as those cited in the present study as Bṛhaspati, Paiṭhīnasi, Yama, and Saṅkhalikhita are practically undatable since these survived only as references and quotations in later writings, as explained by Kane (*History of the Dharmaśāstra*, vol. III [1973], xviii) on references to the Kātyāyanasmṛti which appear in references and quotations on litigation (*Vyavahāra*).

The most important major dharmasmṛtis in which the fundamental ideas, concepts, and themes of the Indian conception of punishment can be found include *Manu*, *Nārada*, *Bṛhaspati*, *Yājñavalkya*, *Kātyāyana*, and *Viṣṇu*--whose dates depend upon the true date of the extant *Manusmṛti*. Kane (Vol. III, [1973], xvii) places them between 200 B.C. and A.D. 100. The *minor* smṛtis such as the *Parāśara*, *Pitamaha*, and *Paiṭhīnasi* incur special problems of dating since, like the minor sūtras, any extant texts are only reconstructions from references and quotations in diverse later writings, and their true authorship is not certainly known. Furthermore, while there are early compilations of sacrificial regulations which are mentioned in the Vedic *saṃhitās* and *brāhmaṇas*--the *Śrautasūtras*--there are others which regulate domestic ceremonies--the *Gṛhyasūtras*--and bear the names of either Gautama, Manu, Āpastamba, or Baudhāyana. Kane (Vol. III, [1973], xvii) dates these between 800 and 300 B.C. Their development may have been contemporaneous with correspondingly named *dharmasūtras*. These somewhat sparingly supplement the abundant references to punishment in the *smṛti*-literature.

Parts of the *Mahābhārata*, including the *Bhagavadgītā* and the *Rāmāyaṇa*, the Kauṭilīya *Arthaśāstra*, and some early major Purāṇas, are properly included in compilations of dharmaśāstra literature. Extensive portions of the *Manusmṛti* in the *Mahābhārata* raise major historical problems regarding the relative datings of both works. Conflicting calculations of either an earlier or a later date for the Arthaśāstra raise problems both for historians of Indian society and culture as well as for workers in the history of Indian ethics. It is probably later than our extant Manusmṛti since it contains a summarization of that smṛti's formulation of the "science of government" (*rājanīti*). As sources of dharmaśāstra, the major Purāṇas are also important; but these incur problems of dating as well. They evidently comprised a distinctive body of smṛti-literature according to a statement of the Yājñavalkyasmṛti (1.3)[a] in

---

[a] "Purāṇanyāyamīmāṃsādharmaśāstrāṅgamiśritāḥ; vedaḥ sthānāni vidyānāṃ dharmasya ca caturdaśa" (Yājñ. 1.3; [1949]).

which they are explicitly named along with the Nyāya, Mīmāṃsā, Dharmaśāstra, and the Vedāṅgas as comprising the five sources of higher knowledge (*vidyā*) and dutiful action (*dharma*). Yet although they are revered sources of moral guidance, they may have lesser authority than the Dharmaśāstra literature inasmuch as pauraṇic references are usually placed by the commentators after quotations and citations of the major smṛti references. Kane (History of Dharmaśāstra, III, [1973], xvii) gives the dates A.D. 300-600 for the earliest of the Purāṇas.

Indications have already been given of the importance of the commentaries and digests as sources of information on early conceptions.[14] Not only did they refer to and frequently quote authoritative sources of dharmaśāstra whose original texts are no longer extant, but in so doing they conserved and continuously contemporized early conceptions and beliefs. The leading interpreters of the Manusmṛti were Bhāruci,[15] Medātithi, Govindarāja, Kullūka, and Nārāyaṇa.[16] Vijñāneśvara, Viśvarūpa, and Aparārka count among the renowned exegetes of the Yājñavalkyasmṛti.

Commentators and jurisprudents also compiled digests of Hindu law. The most widely renowned digests appeared between the twelfth and the eighteenth centuries. Nevertheless, they are valuable sources on early ideas as well as on the history of early sources. The most notable major digests include Caṇḍeśvara's Vivādaratnākara, Vācaspati Miśra's Vivādacintāmaṇi, Ballala Sen's Dānasāgara and Lakṣmīdhara's Kṛtya-Kalpataru, Gopāla's Kāmadhenu (Kane, History of the Dharmaśāstra, I, Pt.II; 618-619) and works by Halāyudha, Hemādri, and Nīlakaṇṭha. Vardhamāna's Daṇḍaviveka, composed in the sixteenth century, earned wide renown throughout India. Its importance is explained by Kane (History of the Dharmaśāstra, Vol. I, Pt.II [1968], xxxix and 854-858).

The value of these compilative and interpretative texts as sources of historical information on early Indian ideas is only partly diminished by the seeming indifference of their composers to the origins and veracity of primary sources. For dependence of the commentators upon authoritative transmissions of ancient schools of interpretation made them instruments of a tradition which they promoted throughout the greater part of India.[17] By repeatedly endorsing the tradition even when explaining its present regional and local applications, they continued to contemporize what otherwise would long have been outdated.

The dharmaśāstra literature, however, is not the only source of the ethical ideas in which the conception of punishment is to be found. For, if it was distinct from other literary traditions in ancient India, this does not mean that the traditions were independent of each other. The standing of the Dharmaśāstra literature in relation to other literary traditions is indicated by its placement within the comprehensive corpus of Vedic studies called the *Vedāṅga*. These stem from the four vedic saṃhitās--Ṛgveda, Sāmaveda, Yajurveda, and Atharvaveda--and comprise not only their respective brāhmaṇas, āraṇyakas, and upaniṣads, but also the regulatory works on public and domestic rituals and social control known respectively as *śrautasūtra*, *gṛhyasūtra*, and *dharmasūtra*. The literary totality accordingly comprises a vast reservoir of references to and expressions of the early Indian conception of punishment which requires only an appropriate procedure for making explicit the underlying assumptions and essential ideas which comprise the conception and for explicating their interrelations in terms of its structure. The procedure followed in the present exploration includes: (a) tracing out the philosophical and theological presuppositions and assumptions relating to the conception of punishment; (b) explication of the retributional bearings of responsible acts; (c) comparing "spheres" and "forms" of punishment with "functions" of punishment; and (d) constructing from the components the reticulated infrastructure of the Indian conception of punishment.

PART I. METAPHYSICAL FOUNDATIONS OF THE INDIAN CONCEPTION OF PUNISHMENT

Early Indian literature in reference to punishment reflects assumptions about the nature of reality and the manner of its manifestation in terms of three metaphysical principles which have retributional bearings: Ṛta, Dharma, and Karma. The richness of the content and meaning of these makes concise definitions difficult and perhaps misinformative. Their retributional bearings, however, can be indicated, while leaving aside more comprehensive explorations of the conceptions such as is found in H. Lüder's monumental study of Varuṇa in Varuṇa: Varuṇa und das Ṛta [1959]. These bearings arise from the conception of Ṛta as Order which is absolute and unconditioned, and of Dharma as its primary manifestation and the substratum of all minor orders such as the order of Nature, the ritual order, the social order, and the moral order articulated or particularized through divine ordinances, moral principles, social regulations, and prescribed sanctions, administered through personal agents or endorsed through the impersonal retributive mechanisms of Karma.

Chapter 1. The Concept of Rightness

A. Ṛta

The appearance of grand metaphysical concept in the very earliest of the ancient brāhmaṇic texts has been a matter of surprise for Indian scholars. It appears to stand far above the rudimentary religious and philosophical expressions which are more common to the Ṛgveda; yet its presence within the matrix of Ṛgvedic ideas suggests long-standing familiarity with a concept which, though central to early Vedic thought, is not apparently a climax of it.[1] In none of its sentential contexts does it appear to have greater prominance than the theistic and cosmological concepts of the Ṛgveda, even though one might have expected a greater prominence to have been given to it on the ground of its being perceived as the locus of all movements and functions of divine beings as well as the "gravitational centre" of the cosmos.

The retributional significance of this grand concept arises from the interpretation of it as "the Way" or the "set order of things." The Ṛgveda repeatedly expresses the belief that all beings or things exist and fulfil their true functions when they follow the courses set for them "according to Ṛta." This grand concept is the ultimate reference behind the Vedic ritual. It was repeatedly affirmed as the infinite and eternal Ground in which the earth and the heavens, the planets and their sovereign deities, and the orderly succession of the seasons subsist and upon which their continuance depends.[2] Its ethical character however, is explicitly indicated by references to the "ordinances of Ṛta" which even the planetary deities are bound to follow for their own survival and to assert against all violators and violations both in the heavenly and the earthly spheres. In relation to them, accordingly, Ṛta is perceived to signify "eternal law;" nothing being outside of its governance, and everything being subject to Ṛta, moving in harmony with Ṛta, and being in "truth" or "falsehood" according to whether or not it is "according to Ṛta."[3]

Yet Ṛta is not a personal being; nor is it a divine instrument.[4] It is the universal Ground of Order, the foundation of "cosmos" and the opposite of "chaos." All beings, divine, human and subhuman, animate and inanimate subsist in Ṛta or through the order of existence which Ṛta sustains. It is like the Sun which does not move but which makes all movement possible as the absolute Energy-Source. Ṛta simply is, and all things live and move and have their beings through Ṛta.

But there are intelligible principles of Ṛta and there are beings which are responsible agents and instruments of it. These articulate through laws, controls and restraints that Order which they serve. The chief agents of Ṛta are the planetary deities or Ādityas, among whom Varuṇa appears as the leader. These are believed to have the power to make effective and to safeguard the Order of Ṛta in the worlds of gods and men and to act against all movements which deserve to be labelled as *anṛta* or falsehood.[5]

B. Agents of Ṛta

The order signified by Ṛta is particularized, manifested, upheld, and protected by agents having retributing powers. In their exercising of those powers, they cause retribution itself to be a manifestation of the counteractive processes of Ṛta.[6] These Ṛta-affirming agents are called in the Ṛgveda "charioteers," "guardians," or "promoters" of Ṛta.[7] It is through their guardianship functions that they manifest the ethicality of Ṛta.

Their functions as "lords of Ṛta" have been mistakenly interpreted by A. Berriedale Keith (The Religion and Philosophy of the Veda, Cambridge, Mass.: Harvard University Press, [1925], 84) as implying that Ṛta is subordinate to the divine agents, a contradictory note which he attributes to a characteristic Indian indifference to logical incongruities. As the absolute principle of Order, Ṛta is not subordinate to anything or anyone. Insofar as Ṛta is "embodied" in finite manifestations such as the Ādityas or "sovereign principles" (Alain Daniélou, Hindu Polytheism, London: Routledge & Kegan Paul, [1964], 112), these may be said to "possess Ṛta." This does not mean, however, without supporting evidence in the Ṛgveda, that Ṛta is, in any sense or to any degree, subject to their wills. Vedic references to "the ṛta of Varuṇa"[a] or "the ṛta of Mitra" in the Ṛgveda (4.56.7) and to "the ṛta of Varuṇa and Mitra" (RV 1.23.5)[b] can only sustain the impression of implying their control over Ṛta if they are interpreted outside of their literary contexts. These do not govern Ṛta so much as immanentalize

---

[a]For example: ". . . ṛtaṃ siṃdhavo varuṇasya yaṃti . . ." (RV 2.28.4; Chowkhamba, No. 99, [1966], Vol. 1, p. 84).

[b]For example: ". . . Ṛtena yāvṛtavṛdhāvṛtasya jyotiṣaspatī, Tā mitrāvaruṇa huve; . . ." (RV 1.23.5, Chowkhamba, 99; [1966], Vol. 1, p. 122).

it through the particularities of divine ordinances and retributions concerning both rewards and punishments. In this sense they do not "govern" Ṛta; they serve it as agents and ministers.[8]

Among the divine retributing agents, Varuṇa is sovereign.[9] His sovereign role as Supreme Judge is indicated by his titles of the Seer (*Kavi*) (RV 1.25.18), as the "All-Seeing One" (*Viśvadarśata*) (RV 1.25.5), and as the "Large-eyed" or the "Many-eyed" (RV 7.34.10). Such references apply to his thousands of spies who never miss any deviation from righteousness even in the remotest corners of the universe. Through their unblinking watchfulness (1.25.13), Varuṇa is kept cognizant of all secrets, both in the supernatural, the natural, and the subterranean worlds, all deeds done or about to be done (RV 1.25.7-11), and all words of truth or falsehood spoken by men (RV 7.49.3). He is said to be present among persons grouped together in private discourse, and the divine cognizor of all that is said (RV 1.25.13). Thus, in the broadest sense he is "the see-er of men" (7.60.2).

A title of Varuṇa is "Lord of Dharma" (MS 2.6.6) in the sense of "guardian of the Law" (MS 3.8.9). This is stated in the Ṛgveda (1.25.10-11) as: "Varuṇa, true to holy law, sits down among his people; he, most wise, sits there to govern all. From thence, perceiving, he beholds all wondrous things, both what hath been, and what hereafter will be done." In a conciser statement the Taittirīya Saṃhitā (1.2.11) invokes the lord of justice as: "Thou art Varuṇa who guardeth law." He is *Dharmapati*, Lord of righteousness (justice),[10] the king (RV 7.34.11) who holds court (Mbh.12.9), and the universal emperor (*samrāj*) (RV 2.25.22) who holds the universe in subjection to Order. It is through his "fetters" (*pāśa*) of rewards and punishments that he restrains all self-willed beings in orderly subjection to rightness. His inflictions alert sinners to unknown faults such as unintended transgressions. His "fetters" evoke in penitents those mental states and longings for reconciliation with Varuṇa which inspired the most moving penitential hymns of the Ṛgveda.[11]

It would be going too far, however, to interpret Varuṇa as a "God of Wrath." Sukumari Bhattacharji (The Indian Theogony, London: Cambridge University Press, [1970], 31) surely misrepresents Varuṇa by stating that "vengeance (i.e. retribution of wrong-doing) is the exclusive domain of Varuṇa; we can almost hear 'Vengeance is mine, I will repay'." Even if sin is said to be "against Varuṇa"[12] this does not mean, for want of contrary evidence, that he is personally affected and moved emotionally by the deeds of men. His "fetters" are perceptible as being automatically or effectually beneficial or hurtful according to men's deeds. As the chief agent of Ṛta he governs the compensatory process even while being distant and aloof from the processes which work out the just consequences of human actions: prosperity and happiness for those who live rightly and do justly, physical deformities, bodily paralyses, and premature aging and death[13] for transgressors of right.

A clear illustration of Varuṇa's judicial role is found in one of the seasonal sacrifices (*cāturmāśya*) described in the Śatapatha Brāhmaṇa 2.5.2.1-48 (SBE XII) which is based on a myth of creation, of original sin, of punishment by Varuṇa, and the healing of mankind through the self-immolation of the Creator, Prajāpati, ensuring that the offspring of his creatures would be born without contamination or blemish.

The offering of the Varuṇapraghāśa oblations first to Prajāpati who freed his creatures "from Varuṇa's noose," then to Varuṇa "since it was Varuṇa who seized his creatures," and "to the Maruts" "for the sake of diversity" and because these would have seized the creatures whom Prajāpati had created, includes not only a substitute ram and ewe fed with "Varuṇa's barley" (*ghās*), but also a ritual act of confession to the priest. A wife who desires "deliverance from Varuṇa's noose through conjugal union" with her husband; that is, the fruition of undeformed offspring, "without disease or blemish," confesses her sins in the presence of her husband. The ritual clearly reflects fear of congenital defects which are instrumented by Varuṇa in punishment of sexual infidelities.

Now when a woman who belongs to any man [i.e., her husband] carries on intercourse with another, she undoubtedly commits (a sin) against Varuṇa.

The woman is invited to confess the name(s) of her paramour(s). The Kātyāyana-śrautasūtra (5.5.7-9 in Eggeling's tr. SBE XII; 397, fn.1) says that she should give the total number or the names of her lovers, or hold up as many stalks of grass, or, according to a commentator, "if she is innocent she is to reply, 'with no one else.'"

The purpose of the act appears to be fourfold:

i. to remove all "secret pangs" in her mind which might have a negative psychological and spiritual effect on her prayer for healthy offspring;

ii. to transmute a negative potential-force (i.e. the sin) into a positive fructifying energy: "for when confessed the sin becomes less, since it becomes truth";

iii. to protect relatives from the evil effects of concealed sins since: "Whatever (connection) she confesses not, that indeed will turn out injurious to her relatives;" and

iv. to bring retribution (for adultery?) to her paramour(s) according to Kātyāyana's interpretation: "Let her declare, N.N. is my paramour, by thus declaring (any one) she causes him to be seized by Varuṇa" (TB 1.6.5.2, in Eggeling's footnote cited, p. 397).

Such a rite clearly not only reflects profound psychological dimensions of the ancient brāhmaṇical ritual, but also reveals the force of conviction of Varuṇa's direct influence in human lives through his role as a divine punisher and rewarder.

In this respect, Varuṇa is, in Bloomfield's words (The Religion of the Veda, N.Y. & London: G.P. Putnam's Sons, [1908], 128 citing RV 10.8.5), "the real trustee of Ṛta." Manu's commentator, Kullūka Bhaṭṭa, put it: "Manu himself has said: '*īśo daṇḍasya varuṇaḥ*' = 'Varuṇa is the presiding deity of Punishment'." This is a reference to Manu 8.336 and compares equally strongly with 9.245 which states that Varuṇa is "the wielder of punishments (*daṇḍadharaḥ*) (even) over kings."[a]

In addition to Varuṇa, several other deities appear in the Vedic, the brāhmaṇic, and epic literature in minor ethical roles usually as agents of Varuṇa and mediators of his retributive operations. The most important of these are Mitra, Agni, Sūrya, and Yama. Frequently they appear as aspects of each other. The Ṛgveda (5.3.1) states that Varuṇa becomes Agni in the evening and rising in the morning becomes Mitra; as Savitṛ (the Sun) he shines in the firmament and as Indra he shines in the centre of the sky. Mitra, like Varuṇa, is invoked as Samrāj, world emperor or lord of all (RV 1.136.1). He also employs spies to seek out the deeds of men (7.63.3). Their names are linked together as guardians of Ṛta "in the highest heaven," (5.63.1) mutually committed to the protection or vindication of Dharma.[14] Both are guardians of the Law (MS 3.8.9), and both (RV 7.66.4-6; 7.40.5) are invoked to destroy sin, to remove ignorance and chastise the deceitful and the untruthful. Both have connections with the proper ordering of the sacrificial ritual though apparently their respective roles are different; badly offered sacrifices are redeemed by Varuṇa and properly ordered rituals are received by Mitra.[15]

In the Ṛgveda (3.59.1; 10.8.4) Mitra is said to be the sustainer of the firmament, as compared with Varuṇa its ruler, though this distinction is not always maintained. But the distinction suggests their respective spheres of ethical responsibility and influence, Mitra upholding the ritual and natural orders, and Varuṇa safeguarding the moral order. Varuṇa certainly seems less interested in rituals, and more concerned with the deeds which gods, men, and demons perform with respect to Ṛta.

In the Rāmāyaṇa (7.56.23-26), Mitra seems to be an assistant of Varuṇa rather than an ethical deity in his own right, for the text explicitly attributes the supreme ethical

---

[a] "īśo daṇḍasya varuṇo rājñām daṇḍadharo hi saḥ" (Manu 9.245, Chowkhamba, 226 [1953]).

authority to Varuṇa, instead of a co-partnership as agents of Ṛta and Dharma. Mitra himself, unlike Varuṇa, does not apparently administer punishments. Mitra accordingly is more naturally associated with light and benevolence, while Varuṇa has an aura of darkness and awe.[16] One place in the Taittirīya Saṃhitā (2.1.9.5) suggests that Mitra pacifies the revengeful Varuṇa, as if according to Mitra a mediatorial role in Vedic theology. This may reflect his connections with the ancient Iranian deity Mithra, the "friend" of man.[17] Whereas Varuṇa is given the title *Dharmapati* or "Lord of Dharma," Mitra is called *Satyapati* or "Lord of truth" (MS 2.6.6). But if Mitra's sphere of authority is ritual and Varuṇa's private and public morality, according to the Śatapatha Brāhmaṇa (5.3.4-5), their functions are complementary inasmuch as both serve as guardians of Order or Right.

Agni, "Ruler of Sacrifices, Guardian of Ṛta, radiant One," also appears in the Ṛgveda closely linked with Varuṇa. He is called Agni's brother (RV 1.1.8; 4.1.2). Rightness or Order is not Agni's primary concern; but whenever he assumes this role he becomes Varuṇa, as the Ṛgveda (10.8.5) says. Conversely, it is said (RV 5.3.1) that Varuṇa becomes Agni in the evening, and rising in the morning he becomes Mitra.[a] But this may be only a poetic expression meaning that Varuṇa rules both the night and the day as distinct from the more limited and specific sovereignties of Agni and Mitra. While Varuṇa's all-encompassing authority extends skylike over all spheres, Agni's sphere of control is the ritual order, for which reason he is worshipped as the divine priest, giver of wealth, lord of the household hearth, and remover of evils (RV 1.1.9). Agni is invoked as the messenger of the gods (RV 5.8.6), and a text of the Śatapatha Brāhmaṇa (1.4.1.30) seems to attribute to him a mediatorial role as one "who carries the sacrifice (of

---

[a] "tvamagne varuṇo jāyase yattvaṃ mitro bhavasi yatsamiddhaḥ; . . ." (RV 5.3.1, Chowkhamba Sanskrit Series, No. 99, 1st Indian edn. [1966], Vol. I, p. 503 [Sanskrit]).

worshipper) to the gods." In epic literature also, Agni is worshipped as the bearer of sacrifices; but through his identification with Śiva, the ethical dimensions of his character become less distinct.

Like Agni, Sūrya also appears to have acquired its ethical personality and functions by his association with Mitra and Varuṇa. Thus (RV 4.13.2), "according to rule go Varuṇa and Mitra when they make rise in the sky the sun (Sūrya) whom they have created to dissipate darkness, being (gods) sure of their habitation and unswerving in intent."[a]

Like Varuṇa, Sūrya is described as the omniscient or "all-seeing one" in the statement (RV 4.53.2-6) that Sūrya is "the see-er of all that moves . . . as a support he touches and guards the vault of the sky," and is "lord of all that stands and goes." Under the name of Savitṛ (or Life-giver) (RV 2.38.2) his functions acquire a more typical judicial character in the statement "the god extends his vast hand, his arms above there--and all here obey him; to his command the waters move, and even the winds blowing cease on all sides."[b] His sovereignty is affirmed in the statement (RV 2.38.9) that "neither Indra, Varuṇa, Mitra, Aryaman, Rudra, nor the demons, impair his law."[c] Prayers for absolution from guilt and for divine favours may be offered to Sūrya (RV 4.54.3; 4.53.6-7) since he is the apportioner to gods and men of retributions for deeds. He is able also to protect men from innocently, through error and ignorance, falling into sin and his divine retributions. Nevertheless, despite his exalted status, Sūrya is not

---

[a]". . . anu vrataṃ varuṇo yaṃti mitro yatsūryaṃ divyārohaṃyati" (RV 4.14.2; Chowkhamba Sanskrit Series No. 99 [1966], Vol. II, p. 384).

[b]"Viśvasya hi śruṣṭaye deva ūrdhvaḥ prabāhavā pṛthupāṇiḥ sisarti; Āpaścidasya vrata ā nimṛgrā ayaṃ cidvāto ramate pari 'ajman" (RV 2.38.2; Chowkhamba Sanskrit Series No. 99 [1966], Vol. II, p. 114).

[c]"Na yasyeṃdro varuṇo na mitro vratamaryamā na minaṃti rudraḥ . . ." (RV 2.38.9; Chowkhamba Sanskrit Series, No. 99 [1966], Vol. II, p. 116).

apparently in his own right the lord of justice, for he performs his ethical functions by the command of Mitra (RV 4.56.7) and by the authority of Varuṇa. In contrast, a larger judicial autonomy appears to be given to Yama.

Yama has an intriguingly mixed personality inasmuch as he appears to be both Lord of the Underworld and Primal Man. A statement of the Atharvaveda (18.3.13) exhorts men to "worship the son of Vaivasvata, the gatherer of men, with oblations," since "he was the first of mortals to die, he who first entered this world (i.e. the world beyond death)."[a] But the name "Yama" itself has ethical and retributional aspects since ascetical restraint or control is one of the word's connotations. According to the Taittirīya Saṃhitā (2.5.11) it was through arduous austerities that Yama "appropriated the power and strength of the gods; hence his name Yama." Since the goal of asceticism is immortality beyond the spheres of reincarnation, this is the meaning intended by the gods who say of Yama that now "Yama here has become what we are." It is not surprising therefore, in view of his achievements in conquering death and gaining immortality in the abode of the gods, that he should be invoked as the Lord of Death (*Mṛtyu*), he who has Death under his benevolent control and who therefore can ward off premature death and lead men through the gates of Death into everlasting life. Yama even became a synonym for Death; and worship, according to the Atharvaveda (6.28.3), became "obeisance to that Yama, Death, who is the master of the two-footed and four-footed."[b]

Particularly in the brāhmaṇas the personality, sovereignty, and work of Yama are developed. In Śat.10.4.3.1-3 Yama is called *Mṛtyu* (Death) and *Antaka* (Ender), and an

---

[a]"Yo mamār prathamo martyānaṃ yaḥ preyāya prathamau lokametam; Vaivasvataṃ saṃgamanaṃ janānāṃ yamaṃ rājānaṃ haviṣā saparyata" (AV 18.3.3.13, Bareilly, U.P. [1962], Vol. II, p. 806).

[b]"Yosyeśe dvipado yaścatuṣpadastasmai yamāya namo astu mṛtyave" (AV 6.3.28.3; Bareilly, UP. [1962], Vol. I, p. 272).

extensive ritual developed solely for ensuring that through Yama, Death will lead men not to repeated incarnations but to immortality. Whereas in the Ṛgveda (10.14.14) he is simply the Lord of immortality, in the brāhmaṇas his sovereignty over the Underworld becomes clear, through his jurisdiction over all souls whose earthly span is complete. Before him (Śat.2.7.33) the scales are mounted wherein men's good and evil deeds are weighed. By them each man enters either to glory or to retribution.

In the Rāmāyaṇa (4.42.66-70), the personality of Yama is depicted by five epithets which are amplifications of different elements of the personality of the old vedic deity. These are Yama, Antaka, Kāla, Mṛtyu, and Dharma. Not all of these signify the ethical role of Yama. The Rāmāyaṇa however fills them out in a vivid picture the splendor of Yama's court. It is a kingdom of light and of beauty, beyond the boundaries of which is a vast darkness. In the heart of "Yama's abode" is a great judgement seat and "there on the Judgement Seat sits Lord Vaivasvata [i.e. Yama] the king." There, he performs a judicial function as the supreme Judge and Retributer of men and by his judgements Yama sifts the good and the evil of men.

Yama's judgement, however, is not always delayed until men are claimed by Death. For in the Mahābhārata (1.68.30-31), Yama also has the title of "the judge within" in the sense of the inward conscience. When all the textual allusions to Yama are thrown together, a richly composite portrait emerges. He is the Lord of justice[18] and the guardian of the world (Manu 5.96). He knows the conduct of all beings (Manu 8.85-6) and he seeks out the wicked for punishment.[19] Evildoers who act in secret do not escape his vigilance nor even do accidental transgressions go unnoticed.[20] He is the Lord of Punishment (Nār.Dhs.1.217) which he administers through hellish attendants.[21] He is the Lord of Death[22] and death means existence in his realm.[23] The statement: "Thou shalt go to the seat of Yama" (AV 2.3.12.7)[a] means: "Thou shalt surely die." But the

---

[a]". . . ayā yamasya sādanamagniduto araṅkṛtaḥ" (AV 2.3.12.7, Bareilly, U.P. [1962], 57).

journey to Yama's place (*yamasya sadana*)[24] need not be terrible; it is even pleasant if the traveller has been virtuous. So also the hospitality of that place is according to the inmates' characters; as each individual is through the deeds of his earthly life, so he eats the fruits of pleasure or of bitterness. To the righteous, accordingly, Yama is a beneficent Lord. As the Mahābhārata (3.11.46, 58) states, as cited by E. W. Hopkins (The Religions of India, NY: Ginn [1895], 380), and as if correcting false notions: "Yama is not death, as some think; he is one that gives bliss to the good and woe to the bad." Put another way, it is said (Mbh.50.74.27; Manu 8.85-86) that Yama removes the sin of him who possesses a good conscience (i.e. presumably one who has made expiation on earth for his sins), but tortures those whose conscience is unclean. The context of this statement suggests the metaphor of a "trial by ordeal" by which Yama ascertains the guilty or innocent state of each person's conscience.

Almost in a summary form, the Mahābhārata (12.92.38) declares "Yama is Dharma, the king of righteousness." Since Yama is also identified with Lord Dharma,[25] he appears as the perfect model of all earthly sovereigns[26] and is the moral exemplar and even the conscience of each individual.[27] He draws near as an attentive witness of every court hearing and is alertly observant of the veracity of witnesses.[28] Thus Yama is also the unseen supreme Judge in every earthly court of law, the true Lord of Justice. Inasmuch as any earthly ruler exercises his office wisely and rules his subjects justly, he emulates Yama; and when he punishes the wrongdoing of his subjects, he fulfills the office of Varuṇa (Manu 9.307-8). In an apparently summary reference to Manu 7.18, Kullūka explains that:

So Yama (the god of death) while discharging the duties imposed upon him, performs them in accordance with the provisions of the law. So Nārada has laid down: persons with the vices unexposed, if not punished by their teachers or the king, are penalized by the rod of Yama and attain the lowliest positions in their future lives.[29]

Kullūka's statement here clearly indicates the limitations of Yama's functions. Although he is "king of dharma" (*dharmarāj*), this is his royal service and he is as much bound by Dharma and its manifest regulations as are earthly sovereigns. His subordinate status is acknowledged even apologetically in a relatively late work from the fourth century A.D. on account of Yama's professed inability to divert the course of Karma by restoring to life a brāhmin boy who had been suddenly stricken with an inexplicable fatal sickness. The Citralakṣaṇa of Nagnajit is manifestly a compilation of earlier works and fragments and therefore represents early ideas about Yama and about his limited role in life and in death. As given in Goswamy's and Dahmen-Dallapicolla's English translation of Berthold Laufer's German edition of the Tibetan text (Early Documents [1976], 66-68), the story goes that when challenged by a "pious and wise king" to restore the boy to life so that he might return to his parents, "the king of the laws," Yama, smiled at the king and "spoke in gentle and majestic words to him":

> My independence is limited and to return or free him is not within my power. All beings are subject to my power because of the reward that their own deeds (*karma*) merit. Because of the time [Tib. *dus* = Skr. *kāla* having two meanings: time and death] and their *karma* they experience fortune and misfortune. Understand, therefore, that it is not I, the King, who exercises powers of reward or retribution. Even if you yourself were to come to me you could be released no more (than this boy) . . . . Superior as you are to all beings, you must still be answerable to your good and bad deeds. The Name [Skr. *nāma* = individuality?] is the basis of *karma*, and this is it that explains the basis of requital.

In the face of the pious king's objections to this plea of Yama, the leader of the gods, Brahmā, comes to Yama's support with the statement:

> The greathearted Yama is truly not to blame. The King of men, the Master of Death (*mṛtyupati*) is not to blame; the blame lies on the other hand with Karma. Because of the good and bad deeds that this boy had committed earlier he was born in the form of a human being, and death has come to him early.

The point of the story is emphatic--that all beings are subject to the principle, rule, or law of Karma, wherefore Yama's role can only be that of its dispenser or administrator. In this regal function as the servant of Law, Yama's office resembles Varuṇa's even to the extent that he "becomes Varuṇa" whenever he implements justice as a guardian of Ṛta having accountability to Brahmā.

C. Ṛta and Divine Punishment

Some penitential hymns of the Ṛgveda appear to express the tenderness of human devotion toward God and aspirations toward enjoyment of peaceable communion with Him. Others reflect recognition of personal afflictions and misfortunes as divine retributions. These reflect a Vedic "theology of punishment" comparable with theologies of divine punishment in Judaic, Christian, and Islamic sacred literature in which God is represented as a personal rewarder and punisher of men.

Attention has already been drawn to S. Bhattacharji's doubtful personalistic interpretation of Varuna's retributive role in which that role is approximated to the Judaeo-Christian theology of the "wrath of God." Unlike the Israelite Yahweh, Varuṇa is not a divine father who knows and cares for His children. Nor is he the divine King who protects and prospers those human subjects with whom he has some kind of contractual relationship. There are no 'first-person' references to Varuṇa in the Vedas. The references and allusions in entirety suggest that the lord of justice performs his justicial functions with an impersonal detachment indifferent to whether the transgressor had committed his transgression deliberately, accidentally, or unknowingly. Yama also, the primordial Man, who proceeded mankind into the underworld, appears to have the same impersonal detachment of that Varuṇa whose partner or agent he appears to be. Justical statements in reference to Yama, even in the Epics, provide little evidence of his personal involvement with those unhappy persons and inmates of Hell whose deeds are being retributed by his hellish attendants. His dispassionate service is of that Ṛta which Dharma manifests and which its guardians uphold. So, any comparison of Yama or of Varuṇa with the Israelite deity is artificially contrived and serves rather to conceal the more significant distinctions. We do not find in Varuṇa, nor in the character and operations of his subordinates, substance for an ancient Indian theology of the wrath of God.

On the whole, the conception of divine punishment which emerges from study of Vedic deities as agents of justice, is that their retributions are purely in the interests of safeguarding a universal order upon which both their own being and that of all creatures necessarily depend. Although certain Vedic deities appear to reward good deeds and to punish transgressions, the instrumentation of punishment stems ultimately, and frequently directly, from Varuṇa. In the Ṛgveda, he is supremely the lord of punishment, a position which appears to be usurped by Yama and by Dharma in the Epics and other literature. Nevertheless, references to divine punishment do not support the notion of it as a means of divine satisfaction, as if the gods themselves had been wronged or injured and needed to be appeased. Their aloofness in justicial administrations is reflective of the exalted order which they uphold and safeguard. In its regard they are truly ethical deities, and their administration of justice only contrasts with, yet never is qualified by, the human warmth of the earnest penitential psalms of the Ṛgveda which their retributions inspired.

Since the pivot of Varuṇa's regality is Ṛta and the essence of his character is in his service of Ṛta, it is to that philosophical concept and its supposed existence as a metaphysical reality that one must look both for the rational source and the spirit of brāhmaṇic ethics, to perceive in it the foundation or ground-concept of ideas which accordingly may be considered as derivative concepts such as *dharma*, *vrata*, *dhāma*, *svadhā*, and *karma* which also are important sources of brāhmaṇical retributional ideas. Theologically also, Professor Bloomfield (The Religion of the Veda [1908], 12ff.) made a justifiable comment that, "from the point of view of the history of religious ideas we may, in fact we must, begin the history of Hindu religion at least with the history of this conception."

Chapter 2. The Concept of Obligation

A. Dharma

The importance of the conception of Dharma in early brāhmaṇic thought is so considerable that it has seemed either that it replaced Ṛta as the leading philosophical and religious conception or that the earlier concept was at some early time absorbed into it. It is probably more true that Dharma was conceived as an aspect of Ṛta which became so useful for framing religious, moral and social regulations, that interest in it and discussion of its applications to social and moral order eclipsed all discussions of metaphysical and theological ideas. Since, moreover, Dharma was made the central subject of a literary tradition which was to become vast and extensive throughout India, while the conception of Ṛta remained largely confined to the Vedas and their commentaries, it naturally took possession of brāhmaṇical thinking even at the expense of older, exalted concepts and conceptions.

Countless references to Dharma in the vast corpus of brāhmaṇic literature resist all attempts at composing a concise and precise definition of the word which would be adequate for all its connotations. An encyclopaedic definition would hardly comprehend the interrelations of the manifold meanings of the word expressed by sentential and contextual references.[1] The ascertainment of the root-meaning of the word as *dhṛ* with the sense of to uphold, support, or nourish, is nearly useless. And discussions of primary and secondary definitions which draw upon religious and moral and judicial uses of the word would be doubtful and highly contentious. For one could only decide arbitrarily that references in the Ṛgveda (e.g., 1.22.18; 5.26.6; 8.43.24; and 9.64.1; etc.) which connote religious ordinances or ritual regulations are earlier uses than those where (e.g., 5.63.7; 6.70.1; and 7.89.5; etc.) the word "dharma" connotes or conveys the sense of "fixed principles" or general rules of conduct. The most fundamental indication is that Dharma is a finite or particularized manifestation of Ṛta inasmuch as it represents that aspect of the universal Order which specifically concerns the mundane natural, religious, social, and moral spheres as expressed in ritualistic regulations, public laws, moral principles, and laws of nature. Since, and insofar as, it is anthropomorphized along with the Ādityas Varuṇa and Mitra in Ṛgveda 8.35.13, it can be assumed to have similar or even identical character and functions with those divine beings which reflect the core-meaning of the word through all its usages.

The setting of its uses and the various views of dharma represented in the literature into a chronological sequence would provide a richly informative account of the expansions of religious and social ideas in brāhmaṇic thought from early times down to the nineteenth century. But although this has been attempted by many scholars the results are doubtful, since too frequently logical sequences are identified with historical successions in the face of the literary evidence that apparently "advanced" connotations are found in early works and are not there simply as interpolations. The variety of sentential and contextual references in any single text in which the word is frequently repeated prevents any trustworthy theory of a linear development in the conception of Dharma. This would be tantamount to arguing that early brāhmin writers were not able to think simply and to think complex ideas simultaneously. All one can do is to recognize diversities of usage-meaning and to distinguish these by some kind of logical comparison. It is apparent, for example, that in the highly ritualistic context of the Atharvaveda, the word commonly carries the sense of the merit which is gained through careful attention to the correct performance of sacrificial rites, as in AV 5.27.5; 6.51.3; 7.5.1; and 11.7.17. Such "ritual connotations" are found in later liturgical and philosophical texts, though here also one finds usages which are appropriate to religious obligations (as in Aitareya Brāhmaṇa 7.17 and 8.13) and to ethical notions such as truth (*satya*) (as in the Bṛhadāraṇyaka Upaniṣad 1.14.14) or to the duties of life connoted by the word *varṇāśramadharma* (as in the Chāndogya Upaniṣad 2.23). Hence, simply because the latter connotation appears to be more explicit and important in that vast literature which comprises social, religious, and moral obligations, or *dharmaśāstra*, there is insufficient justification for accepting Kane's theory (History of the Dharmaśāstra, [1968], Vol. 1, Pt. 1, 3) of the several transitional senses of the word *dharma* which he drew from hundreds of occurrences in saṃhitās, brāhmaṇas, and upanishads, to those of the smṛtis in which it means "the privileges, [the] duties and obligations of a man" occupying a place in a hierarchically oriented society and following a certain vocation in life. An intelligible grasp of the concept itself could be gained by following Medhātithi's example of classifying the meanings of *dharma* just as he classified "the *dharmas* of all the classes" mentioned in the Manusmṛti (1.2) into "caste duties" (*varṇadharma*), vocational obligations (*āśramadharma*) caste and vocational obligations (*varṇāśramadharma*), occasional commitments (*naimittikadharma*) such as the obligation to perform such penances as may be prescribed for confessed sins, and kingly duties (*guṇadharma*). To these might be added qualitative uses of the word "dharma" with distinctions between philosophical, religious, moral, and legal uses of the word which do not assume that any of these uses were attributed to dharma earlier or later than others. As distinct from moral uses of the word dharma, its legal definition is traceable from its usages as being the body of positive and negative injunctions, commands, or prohibitions which are enforceable by judicial action, that is, to which sanctions are attached. Its moral use is then defineable as any rule or order which ought to be obeyed or any injunction whose acceptance involves moral choice.[2] Since there are moral uses of the word in which, apparently inconsistently, court action is envisaged and penal sanctions are prescribed, the definitive distinctions can be seen to be flexible or the boundaries fluid consistent with the recognition of the king as serving a dual role as the guardian of the society and the embodiment of Dharma.[3]

Broadly considered, Dharma appears to have the general sense of "regulation" apart from any specific indications concerning that which is regulated or governed. The ordinances (*pradiśā*) of Ṛta which are said to be the strength of such gods as Indra[4] who obey them are said also to belong to "the dharma of Ṛta." This is tantamount to the statement that dharma, in the sense of divine commands, expresses dynamically the higher order which is signified by Ṛta. As self-willed beings act in accordance with that Order they follow the *pradiśā* of Ṛta or move under the governance (dharma) of Ṛta as in the statement that Soma "flows under the dharma of Ṛta."

An equivalent term for *pradiśā* is *vrata*[5] which has one sense in the Ṛgveda meaning the preordained courses which planetary beings follow, and another sense meaning "divine ordinances" as in the statement (Ṛgveda 1.25.1-2): "Whatever *vrata* of thine, O Varuṇa, we may break today . . . do not reduce us to death." Similarly in an intercession to Soma (Ṛgveda 10.25.3): "O Soma! If I transgress your perfect *vratas*, then in satisfaction (with our sacrifices), pity us as a father (pities) his son."

A third equivalent which is peculiar to the Ṛgveda is *dharman*[6] which is the subject of an extended discussion by Kane (History of the Dharmaśāstra [1968] Vol. I, Pt.I), appears to mean "fixed principles," "rules of conduct," or "religious rites or sacrifices" in different sentential contexts. Other peculiarities include uses of the word dharma as a suffix, as in *vidharman* (in Ṛgveda 1.164.36; 3.2.3; 5.17.2; 6.71.1; 9.4.9; 9.64.9; 9.86.29-30; 10.46.6; etc.), which Kane thinks (History of the Dharmaśāstra [1968] Vol. I, Pt. I, 2) "means the same thing as *vidhartṛ*" which is applied to different deities with the sense of "creator" (as in RV 2.28.4; 7.7.5; 7.41.2 and 7.56.24) as one who brings the universe into being as an unfolding order. Epithetical titles of these deities are also found such as *svadharman* for Agni (in RV 3.21.2) and *satyadharman* for Savitṛ, Viśvedevāḥ, Agni, Mitra, and Varuṇa (as in RV 1.12.7; 5.51.2, 5.63.1; 9.121.9; 10.34.8; and 10.139.3). Kane (History of the Dharmaśāstra [1968] Vol. I, Pt. I, 2) sees these epithets as meaning those deities "whose regulations do not fail."

B. Dharma and Deity

The application of the epithets *vidhartr*, *svadharman*, and *satyadharman* to the Ādityas suggests that the Vedic poets did not merely think of them as natural powers but also as ethical beings. Rudimentary personifications and anthropomorphic representations of Dharma also brought the concept within the Vedic theology and even within the orbit of the Vedic conception of divine retribution. This theologizing of Dharma may have begun even prior to the first millenium B.C. But in the Bṛhadāraṇyaka Upaniṣad (1.4.14) appears the authoritative statement that Brahmā "created still further a better form, Dharma" which is "the power (*kṣatra*) of the ruling (*kṣatra*) class."[a] The statement notably embraces the divine roles of creator, king, and judge within the idea of divinity itself although, not surprisingly, it is the latter two which appear more prominently in Dharmaśāstra literature, especially in later Epic and Paurāṇic literature where Dharma appears in the full glory of a great deity. In the Mahābhārata (1.9.11, Roy's trans., 3rd ed., Vol. 1, p. 51) the phrases "the god Dharma" and "*Dharmarāj*" appear as epithets for Lord Yama. But Dharma is represented as a deity in his own right, in the Manusmṛti, for example (as in 8.16). In the Mahābhārata (12.90.75) Lord Dharma or "Bhagawān Dharma" shares with Yama, Nārāyaṇa, and the Ādityas the governance of the universe and the retribution of deeds. Lord Dharma (Mbh.8.206, Roy's trans.) not only "aids the acquisition and preservation of wealth (*dhana*)" but also "restrains and sets bounds to all evil acts of men." Thus it appears that the full personalization of Dharma into the figure of a divine sovereign

---

[a] "sa naiva vyabhavat tacchreyorūpamatyasṛjata dharmam tadetat kṣatrasya kṣatram yaddharmastasmāddharmātparam nāsti atho abalīyān balīyām̐samāśam̐sate dharmeṇa yathā rājñā evam yo vai sa dharmaḥ satyam vai tat tasmāt satyam vadantamāhurdharmam vadatīti dharmam vā vadantam̐ satyam vadatīti etaddhagyeva etadubhayam bhavati" (Bṛhad.1.4.14; Dasopanishads, [1936] Vol. II; p. 272).

and judge--at the latest by the fifth century A.D.--also resulted in the creation of Dharma as the divine prototype of earthly kingship as well as the ruler and judge of kings. In the Nāradīyasmṛti (18.20 SBE), whose author Kane (History of the Dharmaśāstra [1973], Vol. III, 35) perceives to be a "thorough-going advocate of the divine right of kings," the statement is made that the divine Dharma "personified as a king, roams on earth visibly, with a thousand eyes," hence "mortals cannot live if they transgress his commandments."

The reference to the "thousand-eyed Dharma" reminds one of the Vedic "all-seeing" deities such as Varuṇa (RV 1.25.5 and 16; 7.34.10); Mitra (RV 7.63.3); Sūrya (RV 4.53.2-6); and Yama (e.g. Vaś.Dhs.20.3) who perceive or search out the deeds of men and punish wrongdoers. The metaphors not only suggest the watchfulness of king Dharma over the judicial institutions and moral behaviour, but also support the impression that justice itself is not blind nor are its processes unrelated to that greater Order upon which the social prosperity and human well-being ultimately depend.

The belief that divine Dharma secures creaturely well-being by safeguarding the social order is expressed in the Mahābhārata statement (12.90.75) that Dharma "aids the acquisition and preservation of wealth."[a] The essential role of Dharma may partly explain the preference for the title of "*Dharmaśāstra*"--rather than *arthaśāstra*, *nītiśāstra*, *rājaśāstra*, or *rājadharma*--for the numerous compendia of regulative principles and prescriptions which govern human life. At the same time, by placing divine Dharma within the setting of civil law, social custom, and individual and public morality, the fundamentally religious character of Indian law, and the essential role in society of the religious or brāhmanical class are also emphasized. This point is particularly made in the Mahābhārata (12.90, Roy's trans., p.207) that Dharma has sprung from the Brahman, therefore brāhmins should be honoured by kings who do not

[a]"Adityacandravanilo'nalasca . . . dharmasca jānāti narasya vṛttam" (Mbh.12.90.75).

wish to bring tribulations upon themselves. The religious basis of *Dharmaśāstra*, however, is not limited to the interests of one social class, but concerns all beings. This encompassing role of *dharmaśāstra* is well expressed by K. V. Rangaswāmī Aiyaṅgar (Some Aspects of the Hindu View of Life according to Dharmaśāstra, Baroda: Oriental Institute [1952], 62) in a statement which is tantamount to a religious definition of Dharma, and a religious theory of Law.

> *Dharmaśāstra* is a comprehensive code to regulate human conduct in accordance with the unalterable scheme of Creation, and to enable everyone to fulfil the purpose of his birth. The whole life of Man, considered both as an individual and as a member of groups (small and large) as well as man's relations to his fellow men, to the rest of animated creation, to superhuman beings, to cosmos, generally and ultimately to God, come within the purview of *Dharmaśāstra*. Among the duties that it lays down are both self-regarding and altruistic, those to the living and to the dead, to those who are alive and those who are yet to be born.

This extract which is found in J. D. M. Derrett's book on Religion, Law and the State in India (NY: The Free Press [1968], 100), displays Aiyaṅger's insight into the integrality of religion and law in Hindu culture. Religion provides the transcendent authority of law and its sanctions even where, as Derrett explains (p. 102) that "rules themselves could and in fact did persist by virtue of their own merit and not merely by reason of a superstitious sanction attached to their alleged source."

A striking representation of the divinity of Dharma in his role as the overseer of divine justice appears in the institution of "trial by ordeal" which was accorded a high standing in ancient Indian judicial practice. The justicial character of these, particularly of the "ordeal by Dharma," is discussed later under forms of punishments. They are mentioned here only in drawing attention to the prominant role played by Dharma as the divine judge who presides over all trials by ordeal, even though he is specially invoked in the so-called "ordeal of Dharma." The invocation of Dharma who is believed to be present as the presiding divine judge would have been at least a psychological device to convince the parties in the ordeal that the deities of justice are alert and actively participant in every judicial process particularly against all officers of the court who might be persuaded or tempted to deny justice.

C. Dharma and Sovereignty

Retributional significations of Dharma are expectedly more explicit in contexts bearing upon rulership or kingship than in abstract philosophical contexts. The concept of *samrāj*, the idea of *cakravartin*, and the theories of statesmanship or governmental administration indicated by such words as *rājaśāstra*, *rājanīti*, and *daṇḍanīti*, are major sources for these retributional dimensions of Dharma.

In the Ṛgveda, *samrāj* has both a divine and a human dimension. Kane (History of the Dharmaśāstra [1958], Vol. V, Pt. I, 8) explains that the word is addressed more often in the twelve hymns to Varuṇa than in approximately two hundred hymns to Indra. However it is precisely those deities who exercise ethical sovereignty and who are invoked to make attendance at earthly "trials by ordeal"--Varuṇa, Mitra, Indra, Agni, Viśvadevaḥ, and other deities included among the Ādityas--who are most frequently referred to as "kings" (*rājan*) and emperors (*samrāja*), as in RV 2.41.6; 3.10.1; 3.54.10; 5.85.1; 7.38.4; 8.27.22; and 10.63.5, with authority to institute ordinances, enunciate commands, and impose penal sanctions upon transgressors.

In this respect, the application of the title *dhṛtavrata*[7] in the sense of "one who upholds or supports his ordinances" to each of these deities indicates the distinctive ethical role characteristic of these deities and the high moral level in which they were regarded by the Ṛgvedic sages.

The terms of kingship applied to deities are applied to human rulers also. The word *samrāj* applied specifically to Varuṇa and Mitra in most contexts is given a human regal signification in the Ṛgvedic statement: "O Maruts! The sovereign, protected by you, kills the enemy."[a] The blessing

---

[a] "yuṣmotaḥ samrāḷuta hanti vṛtram pra tadvo astu dhūtayo deṣṇam" (RV 7.58.4 in Kane, History [1958], V.Pt.I.8.note 10).

of the bride in RV 10.85.4--"be you a queen (*samrājñī*)"--indicates this earthly regality. The hymn of King Trasadasyu in RV 4.42 strikingly contrasts divine and human sovereignty by the statement "The gods rely on Varuṇa's might (*kratu*), while I am lord of the people."[a] The statement continues, "Indra and Varuṇa am I, the deep Heaven and Earth am I, I am the son of Aditi" (RV 4.42.3-4). This cultic self-exaltation however should be balanced by such intercessory prayers as RV 1.65.7 and 3.43.5 where the intercessor asks: "Will you make me the protector of the people, the king (*rājan*), O Indra," and in many places in which the word *rājan* applied to Mitra and Varuṇa (as in RV 1.24.11-13; 7.64.2; and 10.173.5 and elsewhere) is applied to earthly rulers (as in RV 1.65.7; 3.43.5; 4.4.1; 9.7.5; and 10.174.4).

Since the *cakravartin* ideal refers to earthly rulership, it is only through earthly conquest (*digvijayas*) that realization is envisaged. According to the Sabhāparva of the Mahābhārata (2.15.2) "that king under whose sole dominion the world abides, he achieves the position of *samrāj*." The Mahābhārata, the Aitereya Brāhmaṇa, and the Śatapatha Brāhmaṇa refer to at least twelve ancient *sarvabhaumas* (lords of the earth) or *cakravartins* (e.g. in Mbh.2.15.15-16, 2.26-32; Śat.13.5.4.1-19).

Kane (History of the Dharmaśāstra [1973] Vol.III, 66) assumes the mythical heroes and emperors who realized the *cakravartin* ideal of world rulership as realizing a purely secular role, since he looks to an early Buddhist source--the Mahāvagga (Selasutta) in SBE 10.102--as providing the earliest formulation of the *cakravartin* ideal in moral and spiritual terms in the Buddha's statement, "I am a king, an incomparable, religious king (*dharmarāj*); with justice (*dhammena*) I turn the wheel, a wheel that is irresistible." But since the idea of sovereignty over many kingdoms implied in the terms *samrāj*, *sarvabhaumi*, and *cakravartin* was fully developed even in early Vedic times prior to any elaborations

---

[a]"kratuṃ sacante varuṇasya devā rājāmi kṛṣṭeḥ . . ." (RV 4.42.1; Kane, History [1973]; III,32).

in succeeding periods, it is not too much to expect that even at that early time the ethical attributes perceived in the heavenly sovereigns were naturally applied to their earthly regents also. This would have also determined the priority of the idea of "righteous rulership" over all other powers of kingship such as military might (*kratu*) and world-conquest (*digvijaya*). Support for this priority of moral over physical powers in kingship can be found in Indian history itself, since when Candragupta, Aśoka, Puṣyamitra, Samudragupta, Harṣa, and other imperial rulers sought to present themselves as those who had realized the *cakravartin* ideal, they published their achievements in inscriptions and on memorials primarily in ethical and religious terms. The emperor Aśoka's rock and pillar inscriptions of the second century B.C. amply reflect both the public self-image he set out to portray and his awareness of popular conceptions of righteous rulership as formulated in the Mahābhārata (12.90.1ff.) that becoming a king "is for the sake of righteousness (dharma), not for pursuing conveniences . . . . A king who acts righteously attains the status of a deity . . *Dharma* depends upon the king; the king who accordingly, upholds dharma is a true king. That king who has a righteous spirit endowed with every kind of grace, is perceived as an embodiment of dharma."

The primacy of ethical over political qualities is also demonstrated by the extensive body of teaching on the theory of kingship (*rājaśāstra*) of which Kane (History of the Dharmaśāstra [1973], Vol. III, 44-55) has given a fairly detailed outline. Of particular interest in Kane's account is the integrality of intellectual aptitudes, practical skills, and spiritual and moral qualities which are required to be developed during the training of princes for rulership according to both the Kautilīya Arthaśāstra (6.1), the Manusmṛti (7.32-44), and the Yājñavalkyasmṛti (1.309-311, 334) and subsumed under the general headings of *dharmaśāstra* (the dharmas of different classes of society), *rājanīti* (civic administration, science of government), and also *arthaśāstra* (general economics). Even more important, however, the authorities distinguished between the inner and the outer qualities of kingship. Kauṭilya, for example, in

Arthaśāstra 6.1 distinguished politically opportunistic qualities or aptitudes (*ābhigamīkaguṇa*) from pragmatic skills (*śakyasāmantaguṇa*) and interior (*ātmasampat*) intellectual and spiritual qualities. These latter generally follow those indicated in the Gautama Dharmasūtra (11.2.4-6) or as detailed in the Saṅkhalikhita with respect to right action (that is, actions supported by the dharmasmṛtis), right speech, personal integrity, self-control, liberal-mindedness, even-handedness, and considerateness toward the king's subjects. The distinction between inward or essential (*antaraṅga*) and outward qualities was followed in the Mitākṣarā on Yājñavalkya Dhs.1.334 and compares with thirty-six such qualities indicated in the Śāntiparva of the Mahābhārata (12.70), nineteen interior (*ātmasampat*) qualities in the Kāmandakīyanītisāra (4.15-19)[8] as cited by Kane (History of the Dharmaśāstra [1973], Vol. III, 45ff.), and forty-four in the twelfth century Mānasollāsa (2.1.2-7, Gaikwad Oriental Series, Baroda), of which the five most essential ones are stated to be truthfulness, valour, forbearance, liberality, and appreciation of others. The Agnipurāṇa (239.2-5) enumerates twenty-one, while the Sabhāparva of the Mahābhārata (2.5.107-109), and the Rāmāyaṇa (2.100.65-67 in the 1933 edition of R. N. Aiyer, Madras Law Journal Office) name fourteen faults to be avoided by rulers.

Whatever may be said for the sciences (*vidyās*) which comprised the formal education of rulers, namely, *ānvīkṣikī*,[9] *trayī* (or the three vedas), *vārtā* (should be *vārttā*, being primarily agriculture and more generally including animal husbandry, mining, and mercantile commerce also?), and *daṇḍanīti*, it is only in the latter discipline that the king's functions as an embodiment and civil guardian of Dharma are explicit. Kane (History of the Dharmaśāstra [1973], Vol. III, 48) even indicates that there may have been a controversy between the juridical schools as to whether or not *daṇḍanīti* is the only requisite *vidyā* for a king and the other *vidyās* only lead up to it. Kane finds evidence for this in the Kauṭilīya Arthaśāstra in the opening statement that the three *vidyas* depend on *daṇḍa* which in turn is based on "discipline" (*vinaya*) or bodily self-control for the prevention of evil tendencies (*śatruṣaḍvargas, ariṣaḍvargas*) and vices due to lusts (*kāma*) and rages (*krodha*).

By the comparison of *vinaya* with *samrāj* it appears that sovereignty was perceived both in personal and in political terms so that once the essential qualities of true rulership were brought into the scheme of princely training, those distinctive qualities of ethical deities were singled out as foundation principles of the "royal science": *rājaśāstra, rājanīti*, or *daṇḍanīti*. The guardians of Ṛta, moreover, were perceived as voluntarily binding themselves to observe their own and each other's ordinances on behalf of the universal Order itself. Accordingly the ethical qualities perceived to belong to their earthly representatives and to true kingship included voluntary self-commitment of kings to the roles of benefactors and protectors of the society. The question of whether and how far Indian rulers did in practice observe the "servant-of-society" ideal is for historians to answer. But there is historic evidence that both Hindu and Buddhist rulers knew of the ideal and the limitations it would place on their powers. One may also assume that whenever they became inclined to forget its restraints, the brāhmin pundits in their courts were able to remind them.

D. Dharma and Daṇḍanīti

If the direction of the royal training of princes in the science of government was the inculcation of the interior qualities of wise and responsible rulership, it follows that its aim was the expression of these model qualities in their day-to-day administration of the state through the science of government. These interior and exterior qualities and skills of government which comprised the "dharmas of kingship" were a species of dharmas which were not included in the *varṇadharma* or "dharmas of all the castes" which had been distinguished prior to Medhāthiti's classification and treated consecutively in the Āpastamba-dharmasūtra (2.9.25.1). The importance of the royal dharma also appears in the specialized sections--the so-called *rājadharma-khaṇḍas*--in the major smṛtis.

Rājadharma is treated extensively in the Śāntiparva of the Mahābhārata (Mbh.12, sections 56-130) which also lists some seven authoritative exegetes of the science of *rājaśāstra*. The Manusmṛti begins a special section (chapter 7) on the exposition of *rājadharmas*, and the author of the Kauṭilīya Arthaśāstra names five schools and seven master exponents, as well as indicating the views of other teachers (*ācāryas*). Kane (History of the Dharmaśāstra [1973], Vol. III, 4) draws attention to the systematization of the science of government in the Mahābhārata, the Rāmāyaṇa, Manu, and Kauṭilya, including their propensity for numerical tables: the seven constituent elements of statehood, the six "ways of polity," the three powers (*śaktis*) of kingship, the four effective means (*upāyas*) of ruling, and so on. This suggests that the science had been formalized even prior to the composition of these early works. Separate treatises on the science may have been composed, in Kane's opinion, "in very early times," in support of which he cites the Śāntiparva (Mbh.12.59) and the Nītiprakāśika (1.21-22, Dr. Oppert's edn.). It is doubtful, nevertheless, that the authors and compilers of the treatises had a purely academic interest in statecraft but rather had a vested interest in preserving the kind of society which was favourable to their classes and in protecting the king's office and role as the protector and leading benefactor of the society. But if the integral relation between public order and social prosperity seemed obvious, the framing of formal rules and guidelines of rulership into a science of rulership called *rājadharma* made the perimeters of that rulership explicit in terms both of its scope and its limitations. Furthermore, inasmuch as the guidelines were deemed to be axiomatic they needed no justification but only explanation with repeated endorsements of their paramount importance through such statements in the Mahābhārata (12.63.25) that "all dharmas are merged in *rājadharma*" or that "*rājadharmas* are at the head of all *dharmas*" inasmuch as they comprehend the totality of smṛti rulings governing valid customs (*ācāra*), litigation (*vyavahāra*), penalties (*dama*) as regulated by penal prescriptions (*daṇḍanīti*), and penances (*prāyaścitta*).

In this connection, the term *rājaśāstra* very early gained currency as a general definition for the extensive literary and exegetical activity related to the science and art (*vidyā*) of government particularly in connection with the names of its renowned teachers. Seven of these are referred to by name in the Śāntiparva as *rajaśāstra-pranetaraḥ*, that is, "expositors of the science/art of government." The named references (noted by Kane, History of the Dharmaśāstra [1973], Vol. III, 4) in the Nītiprakāśikā (1.21-22) are not followed by any explanation of the word *rājaśāstra*, which suggests that its content was sufficiently known and understood. The reference to *nṛpaśāstra*, which should be correctly *nṛpanītiśāstra* or the "science of kingship" in the opening verse of Franklin Edgerton's reconstructed Pañcatantra, is again in reference to the authoritative human exponents of the science, namely, Manu, Bṛhaspati, Śukra, Parāśara, Cāṇakya, and others, as distinct from such legendary divine authors and exponents of the science as Brahmā, Maheśvara, Skanda, and Indra, who are cited in the Nītiprakāśikā.

A positive definition of the science of government as *arthaśāstra* appears in the Kauṭilīya Arthaśāstra (15.1) in the statement: "*artha* is the sustenance of human beings, that is, the earth peopled by men. That śastra which is the mean of acquiring and guarding that earth is *artha-śāstra*" (Kane, History of the Dharmaśāstra [1973], Vol. III, 6). A careful definition in the Śukranītisāra[10] (4.3.56) states,

> that is said to be *arthaśāstra* in which instruction about the conduct of kings and the like is given without coming in conflict with *śruti* and *smṛti* and in which the acquisition of wealth with great skill is taught (Kane, History of the Dharmaśāstra [1973], Vol. III, 7).

Such definitions however are manifestly general; any specificality occurs in the sciences for the different areas of human concern, such as the science of government itself as *nītiśāstra* which is defined in the Śāntiparva (Mbh.12.59.74) as "all those means by which people are prevented from forsaking the right path." The author of the Mitākṣarā on Yājñavalkyasmṛti 2.21 identifies the word *rājanītiśāstra* with *arthaśāstra*.

The main topic of this type of literature is also called *rājanīti* in many places, such as the Śāntiparva (Mbh.12.37.9, 12.11.73) and the Manusmṛti (7.177), though in the Bhagavadgītā (10.38) it is simply *nīti*--translatable as "statecraft"--and is presented as a personalization of Kṛṣṇa in the statement, "Of Punishers I am the sceptre; of seekers of victory I am statemanship (*nīti*); of secrets I am silence; and I am the wisdom of the wise."[a] Other minor definitions for the science of government are *rājavidyā* (as in the Nītisāra 1.8.18), *rājanaya*, *arthavidyā* in the Droṇaparva of the Mahābhārata 6.1, and *naya* in the sense of "law of polity" in contrast to or "bad polity" in the Arthaśāstra (1.2) and in other major works.

A specific term for the science of government is *daṇḍanīti* which is sometimes used synonymously with or approximately close to *arthaśāstra*, and sometimes in contrast to it. Among the four major concerns which are proper for a ruler the Manusmṛti (SBE 7.99-100) states,

> Let him strive to gain what he has not yet gained; what he has gained let him carefully preserve; let him augment what he preserves, and what he has augmented let him bestow on worthy men. Let him know that these are the four means for securing the aims of human (existence); let him, without ever tiring, properly employ them.

Kane (History of the Dharmaśāstra [1973], Vol. III, 5) considers these concerns to be the same as the four objectives which appear in the Kauṭilīya Arthaśāstra (1.4)[b] whose author apparently draws upon the Śāntiparva (Mbh.12. 102.57 and 12.140.5) and the Yājñavalkyasmṛti (1.317) and

---

[a] "Daṇḍo damayatāmasmi nītirasmi jigīṣatām; maunaṃ caivāsmi guhyānāṃ jñānaṃ jñānavatām aham" (BG 10.38; Śrīmadbhagavadgītā [1974], 572).

[b] "Ānvīkṣikītrayīvārtānām yogakṣemasādhano daṇḍaḥ; tasya nītirdaṇḍanītiḥ; alabdhalābhārtā labdhaparirakṣaṇī rakṣitavivardhanī vṛddhasya tīrtheṣu pratipādani ca" (Arthaśāstra 1.4, Kane, History of the Dharmaśāstra [1973], Vol. III, 5, note 8).

the Nītisāra (1.18). In these texts *arthaśāstra* appears to be concerned with the proper means of procuring the "four aims of human life" (*puruṣārthas*), while *daṇḍanīti* appears to comprise all proper means for safeguarding those interests. Hence while the <u>topics</u> which are treated are the same--namely, "the means of acquiring [wealth] and safeguarding the earth" and its produce--it seems by following Kane (Vol. III, 7), that the terms *arthaśāstra* and *daṇḍanīti* manifest different perspectives on those concerns. Therefore, following Kane, "when wealth and prosperity of all kinds is the spring and motive . . . the science of treating of these is called *arthaśāstra*, and when the government of the people and the punishment of offenders is the main idea, the same is called *daṇḍanīti*." In this case *arthaśāstha* comprises the political and economic dimensions of government while *daṇḍanīti* covers the civic dimension of public control.

Several definitions of *daṇḍa* and of *daṇḍanīti* emphasise *dama* or the repressive character of *daṇḍanīti*. In Kane's quotation the Nītisāra (2.15) states that "*dama* is called *daṇḍa*; the king is called *daṇḍa* since control is centred in him; the rules (*nīti*) of *daṇḍa* are called *daṇḍanīti*, and are called rules (*nīti*) because it [they] lead the people."[a] The repressive character of this social control is also evident in the definition given in the Śāntiparva (Mbh.12.59.78) in Kane's rendering (op.cit. page 5). "This world is led (on the right path) by *daṇḍa* (the power of punishment, sanction) or this science carries (or sets forth) the rod of punishment; hence it is called *daṇḍanīti*."[b] Similarly, Vijñāneśvara in the Mitākṣarā on Yājñavalkya 2.26 explains that "the wise have declared that

[a]"Damodaṇḍa iti khyātastātsthyāddaṇḍo mahīpatiḥ; tasya nītirdaṇḍanītirnayanātritirucyate" (Nītisāra 2.15 and Śukranītisara 1.157 in Kane, <u>History</u> [1973], Vol. III, 5, note 10).

[b]"daṇḍena nīyate cedaṃ daṇḍaṃ nayati vā punaḥ; daṇḍanītiriti khyātā trīlaṃlokānabhivartate" (Mbh.12.59.78 in Kane, <u>History</u> [1973], Vol. III, 5, note 7).

the word *daṇḍa* is derived from the root *dam* and hence means punishment."

Beside the definitions, many texts emphasize the importance of *daṇḍanīti*. Some envisage the horrors befalling any society which loses its controls. Without *daṇḍanīti* even "this whole world would break all boundaries" (Mbh.3.150.32). Conversely there are the benefits of the wise science of *daṇḍanīti*. "Daṇḍanīti controls the four social classes (*varṇas*) by compelling the performance of their duties; when properly employed by the ruler, it makes them desist from lawlessness (*adharma*)."[a] Kauṭilya (Arthaśāstra 1.5) perceives *daṇḍa* as the means of stabilizing and promoting the three beneficial sciences: *ānvīkṣikī*, *trayī*, and *vārtā*. On the other hand, the Śāntiparva blames the growth of social and moral anarchy on a king's sole preoccupation with *arthaśāstra*, that is, the fostering of material resources without being concerned with means for safeguarding them. A king whose sole preoccupation is with wealth (*artha*), at the expense of securing morality (*dharma*) and the happiness (*kāma*) of his subjects, causes his wealth to be lost through the pursuit of improper objectives.

Considering all the references to the science of government, it seems that *dharmaśāstra* or the safeguarding of public order was given precedence over *arthaśāstra* or the economy of the state. This precedence is apparent, as Kane shows (*History of the Dharmaśāstra* [1973], Vol. III, 13) even in literature, such as the Kauṭilīya Arthaśāstra, which treats extensively on political strategy and subterfuge for the sake of national and governmental security. Here, even under states of national emergency when public morality might be subordinated to political expediency, this change of precedence is only permitted by the

---

[a]"Daṇḍanītiḥsvadharmebhyaścāturvarṇyaṃ niyacchati; prayuktā svāminā saṃyagadharmebhyo niyacchati" (Mbh.12.69.76 in Kane, *History* [1973], Vol. III, 5, note 7).

Arthaśāstra (1.17) and the Mahābhārata (1.140 and 12.140) as temporary expedients, never as permanent dispensations from the social obligations of public veracity, justice, and community service. The prestige of public morality (*dharma*) over economic prosperity (*artha*) is evident in the fact that while *daṇḍa* is deified as the lord of public order, *artha* is not. According to the Manusmṛti (7.14), "God [i.e. Brahmā] originally created for that very purpose . . . *Daṇḍa* his own son, full of divine splendour, as the (veritable) *dharma*, the protector of all beings."[a] This *Daṇḍa* "punishes all (erring) subjects and protects all (peace-loving) persons and remains awake when everybody else is fast asleep. Hence the wise call *daṇḍa* as *dharma* itself."[b] Also "where *Daṇḍa* with black hue and red eyes stalks about destroying sinners, there the subjects are at peace."[c]

Such metaphors remind one of Varuṇa and even suggest that *Daṇḍa* could be an immanental aspect of the transcendent deity. But beside the occasional indications of the divinizing of *Daṇḍa*, he is fully deified in a major statement comprising two chapters (*adhyāyas*) of the Śāntiparvan of the Mahābhārata. This divinized representation of *Daṇḍa* in the longest interpolation of the Mahābhārata displays the popular conception of *Daṇḍa* by the beginning of the present era. Even the discoördinate manner in which his features are unfolded adds an exhuberant quality to the exalted figure. Adhyāya 121 of the Śāntiparvan of the

---

[a]"Tasyārthe sarvabhūtānāṃ goptāram dharmamātmajam; brahmatejomayaṃ daṇḍamasṛjat pūrvamīśvaraḥ" (Manu 7.14, Chowkhamba, 226).

[b]"Daṇḍaḥ śāsti prajāḥ sarvā daṇḍa evābhirakṣati; daṇḍaḥ supteṣu jāgarti daṇḍaṃ dharmaṃ vidurbudhāḥ" (Manu 7.18, Chowkhamba, 226).

[c]"Yatra śyāmolohitākṣidaṇḍaścarati pāpahā; prajāstatra na muhyanti netā cetsādhu paśyati" (Manu 7.25, Chowkhamba, 226).

Mahābhārata opens with a question about Daṇḍa put by the crown-prince Yudhiṣṭhira to the dying Kuru statesman, Bhīṣma. The ground of the question is that: "it seems that Chastisement occupies a high position and is the lord of everything, for everything depends on Chastisement." Yudhiṣṭhira wants to know (Mbh.12.121, Roy's trans.):

> . . . truly who Chastisement [i.e. Daṇḍa] is? Of what kind is he? What is his form? What is his disposition? Of what is he made? Whence is his origin? What are his features? What is his splendour? How does he remain wakeful among living creatures so heedfully? Who is he that remains eternally wakeful, protecting this universe? Who is he that is known to be the foremost of all things? Who, indeed, is that high personage called Chastisement? What is that upon which Chastisement depends? And what is his course?

In a most grandiose answer, Bhīṣma heaps metaphor upon metaphor to conceptualize *Daṇḍa* as "a great god . . . the individual whose course is irresistible, the Ever-going, the First-born, the individual without affections, the soul of Rudra, the eldest Manu, and the great Benefactor Chastisement is the holy Vishnu." *Daṇḍa* possesses the duality of all attributes and powers: "blessings and curse, . . . righteousness and unrighteousness, . . . merit and demerit, virtue and vice, desire and aversion . . . salvation and condemnation . . . penances and sacrifice and rigid abstinence . . . prosperity and adversity, etc. etc. etc.". *Daṇḍa* indeed is a mighty manifestation of Brahmā, sent down or created by Brahmā "for the protection of the world and for establishing the duties of different individuals."

The manner of *Daṇḍa's* creation from Brahmā, the catastrophic consequences of his withdrawal from the world in pre-primeval times, and his re-creation and exaltation by the "foremost of deities" ("Brahman" referred to here as "the high-souled Grandsire"), comprise the substance of the following section (122) in which *Daṇḍa* is identified in turn with each of the principal Ṛgvedic deities, with the heroes of the Great Epic, and with the patriarchal forebears of the four castes. The poem closes with the instruction that "a virtuous king should rule properly, guided by Chastisement." By the king, "chastisement should be inflicted with discrimination, guided by righteousness and not by caprice. It is intended for restraining the wicked. Fines and forfeitures are intended for striking alarm, and not for filling the king's treasury."

Such a composite depiction of this divine being offered plentiful scope for commentarial interpretation. The rich personalization of *Daṇḍa* in the eulogy from part 13 of the Mahābhārata, following Roy's translation, is breath-taking:

> Chastisement is a great god. In form he looks like a blazing fire. His complexion is dark like that of the petals of the blue lotus. He is equipt [sic] with four teeth [tusks?], has four arms and eight legs and many eyes. His ears are pointed like shafts and his hair stands upright. He has matted locks and two tongues. His face has the hue of copper, and he is clad in a lion's (*mṛgarāja*) skin. That irresistible deity assumes such a fierce shape.

Based on the interpretations of Arjunamisra, Vimalbodhi and Nilakaṇṭha, and on Derrett's essay on Vyavahāra (*Essays in Classical and Modern Hindu Law*, Leiden: Brill [1977], Vol. I, 80-85), the sense of this highly metaphorical passage could be interpreted as:

> Daṇḍa comprehends within himself the dharmas of both parties in a lawsuit and the four modes [tusks?] of punishment, namely, rebuke, fines, mutilation and capital punishment, for the protection of the four-armed society based on the four castes, the eight processes (feet) of an investigation, the varied evidences (eyes) of the parties in the investigation, the two sides (tongues) of the plaintiff and the defendant, the fine and the forfeiture (ears), and the righteous indignation (face) of the ruler clad in dharma (the lion's skin).

In other texts, such as Kauṭilya's Arthaśāstra, *vyavahāra* has the meaning of litigation with respect to both civil and criminal law. But the word appears also to have been used with the wider reference of the regulations and injunctions of brāhmaṇic law: "these are the precepts or injunctions laid down in those sacred books (i.e. smṛtis) for regulating every part of human duty," and also as an equivalent of *kulācāra* meaning ethnic and familial customs where these are not at variance with the established civil and criminal law, or with the regulations laid down in the dharmaśāstras. This implies, however, that the role of *Daṇḍa* in association with *Vyavahāra* is confined to the social and civil law, that is in the context in which the king performs his judicial duties. *Daṇḍa* accordingly is believed to be interiorly present in every lawsuit. With *Vyavahāra*, *Daṇḍa* guides the king's judgements, safeguards the principle of Justice, and protects the eternal Order. As the Śāntiparva puts it (Mbh.12 in Roy's trans., p. 281):

> Although Chastisement is seen to be regulated by Evidence, yet it has been said to have its soul in *Vyavahāra*. It (i.e., Daṇḍa) has Truth for its soul and it is productive of prosperity. That which has been said to be *Vyavahāra* is verily the Veda. That which is the Veda is morality, duty. That which is morality and duty is the path of Righteousness. This *Vyavahāra* it was which in the beginning had been Grandsire Brahman, that Lord of all creatures.

The close linkage of the science of Punishment (*daṇḍanīti*) with the science of government (*rājanīti*) may have resulted in the strongly negative character of the king's office which is presented as governing "all those means by which the people are prevented from forsaking the right path."[11] It is not surprising accordingly that the king is so often represented as embodying Daṇḍa rather than Dharma. In a statement strongly suggestive of Hobbes' "social contract theory," Kauṭilya, in the Arthaśāstra (1.13.5ff.), states:

> People suffering from anarchy . . . first elected Manu, the Vaivasvata, to be their king; and allotted one-sixth of the grains . . . and one-tenth of the merchandise as sovereign dues. Fed by this payment, kings took upon themselves the responsibility of maintaining the safety and security of their subjects, and of being answerable for the sins of their subjects . . . . It is the king in whom the duties of both the rewarder and the punisher are blended, and he is a visible dispenser of punishments and rewards; whoever disregards kings will be visited with divine punishments too. Hence kings shall never be despised.[a]

---

[a]"Mātsyanyāyābhibhūtāḥ prajā Manuṃ Vaivasvataṃ rājānaṃ cakrire; Dhānyaṣaḍbhāgaṃ paṇyadaśabhāgaṃ hiraṇyaṃ cāsya bhāgadheyaṃ prakalpayāmāsuḥ. Tenabhṛtā rājānaḥ prajānāṃ yogakṣemāvahāḥ . . . . Indrayamasthānametadrājānaḥ pratyakṣahedaprasādāḥ. Tānavamanyamānān daivo'api daṇḍaḥ spṛśati. Tasmādrājāno nāvamantaryāḥ" (Kauṭilya, Arthaśāstra 1.13.5-12; Kaṅgle, 1969).

A shorter version of the theory in Manu (7.3) is that: "when these creatures, being without a king, through fear dispersed in all directions, the Lord created a king for the protection of the whole (creation)." But having said in another place (7.14) that: "for the (king's) sake the Lord formerly created his own son, Punishment," Manu explains:

> Punishment [i.e., Daṇḍa] is (in reality) the king . . . the manager of affairs . . . the ruler . . . the surety for the four orders . . . . If the king did not, without tiring, inflict punishment on those worthy to be punished, the stronger would roast the weaker, like fish on a spit. All castes (*varṇa*) would be corrupted . . . all barriers would be broken through, and all men would rage (against each other) in consequence of mistakes with respect to punishment.[a]

This magnification of the king's office has an obvious pragmatic motive since the brāhmanical order itself had a vested interest in the stability of the brāhmanical society which they insisted should be served by kings and not be destroyed or lost through carelessness, greed, or corruption. The divinizing of the king into an embodiment of divine Daṇḍa, however, as well as the exaltation of punishment as the protector of society, reflects a low view of humankind.[12] On the positive side, the jurisprudents recognize the enormous influence for good of a righteous king. Such a king is the earthly incarnation of the divine-cosmic elements,[13] is "a great deity in human form"[14] formed of the lustre of (all) gods.[15] He is ordained to protect this whole world[16] by preserving the sacred order of the society.[17] He is dedicated to "the complete attainment of justice"[18] and never wields in vain the divine instrument of Punishment.

---

[a]"Sa rājā puruṣo daṇḍaḥ sa netā śāsitā ca saḥ; caturṇāmāśramāṇām ca dharmasya pratibhūḥ smṛtaḥ . . . yadi na praṇayedrājā daṇḍam daṇḍyeṣvatandritaḥ; śūle matsyānivāpakṣyandurbalānbalavattarāḥ . . . duṣyeyuḥ sarvavarṇāśca bhidyeransarvasetavaḥ; sarvalokaprakopaśca bhaveddaṇḍasya vibhramāt" (Manu 7.17, 20, and 24, Chowkhamba, 226).

This relation of Dharma and Daṇḍa in Indian jurisprudence however raises the question of whether and how far "sanction" is an essential element of "law." A. L. Goodhart[19] confesses that he is "not at all happy" with the view that sanction or the enforcement of law is "an essential element" in the idea of "law" and therefore part of its definition. The difficulty may lie in the definition of the concept of law. On the one hand it may be defined objectively as something which, of itself or by its own authority, is binding upon its subjects in a manner similar to a "law of nature" upon natural objects, or physical laws on material objects, and moral laws on moral beings. In each case, the law would work negatively on deviant objects and beings as a corrective principle. On the other hand, a subjective definition of law might be preferred in the sense of "a rule which is recognized as binding."

But there are laws which men are not inclined to recognize as binding, but which they must be compelled to recognize by threat of sanctions. Such persons who resist the law are then treated as natural objects rather than as moral subjects. In such cases, the imposition of sanctions is an instance of recognition by the authority which imposes the sanctions, though not necessarily by the persons who are punished, that the laws are obligatory or binding. In this case, the laws are not obligatory <u>because</u> sanctions are attached to them; instead the converse is true, the sanctions are there <u>because</u> the laws are obligatory.

In this light, the glorification of the law, and of the king as the guardian of the law, and of the Order which his justice affirms, make a sufficiently strong impression upon the citizens as to maintain their law-abidingness. Only rarely, such as in anarchical times, would such law-abidingness be disrupted. Accordingly, in normal times, only those sanctions would be needed which would compel any wayward minority to observe the law. It is therefore, only in order to deter this would-be minority of transgressors that sanctions are enunciated and the king and his officers are presented in an awesome aspect. In this case punishment or sanction is not something other than law as if attached to it merely as an afterthought, or on account of weaknesses and faults appearing at a later time in human nature. On the contrary, *Daṇḍa* is a mode of Dharma. As Derrett (Essays in Classical and Modern Hindu Law [1977], Vol. I, 183) states, "*Daṇḍa* [is] the symbol of dharma and the generic name for penalties of all kinds." *Daṇḍa* gave rigour to the authority of law, being perceived to be, in effect, the modus in which the law is manifested in the face of contrary conditions. The same law, accordingly, is either directive or retributive for its subjects. Hence the statements of the jurists which present *Daṇḍa* as the essence of law do not go beyond this assumption that punishment is an aspect of law or that law and punishment are opposite sides of the same coin.

Complementary with this integration of law and sanction in Indian jurisprudence is the integration of religion, morality, and law. Since Sir Henry Maine's essay on Indian Law (Ancient Law, 1861), this "inextricable admixture" has been repeatedly reprehended. But Main would have been fairer to the character of Indian law if he had admitted the comprehensiveness of the idea of law itself with which these could be harmoniously integrated without being confused. As Derrett (Essays in Classical and Modern Hindu Law [1977], Vol. II, 50ff.) says in contradiction of Maine, religious and legal matters were treated by the same Indian jurists because those matters bore upon the same or related concerns of the law, namely, the protection of the citizens, maintenance of the order of the society, and the authority of Right. So when a wrongdoer was expected both to suffer a penalization for his crime, and to perform a penance for his sin, this was because the social interest required the one, and his caste-group community required the other. But where the offender defaulted in the latter matter the social interest demanded that the king should act to compel submission and to uphold the authority of the council or *panchayat* through which the penance was administered.

Similarly, despite the strongly religious character of "trials by ordeal," their utilization in the courts did not entail a confusion of civil and religious procedures.

These instruments of inquiry were utilized only occasionally when legal proofs of innocence or guilt were not available. As instruments of inquiry, they appear to have been quite efficient and rarely were manipulated. They were also psychologically appropriate for the persons who utilized them. Nor did their ritualistic accompaniments confuse kingly and priestly functions. The priests invoked the divinized forms of Law and functioned as experts in law. Religion served Law in Indian society. It provided the metaphysical basis--the standard of Right, and the teleology--the salvation of individuals and the prosperity of the society; it assisted without delimiting the formulation, rationalization, and development of laws. While being the Mother of Indian Jurisprudence, the latter was not tied to her apron-strings; it was no more restricted by its scriptural foundations than were other Vedic "sciences" such as Indian medicine. The assumption that a true science had to be in harmony with the Vedas and not contradictory to them set the boundaries of the jurisprudential science; but the freedom for imaginative interpretation and practical adaptability of the Vedic sources is amply testified by the high prolificity of Indian regulative literature. There, the conception of Dharma embraces a double connotation with respect to morality or virtue in general and the specific obligations or duties of members of the four castes of the brāhmaṇic society. Hence, even when in post-upanishadic writings emphases were placed on one aspect of Dharma or another, Varma's remark (Studies in Hindu Political Thought and its Metaphysical Foundations, Delhi: Motilal Banarsidass, 3rd ed. [1974], 121) is warranted that "the idea that performance of one's duties is a moral task and that moral life is equal to doing one's (*varṇāśrama*) duties is always present."

E. Dharma and Penal Justice

The duty of kings to apprehend and to chastise criminals is a major topic of the science of rulership (*rājadharma*) in the relevant literature where it is frequently treated within the conspectus of *vyavahāra* in the sense of "the administration of justice" which is interpreted by all the miscellaneous regulations which define the correct administration of justice and the protection of society. Kauṭilya's treatise on Hindu polity--the Arthaśāstra--is a notable reflection of the social perspective which dominates the brāhmaṇic perception of the just administration of punishment and the definition of criminal law. The perspective is evident in the peculiar definition of "criminal law" as "the eradication of thorns" (*kaṇṭakaśodhanam*) in Manu (9.252-253) and Kauṭilya (Arthaśāstra 4.1). This epitomizes the utilitarian expediency of criminal law through the investigation of crimes, the apprehension of criminals, the use of torture to elicit confessions, the infliction of bodily mutilations, and administration of capital penalties with or without torture, or prescriptions of fines and atonements (*prāyaścitta*) as substitutes for these.

Kauṭilya's discussion of the rectification of crimes and criminals in the fourth Book of the Arthaśāstra, however, brings into focus the question of how far expediency rather than ethicality determined the Indian treatment of crimes and criminals. One could not defend a thesis of the primacy of ethics in Indian jurisprudence if in fact considerations more than ethical considerations determined its formulations. Admittedly the context of social polity (*nītiśāstra*) in which Kauṭilya set laws of crimes and punishments applies also to the whole corpus of regulations comprised in the dharmaśāstras, inasmuch as obligation or duty and the retributive consequences enunciated for violating these are shown by Kauṭilya to belong within the broad context of *arthaśāstra* as the setting in order of all matters concerning the practical life including those of religion, morality, the technics of administration, distribution of goods, war, and politics, etc. But, the dharmasmṛtis and dharmaśāstra generally regulate the behaviour of individuals while *arthaśāstra*, and more specifically *nītiśāstra*, give greater prominence to politics. Yet it cannot be accidental that this renowned political theorist placed discussion of the concepts of discipline (*dharma*) and punishment (*daṇḍa*) in the first book of the Arthaśāstra and in the fourth book dealt with the practicalities of the "eradication of thorns." If one accepts that in this methodical treatise the order of succession of topics is not haphazard, then one can be sure that his treatment of the *concepts* was primary and fundamental for his conception of social polity. Within Kauṭilya's ordering of themes and topics, his dependence upon authorities behind certain dharmasūtras and smṛtis known to him, and his subjection of polity to ethics in his prescriptions, are plainly apparent both in his opening salutation to Śukra and Bṛhaspati, the legendary promulgators of the science of politics, as well as in his habit of citing different authorities before effecting an harmonization of their directives, or by his uncritical pairing of crimes with punishments without overt consideration of extenuating or other factors relating to justice. In his opening statement, Kauṭilya (following Kāṅgle's translation in *The Kauṭilīya Arthaśāstra* [1972], 1) states:

> This single (treatise on the) Science of Politics has been prepared mostly by bringing together (the teaching of) as many treatises on the Science of Politics as have been composed by ancient teachers for the acquisition and protection of the earth.[a]

Even when, however, some originality in the Kauṭilyan contribution on one point or another is recognizeable, his writing also displays the common recognition of the ground principles of *nītiśāstra* or *arthaśāstra* and *dharmaśāstra* and the priorities of their relationships. Thus, following the ancient authorities, Kauṭilya presents in the Arthaśāstra three senses of the word *Dharma*, namely, social obligations, moral law based on truth, and civil law. The first concerns all observances and duties, whether religious, familial, moral, or social, which it is the king's

---

[a] "prithivyā lābhe pālane ca yāvantyarthaśāstrāṇi pūrvācāryaiḥ prasthāpitāni prāyaśastāni saṃhṛtyaikamidamarthaśāstraṃ kṛtam" (Arthaśāstra 1.1, Kāṅgle's edn. Part 1, 1972).

duty as the guardian of Dharma to protect and uphold. In the sense of moral law rooted in truth and guided by reason and equity,[a] Kauṭilya treats Dharma only in the matter of the king's judgement in reconciling custom (*saṃsthā*) based on tradition with the science of law (*dharmaśāstra*) and the obligation of the king to be guided by truth and justice for deciding when custom should prevail over law or the reverse.

Kauṭilya's textual sources for this form of Dharma in the Arthaśāstra (3.1.40) are mixed. He uses the term quite specifically in the sense of "civil law" as the subject of the third book (*adhikaraṇa*) which is titled "Concerning Dharma" (*dharmasthīyam*). This chapter or section deals with those civil matters such as agreements, property, deposits, ownership, purchases and sales, etc. found in the major authorities whom Kauṭilya cites freely, especially the Manusmṛti and the Yājñavalkyasmṛti. It is, moreover, in these matters that the regulations concerning the suppression of crimes are presented in the fourth section of the Arthaśāstra in the somewhat rambling manner of the Manusmṛti (9.253-293).

Hence, if in any part of his treatise, it is not explicitly Dharma, either in the sense of Justice or of Order, that Kauṭilya is apparently safeguarding, it is only in areas in which it is not the major concern of the authorities whom he cites. Where his concern is to protect the wealth of the community and perhaps his own personal fortunes also, a patently mercenary attitude is expressed as in the statement of 3.1.43 (Kāṅgle's version) that "the king who gives decisions in accordance with Dharma, evidence, settled approved custom (*saṃstayā*) and edict (*nyāyena*) would conquer the earth up to its four ends."[b]

---

[a]"tatra satye sthito dharmo . . ." (Arthaśāstra 3.1.40, Kāṅgle, 1972).

[b]"Anuśāddhi dharmeṇa vyavahāreṇa saṃsthayā, nyāyena ca caturthena caturantāṃ mahīṃ jayet" (Arthaśāstra 3.1.43, Kāṅgle, 1969).

Yet, if the public expediency warranted the development of criminal law even as national expediency warranted development of the technics of war, it cannot be argued that Kauṭilya admitted the primacy of expediency in normal circumstances as setting aside the king's responsibility both to emulate the law which he administered, and to fulfil the dharma of his regal vocation as the guardian of the society's political, moral, and religious structures. It would be a mistake accordingly to view the expediencies assumed in the Arthaśāstra as reflecting a sick society torn by criminality within and enemies without. For the Arthaśāstra is more strongly inspired by an envisionment of a perfect society. Kauṭilya here may have followed Bhāradvāja's teaching as quoted by Bhīṣma in the Rājādharma section of the Śāntiparva [Mbh.12.140.7] that the expediencies of kings and ministers in the matter of all enemies of the state--civilian or military--should not be resorted to in peaceable times but only in times of grave threat or social upheaval. The notion of *Āpaddharma* or "the Dharma of distress" propounded by Bhāradvāja and expounded by Bhīṣma, and known to Kauṭilya, softens any harsh tone in that criminal law which Kauṭilya drew upon, or which had been already mitigated by humane considerations in their implementation. In this regard, D. MacKenzie Brown's caution regarding the "machiavellian realism" of the Hindu political theory, particularly as reflected in Bhāradvāja and Bhīṣma, is applicable also to any estimation of the Kauṭilīya *Arthaśāstra* in general and of his criminal law in particular:

> Unless the modern reader fully appreciates the tenacity and the restraining power of Dharma in Indian traditional government, he may easily conclude that cynicism is the guiding tenet of the author of Śāntiparvan. But behind all the brutal expediencies there remains an ultimate accountability to the rule of Dharma (The White Umbrella, New Delhi: Jaico Publishing House [1953], 37).

Chapter 3. The Concept of Retribution

The importance of the theory of *Karma*, with its correlate doctrine of Rebirth (transmigration, *saṃsāra*, metempsychosis, *punarjanma*), is second only to the doctrine of Dharma among the fundamental conceptions, theories, and teachings of Indian religion and philosophy. Although theories of the moral consequences of human actions, and even of rebirth, are found in other cultures, the Indian formulations of these have acquired unique significance, major importance, and widespread psychological influence in India and in the vast body of early Indian literature.

The Indian theories of Karma and of metempsychosis generated a lively interest among Western scholars. Kane (History of the Dharmaśāstra [1962], Vol. V, Pt. II, 1530, note 2487a) mentions a bibliography of 1913 by E. D. Walker (Rider & Co.) on "Reincarnation" which comprised fifteen pages of references to books and articles by Western scholars on the subject. Kane also noted discussions by Arthur Berriedale Keith (JRAS 1909; 569-606), E. W. Hopkins, A. A. Macdonell, Hermann Oldenberg, and Paul Deussen,[1] as well as to essays on the subject in studies honouring Maurice Bloomfield, whom Kane found to be generally non-accepting of Indian origins of the theory in favour of either ancient Egyptian or early Greek origins. But there is little point in outlining Kane's defence of the Indian origins of the theories beyond mentioning his quotation of Acton's warning to "guard against the prestige of great names" and the substitution of scholarly conjectures for documentary evidence. The abundant literary sources on a distinctive Indian retributive theory in which is presupposed an autonomous principle or self-enacting law of moral operations independent of any divine will warrant explanation and discussion of the theory in relation to the conception of Punishment in early Indian literature.

A. Karma and Moral Causation

Although the word *karma* appears over forty times in the Ṛgveda, it is always used in the sense of "action" or "actions." These are either in the context of exploits of the gods such as the noble deeds of Viṣṇu (1.22.19) or the "ancient deeds" of Indra (1.61.13; 10.54.4) or in reference to pious acts such as hymns of praise (1.148.2) or religious works (8.36.7 and 11.96.11) whose rewards are immortality (*amṛtatva*) and the joys of heaven--"the world of those who perform good works" (*tābhir vahainam sukṛtām u lokam* 10.16.4 cf. AV 3.28.6 and 18.3.71, where the words *sukṛtām lokam*, "the happy world," also occur).

In the ritualistic brāhmaṇic literature, the word *karma* carries a ritualistic connotation which indicated, not an evolution of its meaning, but only an adaptation of its usage-content. There karmas are ritual acts which have the character of "sacred works" and are contrasted with the intellectual effort of sacred study (*vidyā*). The Śatapatha Brāhmaṇa (10.4.4.9) states that those who are to become immortal do so through knowledge (*vidyā*) and through sacred works (*karman*); accordingly (10.4.4.10) he who "knows this, or he who does this holy work, comes to life again and secures immortal life."[2]

In this context, the word *karma* carries no connotation of a "theory of moral causation." The ethical distinction between its ritualistic contexts and other contexts lies in the kind of responsibility or answerability which the word implies in different literary contexts. Whereas in the Ṛgveda it is spiritual and moral actions (*karmas*) which have the nature of "sins" as acts displeasing to the gods because they have transgressed divine ordinances and have drawn down divine sanctions, in the Brāhmaṇas it is careless, indifferent, or faulty ritual acts which comprise the "evil deeds" or "wrong-doing" (*pāpakṛtyā*). These are set in the balance against "good deeds" (*sādhukṛtyā*) "in yonder world" on the day of judgement, according to the Śatapatha Brāhmaṇa (10.6.3.1 and 11.2.7.33).

The manner in which an individual's actions determine and even fashion his future life is more fully outlined in the philosophical and theological treatises of the Upanishads. It is there that the word *karma* appears in the category of a principle or self-operating "law of moral causation" which presupposes the nature of the universe as a universal moral order.[3] In this respect the following words of the Bṛhadāraṇyaka Upaniṣad (4.4.5) as translated by Hume may be considered to be the fundamental text of the classical theory of Karma:

According as one acts, according as one conducts himself, so does he become. The doer of good becomes good. The doer of evil becomes evil. One becomes virtuous by virtuous action, bad by bad action.[a]

The theory of transmigration (*saṃsāra*) is the primary corollary of the theory of Karma. Saṃsāra provides the vehicles through which the principle of Karma effects the fruition of deeds. In general, therefore, the theory of Karma is the belief that a potency exists in actions and survives their performance. The potency is a potentiality for future experience, be it happy or sorrowful, in prosperous or in adverse circumstances. The potency is perceived in the form of merit (*dharma*) and demerit (*adharma*) and even as an attribute of matter, as *punya* and *apunya* respectively. Moreover, the actualization, in form and degree, of this potentiality of merit and demerit is ethically commensurate to moral acts. Furthermore, while this fructification of karmas may take place in the present lifetime of the doer, they are more commonly presented as fructifying in an afterlife in ethically commensurate earthly, heavenly, or hellish realms and conditions.

A more subtle application of the theory of metempsychosis is that not simply is our experience the fruition of past actions, but even the composition of our psychophysical and moral being. Even the very sensitivities of our

---

[a]"Yathākārī yathācārī tathā bhavati sādhukārī sādhurbhavati pāpakārī pāpo bhavati puṇyaḥ puṇyena karmaṇā bhavati pāpaḥ pāpena" (Bṛhad.4.4.5; Daśopanishads; Adyar Library [1936], Vol. II, 449).

sense-organs for peculiar forms of sensory experience, and our intellectual and moral propensities, are conditioned by our inherited karmas. And since we consciously feel our experiences, we are made aware of a compensative or retributive process at work within us and within our lives.

A further development of the Karma-theory is that the world which provides the environment in which our experience is received, is also karmically conditioned. The world is a kind of reservoir or collectivity of karmas. Each individual releases from that collectivity the precise experiential potentialities which correspond to the inherited karmas which are ripe for fruition in his present being and life. Thus, his world and life unfold experiences and conditions of life which ethically correspond to his karmic inheritance.

Since every moment in our human experience is an expiational one, it could be expected that in the course of time the totality of our karmic heritance would be fully compensated. The belief is that we would then die and go to "the place of no return," the *Brahmaloka*, and into the unification-state of "being-consciousness-bliss" (*sat*, *cit*, *ānanda*). But this is our ideal goal, since circumstantially we continuously create new karmas even while annihilating old ones. Hence, by a ceaseless generation of mental and physical acts we perpetuate the cycle of expiational experiences and life-conditions through many life-times.

For the majority of Hindus this theory of Karma is lavishly illustrated by the moral tales of the Epic and Pauranic literature and is doctrinally asserted in the severely uncompromising formulations of the dharmaśāstras. The twelfth chapter of the Manusmṛti is a striking example of the doctrinal mould in which the theory of Karma was framed. The statement falls readily into twelve propositions which would comprise the classical brāhmaṇic theory of moral causation in the conception of Karma.

1. The retribution of deeds is connected with actions of the mind, of speech, and of the body (verse 3).
2. Actions generate good or evil potentialities (karmas) which provide or effect the mental, physical, and

environmental conditioning of human beings (verse 4).

3. In each instance of karmic retribution, this occurs in the offending organ (vs. 8) so that physical disabilities such as lameness, for example, are diagnostic of acts committed in the previous life.
4. Physical acts (i.e. acts done by the body) cause the soul's transmigration into an inanimate earthly existence in the next life; evils of speech predetermine birdlike or bestial forms; and sins of the mind cause men to be reborn into a low caste (vs. 9).
5. Retribution of karmas always takes place in a body whose sense-organs are sufficient for the experiencing of "ripe" and fructifying karmas. Hence there are "hellish bodies" equipped with senses sufficient for the experiences peculiar to the hells (vs. 16).
6. Retribution-bodies only survive as long as their ingredient karmas are being expiated. After this, in the case of hellish bodies, for example, they disintegrate into their five constituent elements which then undergo a new fabrication in an earthly or non-earthly body necessary for the next "transitions of the individual soul (which depend) on merit and demerit" (vs. 23).
7. Earthly bodies however are different from hellish and heavenly bodies inasmuch as they contain karmic attributes which are capable of governing or directing a person's voluntary choices. This means that the nature or character of each individual is a combination of three dynamic qualities (*guṇas*), namely, purity (*sattva*), energy (*rajas*), and lethargy (*tamas*), which are psychical traits tending toward corresponding types of actions (vss. 24-29).
8. The traits accordingly are propensities toward a continuous manufacturing of new karmas and in turn perpetuating the cycle of transmigration (*saṃsāra*) into heavenly, hellish, and earthly bodies (vss. 30-41).
9. For this reason, every human condition and <u>every</u> circumstance in which men undergo experiences of pleasure or pain, and adversity or prosperity, is one wrought by his past actions. All that happens to him is the product of his former virtuous and vicious

actions, while his present willed response to these karmic conditions is producing the potentialities which will condition the nature of his personality and circumstances and fortunes in a future existence.

10. It follows, however, that no condition of finite being is eternal, since it is merely the product of contingent rather than of existent factors. Brahman is that only true or real Existent which is beyond the transitional worlds of Karma. Hence the movement toward the ultimate Existent, Brahman, is the ultimate goal or implicit telos of every process including the life-course of each soul. Hence, the individual soul undergoes the full course of its moral destiny as defined by its inherent karmas, proceeding from one state of existence to another and on "through the whole system of transmigrations" (vs. 51) until it attains the world of Brahman.

11. Karma therefore is one answer to the mystery of suffering. Suffering is not an accident, an unanticipated condition, but a circumstance of our own making. Through sensual indulgences and neglect of duties, "fools become the lowest of men" that are produced by "the vilest births" (vs. 52). On account of grave sins (*mahāpātaka*) men pass "during large numbers of years through dreadful hells"[4] before proceeding via natural births into such earthly conditions as will expiate the moral as distinct from the spiritual elements of their karmas (vss. 54ff.).

12. In the light of this moral interpretation of the conditions and fortunes of men it is possible to diagnose a man's past life by them (vss. 55-72). Theoretically, at least, what a man has been in the past can be determined by his present psychophysical and socio-economic conditions.

The above twelvefold summarization of Manu's description of the brāhmaṇic theory of Karma contains substantially the forms of the theory in Jainism and in Indian Buddhism also. All three traditions included the theory as an interpretation of the life-experiences of mankind. The theory enabled individuals in all walks of life to perceive their circumstances and experiences in moral terms as just retributions of willed acts and to relate their being and experience individually and socially to the larger order of the universe which is based on Dharma and which expresses the absolute Order designated by Ṛta.

These traditions, furthermore, admit the doctrine of "the immutability of ripe karmas," the belief that karmas which have become ripe for fruition on account of existential conditions requisite for them must effect their tale of pain and pleasure; these effects cannot be evaded. This means that each individual's life-experience is already pre-determined by the inherent potentialities of his inherited karmas. It is moreover the karmas themselves which make the conditions for their expiation; the ripening power exists mysteriously within them, or is brought to fruition through the instrumentality of God. Neither rituals nor penances can avert the karmic outworkings. The best that can be done is for one to anticipate the karmic process; one may inflict the pains due from past actions upon oneself through ritualistic, penitential, and ascetical modes of expiation.

All told, however, it is the ethical elements of actions which are causally determinative of future human life and experience. Acts are causally determinative in accordance with their good or evil nature, and their outworkings are inexorable; there is no intrusive or arbitrary factor which might overcome their potentiality for causing retributional effects, or otherwise interfering with the strictly mechanical efficiency of Karma. Since moreover, an individual's fortunes and misfortunes are solely the outcome of his past actions, he has no ground for believing that life is kindlier or harsher than is deserved. He has no cause either for praising God's benevolence nor for lamenting God's wrath.

B. Karma and God

The more prominent form in which the theory of Karma appears in the Upanishads and in dharmaśāstra literature is that of an autonomous dynamic principle or "law of moral causation" which determines the equation of deeds and consequences. The ethical proficiency of the causal mechanisms of Karma is precisely on account of its impervience to any external interferences either from impersonal forces or by personal divine beings. Yet the same literary sources in which the classical formulation of Karma as an autonomous principle of justice is dominant also propound a rich theological system which includes the belief that human fortunes are in the hands of God. In the theistic upanishads particularly, the rewards of virtue and the penalties of evil-doing are presented as coming from God without any apparent reference to statements in those sources which directly contradict the theory of divine punishments by the theory of karmic retributions.

It is not simply that upanishadic statements allow this logical inconsistency, but that they also permit and support theistically oriented rites and practices by which the otherwise inexorable processes of Karma can be avoided, evaded, or circumvented. This contrary view of retribution between the philosophical and the theistic upanishads is carried over into the dharmaśāstra-literature in general. On the one hand, a statement in the Gautama Dharmasūtra (19.5) clearly reflects the upanishadic doctrine of Karma-causation found in the Śatapatha Brāhmaṇa (5.2.2.27), the Bṛhadāraṇyaka Upaniṣad (4.4 and 6.2), and the Chāndogya Upaniṣad (3.14.1) in the statement as rendered by Kane (*History of the Dharmaśāstra* [1953], Vol. IV, 39) that: "Because the deed does not perish, whatever human action it may be, whether good or evil, it cannot be got rid of except by enjoying its consequences." From this stems the frequently reiterated doctrine that the consequences of deeds are certainly reaped, even as if the deeds themselves effected their own compensations according to the metaphor of the Āpastamba Dharmasūtra (2.1.2-7) and the Viṣṇu Dharmasūtra (20.47) as quoted by Kane that "just as a calf finds its own mother among thousands of cows, so actions done in a former life unerringly reach the perpetrator thereof."

On the other hand, upanishadic and smṛti statements

on the mitigation of the consequences of actions are tantamount to a theory of the circumvention of the operations of Karma. The available circumventions stated in Gautama Dharmasūtra (19.11) and Vasiṣṭha Dharmasūtra (20.47 and 25.3) and concisely presented in the Manusmṛti, as in 3.227, include confession, repentance, austerity, recitation of sacred texts, and giving of alms. Their efficiency is suggested by a statement of the Śatapatha Brāhmaṇa (2.5.2.20) as stemming from their power for transmuting negative powers into positive ones, and in effect of neutralizing karmas, "for when [one] confesses, the sin becomes less, since it becomes truth."

The mechanism through which such devices mitigate, transmute, or remove guilt is not as obvious and immediate as Kane's account of them suggest. Nor are they implicitly means of avoiding punishments. For most if not all of the approved acts for dealing with sins which Kane indicates through liberal textual quotations (op.cit. 41-56) have self-inflicted painful accompaniments which imply a punitive element. Like punishments, these painful connections, like divine punitive interventions, produce compensative neutralizing karmas. Where the treatment of a grave sin includes such prescriptions in addition to austerities, they can be perceived to be in effect different complexes of such neutralizing karmas.

Among these additional or alternative expedients to austerities there are *śrāddhas* which are a mode of dealing with sins which is important enough for Kane to have devoted a complete chapter to them in Volume IV of his History of the Dharmaśāstra. *Śrāddhas* are defined by the Mitākṣarā on the Yājñavalkyasmṛti (1.217) as "abandonment with faith of an article of food or some substitute thereof intended for the benefit of the departed." In effect *śrāddha* implies four things: (i) giving up something of value, (ii) the acceptance of that thing by the brāhmins as a fitting offering, (iii) its ritual transmutation through a mantric recitation into a "gratification" for the three most recent generations of male ancestors (*pitṛs*) who are respectively identified with "the superintending *pitṛ* deities, viz. Vasus, Rudras and Ādityas, and (iv) their acceptance of the gratification and rewarding of the performers with such blessings as male progeny, long life, wealth, knowledge, heaven, and final liberation (*mokṣa*).

Kane's contention against *śrāddhas* is that they are irreconciliable with the doctrines of Karma, of Rebirth (*punarjanma*), and of "the fruition of evil deeds" (*karmavipāka*). But it is noticeable that the majority of Kane's references are paurāṇic or commentarial which need not imply a later debasement of the pure doctrine of Karma so much as a different context in which the religious awareness of divine benevolence is stronger than any philosophical notions of karmic retributive autonomy. However, among the *pitṛ*-deities who are active in *śrāddhas*, Varuṇa emerges as the rewarder of food-offerings without detriment to his judicial character and role as the rewarder and punisher of deeds.

Whether or not there are qualifications of the pure Karma doctrine in ritualistic recourses for dealing with sins, the question of the autonomy of the principle of Karma apparently generated among the commentarial writers and theologians lively discussions of the capability of any impersonal metaphysical principle of functioning as an autonomous intelligent being. Any "rational principle" would be thought of as a mental object, something in the minds of men or in the mind of God. Its outworkings could also be perceived as manifestations of the will of God. That a relation exists between Karma and the will of God is a specific dimension of the Karma-theory in the theistic upanishads which medieval exegetes were compelled to explain in defence of upanishadic teaching and vindication of the wisdom of its authors.

In the earliest adumbration of the doctrine of Karma in the Chāndogya Upaniṣad (5.3-10) the path of transmigration created by one's deeds is towards the gods and on to Brahmā or downwards away from the worlds of the gods to terranean and subterranean wombs and existences. This movement of the soul is perceived as taking place within the crematory *Agnihotra* sacrifice. Although King Soma presides voicelessly over the ritual, the indications are that the gods actively witness and somehow even determine the course of the soul's journey into the after-world according to its deeds. But the "way of works" implied in the *Agnihotra* sacrifice is not the only recourse for making the soul's ascent or its descent. In the theistic upanishads the path of knowledge (*vidyā*) is also recognized as a way of dealing with karmas and rebirths in the theocentric sense of the Śvetāśvatara Upaniṣad (1.11) that "by knowing God there is a falling off of all fetters; with distresses destroyed there is a cessation of birth and death." However, whether through the way of sacrifice or the way of higher knowledge, God actively directs the outworkings of karma even in the course of leading each soul towards its destined goal.

Such an interpretation does not substitute an autonomous Karma theory by a theory of divine causation theologized as the Will of God. Rather, it reflects a skillful reconciliation of early upanishadic statements on the autonomy of Karma with other early upanishadic statements on the sovereignty of the divine Will. The interpretative skills of the theologians, notably from Rāmānuja onwards, ostensibly aimed at explaining the ancient teachings rather than evolving new ones. They did not believe that their reconciliations of seemingly contradictory statements was new in the sense of being attempted for the first time rather than an exegetical exercise engaged in by members of ancient schools of interpretation from early times.

In the Śvetāśvatara Upaniṣad (6.1), particularly, it is Brahmā who is presented as creator and lord of the universe. The universe is "this Brahmā wheel" which His power has "caused to revolve."[a] According to that upanishad, it is Brahmā who distributes finite beings throughout the world according to their karmic constituents of *sattva*, *rajas*, and *tamas* (6.2-4). He is therefore the first and

---

[a] "Svabhāvameke kavayo vadanti kālaṃ tathānye parimuhyamānāḥ; Devasyaiṣa mahimā tu loke yenedaṃ bhrāmyate brahmacakram" (Śvet. 6.1 in Swāmī Tyāgīśānanda's ed. Mylapore, Madras [1957], p. 117).

the efficient Cause of all beings (6.5). As Lord of all heavenly, earthly, and hellish rulers (6.7, 9), he is also "guardian of this world" who "constantly rules this world" (6.17). This rulership imparts to Brahmā the role of an ethical Deity, "the bringer of right" (*dharma*), the remover of evil (*pāpa*), and the lord of prosperity."[a] He is the overseer of all deeds (6.11) and the adorable Bestower of divine favours (6.13). He is the cause of the transmigrations of souls and of their liberation. He causes their continuance in bondage and their eternal release from bondage. Brahmā is that Lord who (following Hume, *Upanishads* [1931], 410, note 6), "through His own grace lets himself be known," thereby being found as the true heaven of all who seek Him in desire for liberation.[b]

This sixth adhyāya (section) of the Śvetāśvatara Upaniṣad comprises a compendium of religious teaching on Brahmā whose powers clearly include those attributable to a "Lord of Karma" in the sense of One who safeguards and guarantees its otherwise self-generating processes. But it is difficult to reconcile inferences from this Upanishad which appear to make Karma dependent upon the Will of God with those which imply its autonomy and independence of any deity. The absoluteness of Karma is logically contradicted by the absoluteness of the divine sovereignty. The absoluteness of one demands the conditionedness of the other. The autonomy of Karma even appears to be denied by a statement of the Kauṣītaki Upaniṣad (3.8) that even the

---

[a] "Sa vṛkṣakālākṛtibhiḥ paro 'nyo yasmātprapañcaḥ parivartate yaṃ; Dharmāvahaṃ pāpanudaṃ bhageśaṃ jñātvātmasthamamṛtaṃ viśvadhāma" (Śvet. 6.6, Tyāgīśānanda, Mylapore [1957], 123).

[b] Sa viśvakṛviśvavidātmayonirjñaḥ kālakāro guṇī sarvavidraḥ; Pradhānakṣetrajñapatirguṇeśaḥ saṃsāramokṣasthitibandhahetuḥ" (Śvet. 6.16, Mylapore [1957], 132).

deeds which cause the retributive processes of Karma are divinely determined:

This One, causes him whom He wishes to lead up from these worlds, to perform good actions . . . whom He wishes to lead downward, to perform bad action.

This power of God is the exercise of his right as the world-protector (*lokapāla*) and as the world sovereign (*lokādhipati*). From an ethical point of view it appears to be an outright declaration of the arbitrariness of God and his transcendence of all ethical discriminations. From that point of view Karma is meaningless or is only a symbol for the Will of God. Nimbarka (d.c.1162) appears to have accepted this view in recognizing that the absolute sovereignty of God properly and necessarily implies the dependency of Karma upon the divine Will. On the other hand, the expression of that sovereignty as providence shown through divine grace to some extent resolves the difficulty, inasmuch as God is perceived as a protector of the operations of Karma in order that its processes might purify and bring His devotees speedily to Himself. Such an interpretation, which affirms both the power of God and the power of Karma, is perceptible in the words of a thirteenth-century disciple of Rāmānuja that the loving Father "does not force His presence on the soul (which is) not yet ripe to receive Him, (but) with infinite patience He waits and watches the struggle of the soul in *Saṃsāra* since the struggle is necessary for the full unfoldment (*vikāsa*) of the faculties of the soul."[5]

Such a statement places the operations of Karma and of divine Grace in tandem. It even reconciles them by making the operations of Karma and the cycle of transmigration a divine teleological process graciously directed toward the salvation of souls.[6] A converse and yet equally feasible argument is that while God's Will is absolute it becomes finite in and through human experience. This limited expression and outworking of the divine Will is Karma and the believer in God benefits from the processes of Karma when he recognizes and accepts them as a mode of divine Grace. One cannot pursue the history of the Grace and Karma debate without going beyond the perimeters of this study, but can only indicate its importance in recognition of the probability that it was one which had already a long history in philosophical circles in India even many centuries prior to Rāmānuja's contribution to the resolution of the problem in the eleventh century. On the whole it appears that the theologians sought a theological reconciliation between the sovereignty of God and the autonomy of Karma without overcoming the logical exclusivity of two absolutes which might have betrayed the Upanishadic teaching by some kind of "qualified-Karma" theory or some kind of doctrine of "limited divine grace."[7] Rāmānuja argued for Karma as a mode of God's gracious operations. The twelfth-century Telegu brāhmin, Nimbarka, simply rejected the notion of Karmic absolutism by declaring that God is not bound by Karma since He might overrule its operations whenever He pleases. Jīva Gosvāmī argued for the self-restraint of God. Whatever God does is entirely of His free, unconditioned Will; but He expresses His Will in human individuals always in accordance with their past good and evil actions.[8] Gosvāmī's argument as rendered by S. N. Dasgupta (A History of Indian Philosophy, Cambridge: The University Press [1922-55], Vol. IV, 412) reads:

The inscrutability of God's behaviour in the fulfillment of His devotee's desires is to be found in the inscrutability of the suprarational nature of the essential power of God. Though all the works of God are absolutely independent and self-determined, yet they are somehow in accord with the good and the bad deeds of men. Even when God is pleased to punish the misdeeds of those who are inimical to His devotees, such punishment is not affected by the rousing of anger in Him, but is the natural result of his own blissful nature operating as a function of his *hlādinī* (essential power).

Contrastingly, in Śaiva Siddhānta, the Will of God which was sometimes identified with the Karma was sometimes also identified with the "law of Nature" as S. Sabāratna Mudaliya (Essentials of Hinduism in the Light of Śaiva Siddhānta [1913], 176) explains:

The Hindu Siddhānta School . . . very aptly lays down that the Great God rewards our karmas or actions. This rule of our God is so fixed and inviolable in itself that the agency is forgotten and the rule is considered the regulator of our destiny. In fact, the rule of God is what we call

Nature, and Nature is nothing but the design planned by the Great God in His sublime wisdom for the salvation of souls.

It is doubtful however if this is in effect a genuine reconciliation. The fixity and inviolability of the "Rule" of God which impart to it an autonomy as "the regulator of our destiny," whether called "Nature" or Karma, still leaves us with a dualistic relationship in which the divine Will and Karma are not reconciled even when subsumed under the notion of divine Grace. Indeed, Sabapathy Kulandran (Grace in Hinduism and Christianity, London: Lutterworth Press [1964], 257) surely has a point that Śaiva Siddhānta itself is a dualistic religion. "Siddhānta is a Bhakti religion, but is also a religion of Karma." Bhakti and Karma appear to function salvifically in their respective ways, and both are reconciled insofar as both are perceived as divinely gracious activities and operations, with Karma working within God's "general mercy" which He shows to all mankind and Bhakti working within the "special mercy" which God shows to those who love and serve Him. Karma is not the only expression of God's "general mercy." This is represented as having five manifestations, namely, creation, preservation, destruction, retribution or Karma, and concealment which is the hiding of the difficulties of human existence from souls so that they may not despair.

Such an interpretation of God's general mercy clearly preserves both the doctrine of the love of God and of the justice of God or rather of the inviolability of Karma, and spares Śaiva Siddhānta from any argument that its doctrine of divine grace implies an evasion of the principle of just retribution. Even the Śaivite hymn of Thāyumānavar which contains the following lines, which are "often taken as declaring that grace cancels Karma," are mistakenly interpreted, as S. Kulandran (Grace in Hinduism and Christianity [1964], 218) explains:

> A single stone is strong to scatter
> In hasty flight a crowd of crows.
> So all past deeds, the sum of Karma
> Cause never hurt nor harm to those
> Who for thy Grace love-thirsty longing
> Its fruition and its fulness find.

Here the poet looks forward to the day of his own salvation when, having reached the goal of self-realization, his past will be left behind forever because now his soul is completely purified of earth-binding karmas. In the meantime, he is able to accept serenely the processes of Karma as outworkings of God's "general mercy" even while tapping the infinite resources of the divine Love which God makes available to His devotees through his "special mercy." Clearly, insofar as the Śaiva Siddhānta has brought the retributive processes of Karma within the orbit of divine Grace, it has brought Hindu theology within the closest approximation to Christian soteriology and the "gospel of the Wrath of God."[9]

C. The Ethicality of Karma

Karma could not be a "just" retributional principle in the Idealist brāhmaṇic philosophy if criticisms of its ethicality were substantially true. The theory of Karma is an ethical one in the sense of accounting for the manner in which acts are justly compensated. It is also a metaphysical theory inasmuch as Karma is perceived to be a cosmic principle having a real but transcendental identity and manifested in nature and in human life as a "principle of moral causation." Karma is also a moral idea since there are karmas which are perceived to be meritorious on account of being right, proper, or good actions, and others which are demeritorious on account of being wrong or evil. Yet strong criticisms have been raised against the adequacy of the theory of Karma as a moral explanation of human experience. For although it is purported to provide a moral explanation of the totality of that experience, there are kinds of human experience, including human suffering, which are accounted for by other theories such as Fate and divine retribution.

The ethicality and logicality of the theory of Karma have been challenged on several grounds. A fundamental premise of the theory, as stated in the Mahābhārata (12.291.12) is that every man reaps the consequences of his own actions; no man bears the sins of someone else.

But this premise appears to be denied by textual statements which amount to what E. W. Hopkins (JRAS [1906], 581-593 and [1907], 665-672) called "modifications of the Karma doctrine," which imply that the retribution of an action falls, not on the doer of the act, but upon someone else. The premise appears to be contradicted also by śāstrika statements pertaining to shared guilt and collective suffering, and to vicarious suffering in the sense of suffering accepted on behalf of others as an expiation of their sins. The theory appears inadequate for an ethical explanation of suffering which is self-inflicted as a voluntary, purificatory discipline, or of suffering which arises in the performance of difficult and unpleasant duties. The theory appears unsuitable as an ethical explanation of sufferings experienced by innocent persons such as children through diseases and deformities transmitted to them by immoral acts of their parents, or sufferings inflicted on the innocent by the willed malice or greed or selfishness of others. There is a problem in the theory inasmuch as definitions of it allow that acts are retributed even though the doer has no memory of them either because he performed them in the previous life and the memory was erased by the rebirth process or because he performed them during his present life unknowingly and accidentally. The notion of "transferred karmas" according to which certain interpersonal relationships permit transfer of karmas from wrongdoers to someone else who subsequently undergoes retribution for them, violates the fundamental premise of the Karma-theory. Finally, ideas of collective identity, responsibility, and guilt which are found in śāstrika statements permit a conception of public retribution in which the totality of sins of past generations are visited upon later generations in the forms of famines, pestilences and social calamities.

On the other hand, the textual statements which present problematic qualifications of the Karma-theory occur in contexts which meet these ethical problems. Inasmuch as any suffering is a perceptible consequence of sinning, it is interpretable as a demonstration of the outworking of Karma. The doctrine that all suffering is a consequence of sins could then be stated more precisely as the doctrine that all sins cause suffering. The doctrine is then an expression of belief that the principle of Karma causally related deeds to consequences.

Further, inasmuch as the śāstrikas sometimes wrote of the society as a kind of "corporate person" they could think of the past "acts" of the society as being retributed in the form of general social calamities in the present age. By perceiving society as a joint enterprise, then the past and present members of the society could be perceived as joint-participants in the enterprise and as having mutual liabilities for its outcome.

Suffering accepted on behalf of others, particularly for the expiation of their sins, is consistent with the theory of Karma, inasmuch as the principle is affirmed that acts effect consequences, though not in the doer of the act, but in a person closely related to him. This implies however, an intimate relationship between the sinner and the expiator of his sin through the kind of "extended personality" which is thought to exist between a teacher and his disciples, a king and his subjects, a father and his sons, a husband and wife, a society and its members, and so forth.[10] What is referred to as "transferred karma" is really thought of as an inferior expiational process at work within the experience of a "corporate person." The process is also perceived in the relationships of parents with their children particularly when the children inherit the disease-consequences of immoral acts which were committed by the parents. The belief that the fathers are reborn in the sons lends another facet to the notion of extended personality in terms of which the karmic process is not really a "transfer" of karmas but the outworking in a person's present life of acts of his former life. But since, in the end, the principle of Karma is perceived to apply to the retribution of <u>deeds</u> (rather than of persons), then whether the deed was remembered by the doer or he was aware of committing a transgression is irrelevant; and it is theoretically admissible without ethical incongruity that, whether or not the doer of the act and the experiencer of its retribution are the same individual, the principle of Karma is asserted. The problem of the ethicality of Karma becomes transferred therefore to ethical problems in the notions of corporate personality, and of corporate responsibility and guilt, entertained by the śāstrikas.

PART II. ETHICAL DIMENSIONS OF PUNISHMENT

Numerous statements in early Indian literature have retributional bearings which include the supposition that all acts and actions are "responsible," "culpable," "answerable," and therefore deserving of retributions. The conception of Punishment in early Indian literature reflects a perception of self-willing beings as moral persons, and of the moral character of their actions. The numerous statements which reflect these perceptions do not admit, however, that there could be wrongful acts, that is, acts which are contrary to what is right and/or good for which the doer might not be responsible on account of infantility, senility, imbecility, or unknowing accident. We could think of acts motivated by good intentions but which "go wrong" through causes beyond our control and for which we could hardly be "held responsible." But it is not apparent that the śāstrikas thought that there could be such acts which would be altogether outside of the responsibility of the doer.

This means that Indian writers on human conduct did not think that there are any amoral acts in the sense that the doer of them could not be held to be blameable, answerable, or responsible. Instead, they made distinctions in the nature of the responsibility, that is, would a deed properly be answerable in a court of law or before some other authority and would its retribution properly rest in the king's hands or in some other authority? They also distinguished "degrees of responsibility" which could run from the lowest to the highest levels.

A judge, for example, would be totally responsible for the penalty which he prescribed for a crime; but he would be totally unresponsible for any effects of the sentence which caused harm to the criminal. Bhavadeva Bhaṭṭa is quoted in the Daṇḍaviveka (Bhattacharya trans., p. 63) as saying that "When a culprit, having been penalized with admonition, fine or any form of corporal punishment, appropriately applied to him for his specific

16th century Hindu law digest (see p. 25 above)

offence, commits suicide by tying a noose around his neck, (the king or the judge) thereby incurs no fault whatsoever, as even though punishments enrage criminals, there is no valid reason for withholding them."

The idea of "zero" responsibility appears to be addressed in the same passage to those servants who do criminal acts which are ordered upon them by their masters, in which case the full responsibility is taken by the employer and not by the servant. But where the servant is excused from any criminal liability he may not be excused from moral responsibility if he acted against his conscience or against his caste purity. The śāstrikas, in other words, appear to have entertained no notion of "amoral acts," unless one were to argue that if there were such acts they were not interested in regulating them! The idea of "degrees of responsibility" enabled them to regard all acts as responsible and to lay down criteria by which degrees of responsibility or guilt could be ascertained as the precondition for pronouncing penalties.

In addressing the question of responsibility to acts which are punishable, the śāstrikas analytically distinguished all kinds of acts which come within the broad category of "transgressions," whether these include sins against God, defilements of caste purity, violations of laws, and trespasses against that order of society or order of Nature which it is the duty of kings or the duty of the divine guardians of order to protect. The development of a sophisticated definition and analysis of all human acts was preconditional for the development of the systems of penalization by which different kinds and degrees of guilt could be compensated. It is these definitions of responsible acts, and the idea of "responsibility" itself, both of individual and of corporate responsibility, which have bearings upon the conception of Punishment, which warrant here a reasonably brief examination.

A. Imputable Actions

There are certain acts which, ethically considered, ought not to be regarded as deserving of praise or blame inasmuch as the doer is compelled under constraints for which he cannot be regarded at all responsible. The fact that the śāstrikas apparently did not recognize any acts which are totally unblameworthy is in surprising contrast to the numerous different kinds of acts which were not only deemed meritorious or demeritorious but for which the doer could be held publically answerable, and for which compensation or retribution could be administered. Many of these acts, indeed, would not be considered ethically significant outside of the brāhmaṇic tradition of the śāstrikas.

Responsible acts may be "formal" or "informal" in the sense of being regulated by the smṛtis or not regulated. They may be enjoined (*siddha*) by the śāstras, or prohibited (*nisiddha*), or they may be "indifferent" (*udāsa*) in the sense that they are not contemplated by the śāstras. Since all these kinds of acts effect merit or demerit insofar as they conform to Dharma or do not, they are ethically significant.

Acts are good or evil. That is to say, they carry positive or negative potentialities for pleasant or unpleasant experiences. Acts may also be pure, or impure, that is, free from egoistic impulses or passions (*kleśa*) or egoistically motivated. Impure acts are further distinguished as proper (*kuśala*), improper (*akuśala*), or undeveloped (*avyākṛta*) in the sense that one may do right acts for wrong motives, or do good acts but in an impulsive, uninformed, misguided, or incomplete manner. Impure acts however may be meritorious; but their rewards are in "the sphere of desires," that is, one of the heavens. Other categories formally distinguished include "fixed" (*nitya*) acts, namely regular religious ceremonies, "occasional" (*naimittika*) acts comprised of periodical ceremonies or observances, and acts of propriety (*sahaja*-karmas), that is, works innately appropriate for individuals on account of their being in harmony with their temperaments or innate nature (*svadharma*) and with their station in life. Other acts come within a general category of acts called "obligatory" or "necessary" known as *niyata* or "determinate" acts.

Acts which are contrary to these are unclearly distinguished as either or both "sins" and "crimes." W. D. P.

Hill indicated in his introduction to the Bhavagadgītā at least six different senses in early Indian literature in which an act could be called a "sin." "Sin is a defect (*doṣa*), a stain (*kalmaṣa*), a crooked thing (*vṛjina*), that causes man to fall (*pātaka*), an offence or injury (*kilbiṣa*) against the order of the world; to prefer the indulgence of the senses to the performance . . . of one's duty in the world is sin. Sin, in short, is *adharma*, defiance of that duty for which the nature of man fits him."

The long list "by way of example" of Sanskrit terms which Julius Jolly (Hindu Law and Custom, Delhi: Bharatiya Publishing House [1928 and 1975], 251) explains as belonging to "the general concept of crime, transgression" are admitted as being "mostly of a religious nature." But his list shows that nouns and adjectives like *agha*, *āgas*, *enas*, *pāpa*, *pāpman*, *aśubha*, *kalmaṣa*, *paṅka*, *mala*, *duṣṭa* have both religious and civil connotations applicable to spiritual transgressions as sins or offences against God, to ritual--faults or defects in ritual procedures, to moral offences or injuries to others, or to crimes or acts punishable by law. Frequently, however, the religious, ritual, moral, judicial, or social connotations are only ascertainable from the types of penalties or expiations which are recognized for them. The word *enas*, for example, appears to have a religious connotation in the statement of Kātyāyana (Kāty.Dhs.961; Kane's trans.) that "kings and ministers specially incur sins from the non-restraint of the vicious and infliction of punishment on the innocent."[1] The religious connotation of the word is supported by a statement of Vasiṣṭha who prescribes specific penances for acts of withholding punishments from deserving persons and for punishing innocent persons. Yājñavalkya (2.307) also indicated the religious or spiritual connotation of this word or for acts of that kind by ordaining a heavy pecuniary penance amounting to thirty times any fine which is wrongly imposed to be dedicated to Varuṇa and then distributed to brāhmins.

The word *pāpa* is not always used with the sense of "sin." Kātyāyana frequently uses it in contexts for which one would expect the word *pātaka* or its derivatives to be used and which in the Viṣṇu Dharmasūtra has the general sense of "crime." Thus in the Kātyāyanasmṛti (783) appears the statement that "no pecuniary punishment is to be inflicted on untouchables, cheats, slaves, outcastes (*mlecchas*), and persons born of the *pratiloma* form of union, when they are bent upon committing crimes (*pāpakāriṇām*), but they should be harassed physically."

The closest the Hindu jurists got to a systematic definition of crimes appears to be that of the Viṣṇudharmasūtra but which, as Julius Jolly (Hindu Law and Custom [1928 and 1975], 253) remarks, "does not claim to be exhaustive." The tabulation does at least indicate the scale of criminality recognized by the jurists in terms of social reprehensibility and with respect to the kinds and degrees of severity of punishments required for their expiation. Conversely, the degrees of reprehensibility are calculable from the size of any fines which are prescribed for them and in the light of any indications of the equivalence values of fines to corporal punishments such as are found in the Arthaśāstra.

In the Viṣṇudharmasūtra (33) the species of crimes are (i) those which are dangerous to householders; (ii) crimes effecting loss of caste, i.e. excommunication; (iii) crimes effecting degradation of caste; (iv) crimes adversely reflecting on the honour of a caste; (v) crimes which effect personal impurity or defilement of caste purity, and (vi) minor offences.[a]

These are specified in that sūtra (SBE VII, XXXIV-XLII) in the order of criminality as follows:

---

[a]"atha puruṣasya kāmakrodhalibhākhyaṃ riputrayaṃ sughoraṃ bhavati; parigrahaprasaṅgādviśeṣeṇa gṛhāśramiṇaḥ; tenāyamākrānto 'tipātakamahāpātakānupātakopapātakeṣu pravarttate; jātibhraṃśakareṣu saṅkarīkaraṇeṣvapātrīkaraṇeṣu ca; malāvaheṣu prakīrṇakeṣu ca" (Viṣṇusaṃhitā, 33.1-5, The Dharmaśāstra, Calcutta [1909], Vol. II, 596).

atipātakas, crimes of the highest degree of reprehensibility and punished by the extreme penalty. These are sexual acts with one's mother, daughter, or daughter-in-law;

mahāpātakas, high crimes requiring the costly horse-sacrifice (*aśvamedha*) followed by lifelong penitential pilgrimage. These are brāhmin-murder, drinking spiritous liquor (*surāpānam*), stealing a brāhmin's gold, sexual union with a Guru's wife; and association with perpetrators of such crimes;

anupātakas, "comparable" crimes, that is, crimes equal in reprehensibility to the *mahāpātakas*. Thus, comparable to slaying a brāhmin are: slaying of a kṣatriya, a vaiśya who performs a sacrifice; slaying of a menstruous or of a pregnant brāhmin-woman, instrumenting or causing an abortion, or slaying of one who seeks refuge. Comparable to drinking liquor are giving of false evidence and incriminating a friend; and to stealing a brāhmin's gold are misappropriation of a brāhmin's land or embezzling a brāhmin's deposit. Comparable to sexual union with a Guru's wife are any incestuous acts with a relation, or with one's social superior such as the king, a pious elder, or an ascetic, or with the relation of a friend;

upapātakas, minor offences relating to speech-manners, reverences, and discipline. These include: bad speech (bragging, accusing, denouncing, and reviling), acts of irresponsible neglect or omission of proper reverences toward parents, son, wife, or the sacred fire; improper bodily acts such as imbibing forbidden food and drink, wrongful possession of property, improper gainful employment (such as dancing), adultery in general, "unlawful presents," studying irreligious books, atheism, etc., altogether thirty-three cases being cited in this category.

jātibhraṁśakara-karma, acts causing loss of caste, particular sexual acts contrary to nature such as unions with cattle, homosexuality, and lesbianism;

saṁkarīkaraṇa, crimes degrading caste such as killing of domestic and wild animals, or the taking of life (*hiṁsā*);

apātrīkaraṇa-karma, dishonourable acts rendering one unworthy to receive alms. These include accepting presents from despicable persons, engaging in business partnerships with these, and all deceitful and degradingly servile acts;

malavaha-karma, acts causing defilements such as killing of lower animals and concocting alcoholic and other intoxicating beverages;

yadanuktam tatprakīrṇakam, "miscellaneous" non-aforementioned crimes. Jolly (*Hindu Law and Custom* [1928 and 1975], 253) is of the opinion that this category suggests that the author knew either the existence of other lists of crimes or of ancient authors who had prescribed penances for sins both of commission and omission but which had not been listed under the above categories or could not for reasons of his own, be listed in his own lists. Moreover, neither the author of the sūtra nor later redactors supplemented the lists of crimes with different categories of sinners (*sūryabhyudita*, *brahmaha*, *bhrūṇahan*, *parivitta*, *diddhiṣūpati*, *agredidhiṣū*, and others). This is probably because there already existed from earlier times a definition of crimes and punishments as evidenced by ancient texts as the *Kāthakagṛhyasūtra* (31.5), the *Atharvaveda* (6.112.3), and the *Taittirīya Brāhmaṇa* (3.8.11ff.) with its reproduction "almost literally" in the *Āpastamba Dharmasūtra* (2.12.22) by which degrees of responsibility and commensurate severities of punishment could be calculated.

Since, however, the primary source of reference for any kind and severity of punishment is that Order which the punishment is presumed to vindicate, assert, or uphold, it is this which supplies the rationality of the disconcerting and almost fantastic forms of sin and criminality which Jolly (op. cit. 253) observed in the literature. The sins and crimes which are most serious despite their interrelational incongruity are *brahmahatyā*, *strīhatyā*, *balahatyā*, *gohatyā*, and *agamyāgamana* which are respectively the slaying of brāhmins, women, children, and cows, and sexual relations which violate caste restrictions. But whether or not these and other unlawful acts are properly identified as either "sins" or "crimes" or simply as moral failings (*adharma-karma*) against which the "law of moral causation" (Karma) will become operative, is only generally ascertainable by reference to the forms of sanction which are prescribed for them. For example, the threat of a hellish incarceration, or of a sudden judgement of God, would immediately suggest a sinful act; rebirth in a lowly human or an animal earthly form would suggest a moral (karmic) act; a corporeal punishment or a fine would imply a criminal or a civil act. Given the interrelation of the three worlds of experience within the Indian cosmography, the distinctions must be treated cautiously. Nevertheless, the threat of hell attached to the king's failure to exercise responsible rulership suggests that the dharmaśāstrikas regarded this as a spiritual fault, not a civil one. Inasmuch as perjury is both an act against Justice itself and the misuse of a civil court, it is not surprising to find that both spiritual and social sanctions are attached to it. In the Mahābhārata (2 [Vanaparva], Section 209; 29-32) sinful acts, for example, as distinct from moral and social offences, cause one to be cast into hell.[2] Hence where the character of an act, whether it is a simple deed of a religious nature such as a ritual fault, or a complex act having spiritual, moral, and social dimensions, cannot be discerned by its culpability and liability for retribution, this can be discerned by the form or forms of sanction prescribed for it. But since there are few acts which are simply in one or other category, and most could be criminally, morally and religiously culpable simultaneously, they would be liable for double or triple retributions at each of the levels of culpability. In this light it cannot be said that the dharmaśāstrikas described either a "criminology" or a "penology" or a theory of sin and its consequences in their writings.[3] Nor, on account of prescribing different modes of punishment for different dimensions of any one act, can it be said that they admitted an unethical "theory of double retribution" into their prescriptions.

A word which bears a strictly criminal connotation in the literature is *sāhasa*. In its broadest sense a *sāhasa* is any act of infraction, violation, or transgression of a law of the society. One who so transgresses is a *sāhasam kārayah*, "he who commits a *sāhasa*."[4] While a *sāhasa* is simply any act for which the doer is legally liable for punishment, Manu (8.332) explicitly confines it to any act "done with force"[a] in the sense of any violent crime such as robbery as distinct from an act such as theft (*steya*) which is done without force. Or more strictly, theft, whether done openly or surreptitiously, is one kind of *sāhasa* and the several kinds of theft from simple shop-lifting through house-burglary to robbery and the more sophisticated kinds of fraud (*chala*) are all respectively different degrees of *sāhasa*.

In contrast to Manu and yet on the basis of his statement, both Nārada and Kātyāyana delimit the connotation of the word *sāhasa* to any heinous or forceful crime.[5] Nārada (14.2-6) distinguished *sāhasas* into four kinds: homicide, robbery, bodily assault, and abuse. The author of the Daṇḍaviveka, on the basis of Nārada 5.12, judged any injuries done to persons forcefully to be *sāhasas*. In this case, the word is not the Sanskrit equivalent of the English word "crime," but is limited to Nārada's four categories and their amplification into the ten violent acts (*daśāparādha*). These are classified by Nārada in 5.2 as being violation of royal commands, several kinds of homicide, robbery, sexual molestations, two kinds of "rudeness" (*pāruṣya*), namely, abuse and defamation (*vāk-pāruṣya*), illicit intercaste sexual relations, human abortions, and physical assaults causing bodily harm (*daṇḍapāruṣya*).

Following this classification, Nārada explains the relation between such *sāhasas* and forms of *steya* or theft as being the difference between physical assault and the absence of such assault. Inasmuch as a theft includes physical assault it is a *sāhasa*; on the other hand, fraud, which is a form of theft, does not entail physical assault and therefore is a simple *steya* which is a civil offence.

---

[a] "Syātsāhasaṃ tvanvayavatprasabhaṃ karma yatkṛtam; niranvayaṃ bhavetsteyaṃ hṛtvāpahlūyata ca yet" (Manu 8.332; Chowkhamba 226; 457).

In the light of this, and following the Bṛhaspati Dharmasūtra (2.5-10), a positive distinction can be made between cases involving wrongful acquisition of property and cases of violence against persons, particularly since the jurisprudents prescribed different kinds of penalties and different degrees of severity for acts in either or both categories.

Even so, in this connection, the question of whether brāhmaṇic law as relating to offences and their punishments is a law of <u>crimes</u> or a law of <u>torts</u> (wrongs) appears to break down. For, after considering Dr. Priya Nath Sen's examination[6] of Sir Henry Maine's dictum (<u>Ancient Law</u> [1861], 307) that "the penal law of ancient communities is not the law of crimes; it is the law of wrongs, or, to use the English technical word, of torts, [since] the person injured against proceeds against the wrongdoer by an ordinary civil action, and recovers compensation in the shape of money damages if he succeeds . . . ."[7] Rāmprasād Das Gupta (<u>Crime and Punishment in Ancient India</u>, Varanasi: Bharatiya Publishing House [1973], 8ff.) explains that since in many cases where fines are imposed, prescribed <u>compensations</u> are purely secondary, and often are not prescribed at all, it cannot be said that Indian law is a law of torts. The primary object of Indian law is "the punishment of offenders and the suppression of crimes." So Indian law is essentially criminal law, and the purpose of the state in becoming party to a cause is to apprehend the criminal, to bring him to justice, to detect and to punish the offender. Only in the case of injury to persons through theft or damage to property do laws of compensation appear in the jurisprudential writings. In no sense are fines indicated as being compensations to the state which was considered to have been injured by criminal aggressions. But since injuries to the state could come from a wide range of actions of which many would not, nowadays, be regarded as crimes, Indian law can only be regarded as criminal law in the widest sense of the word "crime." In this case the broader term "transgression" conveys more adequately the early Indian conception of a culpable act as being any violation of laws, approved customs and sacred traditions. It can be seen moreover, that when calculating the gravity of punishable acts, the śāstrikas frequently applied exterior rather than interior criteria. They apparently considered sleeping after sunrise as reprehensible as cow-slaughter. On this particular point, Derret (Essays in Classical and Modern Hindu Law [1976], Vol. I, 185) remarked:

> What made an act sinful, and therefore fit for an accusation tending towards penance or excommunication in default of performance of penance, was not the nature of the act when analyzed by a rational man, but the fact that the act was prohibited. Killing is sinful, not because of the killing, but because of the prohibition.

Hence in terms of the prohibitions any act could be simultaneously sinful, immoral, and criminal. Theft could lawfully be subject to penal impositions; but since it is also sinful, the judicial penalty could not totally expunge it; a moral recompense would need to be made, and a spiritual expiation would be necessary in order to effect a purification and caste-restoration. Only under certain conditions could a civil penalty count also as a penance, and thereby atone for both the civil and the spiritual dimensions of an act. This particularly refers to acts for which the penalty prescribed is capital punishment.[8]

In one instance (Manu 5.110), however, it appears that acts could be punishable even where no written prohibition was violated. These are acts which are contrary to those customs of the twice-born which are declared to be authoritative as usage (*samācāra*) and bound to be observed by others whether or not support for them can be found in any smṛti.[9] According to Manu (2.12) these practices of the "twice-born" are a limb of the fourfold source of Dharma comprised of the Veda, the sacred tradition (i.e. *smṛti*), the customs of virtuous men, and "one's own pleasure" (*priyam ātmanaḥ* = conscience?).[10]

It is likely that a precedent for this smṛti text is a statement of the Taittirīya Upaniṣad (1.11.4) in which virtuous men are defined as "brāhmins competent to judge, apt, devoted, not harsh, lovers of *dharma*" such that as "they would behave themselves in a case, so should you behave yourself in such a case."[a] But Manu (2.18) defined "the conduct of virtuous men" as being "the custom handed down in regular succession (since time immemorial) among the (four chief) castes and the mixed (races) of that country."[b] Thus even śūdras (Manu 10.126-128) "who are desirous to gain merit, and know (their) duty, commit no sin, but gain praise, if they imitate the practice of virtuous men . . . . The more a (śūdra), keeping himself free from envy, imitates the behaviour of the virtuous, the more he gains without being censured, (exaltation in) this world and the next."[c]

Such regulations are sociologically significant inasmuch as they reflect brāhmanical moves toward bringing non-Hindus within the compass of Hindu law and in effect bringing these and even non-Aryan groups into the fold of the brāhmaṇic society. Furthermore, smṛti regulations which might not have been enforceable upon socially excluded persons were now made legally binding.

B. Criminal Motive

The ascertainment of whether or not any act is a criminal act would reasonably turn upon the presence or absence of "evil design" or "criminal intent." On the other hand, "motive" in the sense of that which compels a person to act through desire, fear, or compelling circumstance could be considered less significant than "evil design" in a measurement of the guilt of an act. In Indian

---

[a]"Ye tatra brāhmaṇāḥ saṃmarsinaḥ; yukta ayuktaḥ; alūkṣā dharmakāmāḥ syuḥ; yathā te tatra varteran; tathā tatra vartethāḥ" (Taitt.1.11.4, Daśopanishads, [1935], Vol. I, p. 340).

[b]"Tasmindeśe ya ācāraḥ pāramparyakramāgataḥ varṇānāṃ sāntarālānāṃ sa sadācāra ucyate" (Manu 2.18, Chowkhamba, 226; 31).

[c]"Dharmepsavastu dharmajñāḥ satāṃ vṛtimanuṣṭhitāḥ; mantravarjyaṃ na dūṣyanti praśaṃsāṃ prāpnuvanti ca. Yathā yathā hi sadvṛttamātiṣṭhatyanasūyakaḥ; tathā tathemaṃcāsuṃ ca lokaṃ prāpnotyaninditaḥ" (Manu 10.127-128, Chowkhamba 226; 592).

literature numerous specific cases of guilt show that the presence or the absence of either evil design, criminal intent, or compelling motive were not determinative of the fact of guilt but only of the degree of guilt for which a corresponding severity of punishment would be warranted; diminished guilt and lighter penalties are warranted for acts due to insanity, bodily weakness, infancy, poverty, senility, and ill-health.[11]

Although a distinction is made between "intentional" (*kāmataḥ*) and "non-intentional" (*akāmataḥ*) acts in the matter of calculations of guilt, the śāstrikas do not appear to agree on the modes of treating deliberate and accidental offences. Yājñavalkya (Yājñ.Dhs.3.226) made penances the proper resort for treating unintentional transgressions, and penalties for intentional acts. Manu (11.46) permitted prayers or mantras (*vedābhyāsa*) for "unintentional sins" (*akāmataḥ kṛtaṃ pāpaṃ*), but ordered penances for intentional acts which are not of a criminal nature. Since, however, an act performed deliberately is presumably graver than if done unintentionally, the commentators were justified in interpreting the prescriptions of the ancient śāstrikas to mean that the heavier penalties are for intentional acts and the heaviest penalties are for intentional acts which are repeated (as in Āpast.Dhs.2.27.11ff.; and Manu 9.277).

Since intention or motive affects the degree of guilt, not the fact of it, it follows that motivational criteria would need to be considered when assessing that guilt. Since intentionality, however, can range from deliberate or fully conscious purpose through reluctant submission to compulsion, enforced submission to coercion, to the innocent willing of ignorance or stupidity and to accidental non-willing, the guilt of any criminal act could fall under one of several degrees of criminality. An act of perjury, for example, could fall, according to Manu (8.118-122), into any of eight categories insofar as its performance was extenuated either by covetousness, distraction, terror, friendship, lust, wrath, ignorance, or childishness (*ajñānāt*). Although the prescribed "amercement levels" of fines varied with the authority, the lowest for criminal perjury being set at 250 paṇas (copper pieces), the middle amercement at 500 and the highest amercement at 1000 paṇas, calculations based on the factor of extenuating circumstances in the Manusmṛti yield the following table of gravity:

Childishness (innocence, juvenility, senility, or imbecility) (*ajñānāt*)	100 *paṇas*
Ignorance (*mohāt*)	200 *paṇas*
Infatuation (temptation?) (*bāliśyāt*)	250 *paṇas*
Fear (two middle amercements, that is)	2x500 *paṇas*
Friendship (*sa-bandhavam*)[12]	4x250 *paṇas*
Covetousness (improper gain) (*anyāyena*)	1000 *paṇas*
Wrath (rage)	3x250 *paṇas*
Lust (wilful personal ends)	10x250 *paṇas*

Despite the uncertain meanings of *bāliśyāt*, *ajñānāt*, and *mohāt*,[13] the scale of fines provides degrees of criminality in an order of severity determined by motive.[14] Since any motive could be determined by a good or an evil will, it is possible for wrongs to be committed from noble and pious motives. To what extent would these mitigate the criminality of an act? Manu (8.103-4) appears to have recognized the mitigation of guilt through pious motives.

In some cases a man, though knowing (the fact to be) different, gives such (false evidence) from a pious motive, does not lose heaven; such evidence they call the speech of the gods. Whenever the death of a Śūdra, or a vaiśya, of a Kṣatriya, or of a Brāhmaṇa would be (caused) by a declaration of the truth, a falsehood may be spoken, for such (falsehood) is preferable to the truth.[a]

This special case, on the other hand, reflects only diminished guilt not the excusing of guilt entirely. For, immediately following Manu's statement (8.105) he states that "the best penance" is to be performed "in order to

---

[a]"Tadvadandharmato'rtheṣu jānannapyanyathā naraḥ; na svargāccyāvate . . . Vāgdaivatyaiśca carubhiryajeraṃste sarasvatīm; anṛtatyainasastatya kurvāṇāniṣkṛtiṃ paraṃ" (Manu 8.103-5; Chowkhamba 226; 401-2).

expiate the guilt of the falsehood." This stipulation implies a distinction between the legal, moral and religious references of any guilty act. For if it is legally and morally permissible to commit perjury "for conscience sake" where the life of a brāhmin is at stake, the permission is not without an entailment of sin which must be expiated by prescribed penances under threat of consequences befalling the perjuror through Karma or from retributing deities. In this light, the sanctions against perjury are such that it normally incurs heavy fines and/or banishment, according to Manu 8.118-124. If it is committed from a pious motive, the punishment is reduced (Manu 8.103) or dispensed with altogether in a few specified cases (Manu 8.104). Since, however, a transgression has nevertheless been committed, the perjuror must expiate this by stipulated penances. Whenever acts such as errors are committed accidentally and therefore without any evil will, since these are transgressions they must be expiated either by lighter penalties or lighter penances than those prescribed for wilful criminal acts.[15] Manu (11.44-46) illustrates this distinction in the following statement, though it must be admitted that some of his contemporaries and near-contemporaries do not support his opinion:

> A man who omits a prescribed act, or performs a blameable act, or cleaves to sensual enjoyments, must perform a penance. (All) sages prescribe a penance for a sin unintentionally committed; some declare, on evidence of revealed texts (*śruti*), (that it may be performed) even for an intentional (offence). A sin unintentionally committed is expiated by the recitation of Vedic texts, but that which (men) in their folly commit intentionally, by various (special) penances.[a]

---

[a] "Akurvanvihitaṃ karma ninditaṃ ca samācaran; prasajaṃa-ścendriyārtheṣu prāyaścittīyate naraḥ. Akāmataḥ kṛte pāpe prayaścittaṃ vidurbudhāḥ; kāmakārakṛte 'pyāhureke śrutinidarśanāt. Akāmataḥ kṛtaṃ pāpaṃ vedābhyāsena śudhyati; kāmatastu kṛtaṃ mohātprāyaścittaiḥ pṛthagvidhaiḥ" (Manu 11.44-46, Chowkhamba 226; 604-605).

The Gautama Dharmasūtra (19.7-10) also quotes vedic texts which prescribe penances for wilful offences, and the commentators adduce a Brāhmaṇa text (Āit.Br.7.28) in support of this. Unintentional or accidental sins and their expiations are treated in the dharmasūtras of Yājñavalkya (3.30) and Gautama (24.1) as well as in Manu's code (11.248ff.). The Śāntiparva section of the Mahābhārata (12.37) in Roy's translation (p. 79) also emphasizes the distinction and the necessity of expiation for both. "As regards sins . . . they are of two classes, viz., those committed consciously and those committed unconsciously. All sins that are committed consciously are grave, while those that are committed unconsciously are trivial or light. There is expiation for both."

Āpastamba (1.10.29.2-5) admits that non-culpable ignorance mitigates but does not remit the penalties of the law, since he who slays unintentionally, nevertheless reaps the consequences of his sin. An exception occurs according to Baudhāyana (1.1.2.6) citing Manu 11.90 for the murder of a brāhmin. "The sages declare that he may be purified (if he did it) unintentionally. But no expiation (*niṣkṛti*) is found for a wilful murderer."[a]

C. Moral Responsibility

"The free will problem" was a lively topic of debate between brāhmanical and Buddhist schools in India, although there is no need to record it in detail beyond the observation that, as far as ethical theory and moral conduct are concerned, theorists of all schools and sects, other than the little-known Materialist (*Cārvāka*) School, accepted a form of "qualified determinism." They understood human life to be biologically and environmentally conditioned on

[a]"Amatyā brāhmaṇaṃ hatvā duṣṭo bhavati dharmataḥ; ṛṣayo niṣkṛtiṃ tasya vadantyamatirpūvake; matipurvaṃ ghnatastasya niṣkṛtirnopalabhyate" (Baudhāyana Dharmasūtra 1.1.2.6, Chowkhamba 104 [1934], p. 108).

account of Karma but each individual to be spiritually and morally free with respect to his capability for rational judgements and moral actions whereby he is morally answerable for his decisions and actions and their moral consequences are justly warranted. The notion of individual responsibility for acts and their consequences is asserted by Manu (4.23-24) and the Mahābhārata (12.291.21) in the statement that "as a man himself sows, so he himself reaps. No man inherits the good or evil of another man." Roy translates this statement of the Mahābhārata as, "One never has to enjoy or endure the good or bad acts of another. Indeed, one enjoys and endures the fruits of only those acts which one does oneself."

Such an insistence rules out the possibility that one could justly suffer the consequences of someone else's actions. But there are notions of "corporate personality" or identity and of "shared individuality" expressed in the literature which qualify somewhat the exactness of the above statements. The idea that persons might be guilty of acts they did not commit on the ground of a real or imagined connection with the doer of an act goes strongly against the convictions of Western proponents of the idea of "individual responsibility" as being "fundamental to the whole subject of ethics." These words of H. D. Lewis (Morals and the New Theology, London: Gollanz [1947], 76 and 92-95) were asserted against all "modern forms of the primitive attitudes which regard the innocent with the guilty as uniformly responsible for so-called 'collective crimes.'" But the conviction would need to be modified if in any instance of a criminal act the "innocent party" were to stand in some kind of relationship in which a transfer of responsibility could be perceived ethically as taking place. The point is that the śāstrikas recognized a significant range of relationships in which such transference of guilt might occur, in some of which the transferee would certainly have been innocent of any moral involvement or action through which such transference could have been ethically warranted and the consequences justly deserved. An oft-mentioned relationship is between a judge and a criminal, in which any failure of the judge to prescribe a penalty which is strictly related to the offender's guilt would cause the "remainder of that guilt," presumably some unexpiated part, to transfer itself to the judge with magnified consequences arising from the judge's exalted responsibility for his juridical decisions. But there are other standing relationships between individuals recognized by the śāstrikas as being so close that in the processes of justice both are affected as if they had a single identity or dual personhood. Among these special and intimate relationships indicated in the literature are those of a guru and his disciples,[16] a husband and his wife,[17] a brāhmin guest and his host,[18] a perjuror and the one injured by his perjury,[19] a father and his eldest son,[20] and a master and his servant.[21]

That a father may be punished by law for the delinquencies of his sons is assumed in the smṛtis; but that the father may formally transmit his own guilt to his forebears is a strange motive for begetting sons in a statement of the Taittirīya Brāhmaṇa (1.9-11). For "he who in his lifetime rightly continues to spin the thread of posterity, thereby transfers his guilt to the fathers, for it (i.e. begetting) is the transference of guilt." A more intelligible interpretation of this idea is supplied by the Bṛhadāraṇyaka Upaniṣad (1.5.17) in the statement, "whatever wrong has been done by him (i.e. the father) his son frees him from it all." For as Manu (9.137-138; and Mbh.1.74.39) explains in the light of this guilt "transmission" ceremony illustrated by the Kauśītaki Upaniṣad (2.15) the very name "son" (*putra*) means "expiator" "because a son (*putra*) delivers (*trāyate*) his father from the hell called Put, therefore he is *put-tra* (deliverer from Put by the Self-Existent Svayambhuvā) himself."[a]

The ground of such a rite of transference may be the ancient belief that a father is "reborn" in his sons who thereby effect a continuance and extension of his personhood.[22] The rite therefore is in striking contrast to any

---

[a]"Putrāmno narakādyasmātrāyate pitaraṃ sutaḥ; tasmātputra iti proktaḥ svayameva svayambhuvā" (Manu 9.138, Chowkhamba 226; 513).

formal act of self-excommunication through which a father who has sinned grievously may dismember himself from his sons and from his caste in order that they may not share in the disgrace and social and religious retributions which the sin has brought upon him.[23] On the other hand, once earthly ties are formally severed by a dismemberment ritual, or naturally through death, then responsibility for any subsequent actions devolves entirely upon the doer, as explained by Āpastamba (1.10.29.1-10) in Buhler's translation (SBE II):[24]

These (sons) who live, fulfilling the rites taught (in the Veda) increase the fame and heavenly bliss of their departed ancestors. In this manner each succeeding (generation) increases (the fame and heavenly bliss) of the preceding ones . . . . (But) those among these (sons) who commit sin perish alone, (but not their ancestors), just as the leaf of a tree which has been attacked by worms falls without injuring its branch or tree). (For) the (ancestor) has no connection with the acts committed (by his descendant) in this world, nor with their results in the next.

For this reason, fathers may transfer their merits and demerits to their sons; and sons can add to the merits of their ancestors. But sons cannot transfer their sins to their ancestors or their forebears.[25] For these the sons must bear their own responsibility until they too, by becoming fathers, are able to enact the formal transference of their merits and guilts to their children. It is here that the principle arises of the transfer of retributions even to the third and fourth generations, as Manu (4.172-173) explains:

Unrighteousness practiced in this world does not at once produce its fruit . . .; but advancing slowly, it cuts off the roots of him who committed it. If (the punishment falls) not on (the offender) himself, (it falls) on his sons; if not on the sons (at least) on his grandsons. But an iniquity (once) committed, never fails to produce fruit to him who wrought it.[a]

---

[a]"Nādharmaścarito loke sadyaḥ phalati gauriva; śanairāvartamānastu karturmūlāni kṛntati. Yadi nātmani putreṣu na cetputreṣu naptṛṣu; na tveva tu kṛto 'dharmaḥ kartturbhavati niṣphalaḥ" (Manu 4.172-173, Chowkhamba 226, 219).

Here the words, "in this world" are significant with respect to the theory of Karma which implies that sins committed on this earth in a physical body can only be expiated in an earthly and physical existence. Corporate personality embracing the physical re-existence of the father in his sons meets this karmic requirement in a convenient way. The above passage, on the other hand, may be contrasted with a passage in the same chapter of the Manusmṛti (4.238) which states the necessity of spiritual retribution, that is, retribution for religious offences in the spiritual world which is in the next world. Such spiritual acts which produce spiritual retributions include egoistic austerities, false-motivated sacrifices, ill-will toward brāhmins, vain charity, and cruelty to animals. These are said to deprive a person of merit to take him "into the next world." Explains Manu (4.239-240, SBE XXV):

> . . . in the next world neither father, nor mother, nor wife, nor sons, nor relations stay to be his companions; spiritual merit alone remains (with him). Single is each being born, single it dies; single it enjoys (the reward of its) virtue; single (it suffers the punishment of its) sin. Leaving the dead body on the ground like a log of wood or a clod of earth, the relatives depart with averted faces; but spiritual merit follows the (soul).[a]

According to this statement, shared guilt and transferred responsibility are possible in this world where natural and voluntary inter-personal identifications are possible. But in the next world where only "souls" or spiritual beings abide, they suffer alone the deserts of their past spiritual actions. In the earthly sphere, moral acts are expiated; in the heavenly or hellish spheres, spiritual or religious acts. Each kind is expiated in its ethically appropriate sphere, save that in the spiritual spheres no transference is possible. In either case, however, retribution is declared to be inevitable; no one

---

[a]"Nāmutra hi sahāyārthaṃ pitā mātā ca tiṣṭhataḥ; na putradāraṃ na ĵñātirdharmastiṣṭhati kevalaḥ. Ekaḥ prajāyate jantureka eva pralīyate; eko 'nubhunkte sukṛtameka eva ca duṣkṛtam" (Manu 4.239-240; Chowkhamba 226; 238).

can escape the moral consequences of his deeds.

The ethical implications of "shared responsibility" and "guilt-transference" become more significant when the partnership in which these occur is a vocational or moral one rather than a physical or natural one. For example, Manu (4.200) says that one who pretends to be a student (*brahmacārin*) takes upon himself the collective guilt of all students. But this should not be understood as implying that in this case the guilt of those other students is removed from them. Rather, on the analogy of an infectious disease, the hoaxer acquires contagions from his false relationship to students; he enters into the totality of their demerits without reducing their continuing liability for their own demerits. He becomes a participant in or partaker of their guilt. Similarly, Manu (4.201) and others declare that one who bathes in a holy tank which does not belong to him is "tainted by a portion of the guilt of him who made the tank."[26a] In both cases, the offender effects a kind of personal identity with the owner and a participation in his guilts but not in his merits. It is accordingly, only a negative participation. Furthermore, while this intrusion in no sense diminishes the guilt of the owners, it enormously enlarges the offender's.

This kind of transference, however, is less apparent in the case of the relationship between a saintly ascetic and his enemies. The statement in the Manusmṛti 6.76-96 appears to be a ceremonial ritual of disengagement by which the *saṃnyāsin* disowns his own guilt and transfers it to his enemies in a moment immediately preceding his passage into the state of final liberation. "Making over (the merit of his own) good actions to his friends and (the guilt of) his evil deeds to his enemies, he attains, by the practice of meditation, the eternal Brahman."[b]

---

[a]". . . nipānakartuḥ snātvā tu duṣkṛtāṃśena lipyate" (Manu 4.201; Chowkhamba 226; 226).

[b]Priyeṣu sveṣu sukṛtamapriyeṣu ca duṣkṛtam; visṛjya dhyānayogena Brahmābhyeti sanātanam" (Manu 6.79, Chowkhamba 226; 311-312).

The plain sense of this statement is that the ascetic has simply rid himself of the residue of his guilt. But several considerations throw doubt upon this understanding. For example, it is difficult to imagine that the ascetic had reached the stage of entry into "the world of Brahman" as long as there remained karmas needing to be expiated. In this case, he would not have a remainder of merits to bequeath to his friends or of demerits to transfer to his enemies. Unfortunately, the statement is too ambiguous and its intention too unclear to provide certain information on early Indian notions of guilt-transference. Since neither Govinda nor Medhātithi nor other commentators shed light on this particular statement of Manu, they cannot be cited as authorities on the general theory of guilt transference from a saintly to a sinful person. The statement of Manu 6, being unlike that of Manu 4, may only be a metaphorical statement rather than part of a doctrine of guilt-transference. In Manu 6.85 the ascetic's liberation is called "shaking off sin here below;" in 6.95 as "throwing off the guilt of his acts;" and in 6.96, he "destroys guilt by his renunciation." All three statements imply the purification of the ascetic by his own actions with this added implication--that those who aid his spiritual endeavours, i.e. his friends, share in his accomplishments, while those who oppose him and resist his high endeavours participate only in evil actions which bring them demerit.

The transfer of karmas, however, is not voluntary in the case of the special relationship of a magistrate with a criminal offender; nor is it voluntary in the specific instance of connivance between parties in a law-suit and the law-administrators to thwart the processes of justice. Manu (8.18-19) says of such connivances that:

> One quarter (of the guilt of) an unjust (decision) falls on him who committed (the crime), one quarter on the (false) witness, one quarter on all the judges, one quarter on the king. But where he who is worthy of condemnation is condemned, the king is free from guilt, and the judges

are saved (from sin); the guilt falls on the perpetrator (of the crime alone).[a]

Superficially this statement suggests that where there has been a joint contrivance to thwart justice, the criminal transfers his guilt, or at least three-quarters of it, to the others. But where there is criminal evasion of justice, that too is an act of guilt which is shared between the parties to it. The criminal, however, having perhaps escaped the civil arm of the law carries his guilt with him even into his next life, where through the operations of Karma he reaps its fruitions in his own body by suffering the criminal injury which he caused to others. Similarly with respect to other joint criminal ventures, the guilt allotted to each participant is not a partitioning of the total guilt but a proportional enhancement of it on the ground that a joint criminal enterprise produces the composite of guilt which is a "gestalt" of the individual parts.[27]

Furthermore, as Āpastamba shows (2.11.21.1-2), all parties in a joint criminal enterprise are not necessarily equally committed. "He amongst these who contributes most to the accomplishment (of the act obtains) a greater share of the results." Elsewhere, those who "aid and abet" a crime are declared to be twice as guilty as if each had committed identical crimes separately.[28] If a joint criminal act requires a larger determination and planned effort showing a greater will to do evil, then the guilt of the act must be considerably enhanced and therefore be deserving of larger penalties than if undertaken by each member alone.[29]

The manner in which this enhanced guilt is calculated might be ascertained from records of past cases of joint criminal acts and the punishments given, or from hypothetical

---

[a]"Pādo 'dharmasya kartāraṃ pādaḥ sākṣiṇamṛcchati; pādaḥ sabhāsadaḥ sarvānpādo rājānamṛcchati. Rājā bhavatyanenāstu mucyante ca sabhāsadaḥ; eno gacchati kartāraṃ nindārho yatra nindyate" (Manu 8.18-19; Chowkhamba 226; 378-379).

cases in which the criteria of assessment of proportionate responsibility are indicated. It is probable that hypothetical cases were discussed in the jurisprudential schools; but at least three tangible instances of joint criminal enterprises have prescriptions legislated for them in the literature. These are homicide, theft, and assault.[30] But while sufficient illustrations of joint criminal acts are provided, no clear principles for their assessment are enunciated. They appear more as standards of reference than as case studies on juridical principles. One has to accept on authority the prescriptions provided for joint criminal actions for the leader, his aiders, and his abettors.

The penalty which is usually prescribed for murder is capital punishment. The implementation of this sentence, however, is dependent upon extenuating circumstances.[31] In the case of a joint action of homicide, different factors operate. Bṛhaspati ruled on the specific instance of several persons who violently beat a person to death, that the member of the group is to be singled out as the murderer who is found to have delivered the mortal blow. He is to be penalized as if he had committed the murder singlehanded, subject to the extenuating circumstances which are normally allowed. "The beginner and the assistant," on the other hand, are to receive half the penalty prescribed for murder[32] subject to the usual extenuating conditions.

Unfortunately, the real conditions of any real lynching-case could be extremely complicated and it may not be possible to establish which one of many blows was de facto the fatal one. Just why are the aider and the abettor provisionally regarded as only half as guilty as the deliverer of the fatal blow? One would assume that they were equally as committed both to the process of the lynching and to its intended outcome? And what of the one who planned the lynching or roused and led others to perform the act while he stood in the sidelines urging them on?

It is not evident that the śāstrikas are unaware of these distinctions, though they provide only general indications of their respective guilt and the degrees of just punishment proper for each of the participants in a joint criminal enterprise subject to any mitigating factors already indicated. Yājñavalkya and Kātyāyana in particular refined Āpastamba's directive by a careful ascertainment of the specificalities of the composite guilt devolving from any joint criminal enterprise. Moreover, Yājñavalkya, for example, prescribed twice the stipulated penalty for murder or any other rash act (*sāhasa*) which occurs within a joint criminal action, but added that should the "instigator" take out a contract upon the victim by stipulating that he would make payment of money to the one who commits the offence, then he should get four times the prescribed punishment.[33]

But one may question the yardstick of Yājñavalkya's apportionments. Just what makes simple instigation versus contracting to kill respectively twice and four times as guilty as unpremeditated homicide by a private individual? Here, too, the principles or guidelines for such determination are not explicitly given even if the cited cases provide guiding precedents. These reflect the concerns of the legislators and their commentators that in any and every case the punishment should befit the crime and should neither be more nor less than this. Behind this concern lies more than the belief that justice is in the social interest, because justice itself has a reference to divine powers who are invoked by justice to act harshly against careless and corrupt law-administrators. This belief may have led the jurisprudents into ever sharper scrupulosity as their categorizations of crimes and punishments, and their distinctions between the different parties in joint criminal enterprises, became increasingly refined. Kātyāyaṇa (832-834), for example, distinguished the commencer, the assistant, the adviser (or planner of the scheme), the person providing asylum to the culprits, the provider of food, implements or other supplies, the instigator of the scuffle (*yuddhopadeśaka*), the deviser of the method of the victim's murder, the winker or bystander who "turns a blind eye," and so forth. Vyāsa distinguished the partners or assistants (*sa-sahāyam*) from the friends and supporters of the wrongdoer (*sa-bāndhavam*).[34] Yet while Yājñavalkya apparently led the way in deciding the criteria for ascertaining proportionalities of responsibility and guilt for the respective participants of any joint criminal enterprise,[35] Bhattacharya notes that the jurisprudents generally understood the criteria as guidelines which could be followed in determining culpabilities even in the absence of positive legislation on specific joint crimes in the knowledge of the salutary effects of this determination on those criminals who are duly punished.[36]

Theoretically there is no limitation on the size of a joint criminal enterprise. Yet, if the dharmaśāstrikas did not discuss the relationship of size and responsibility, they did envisage the possibility and terrible prospects of a whole community turning to crime or rather becoming a kind of joint criminal enterprise accountable at least to the sovereign deities as a single "corporate person" expressing a single reprobate will. Recognition of this "corporate personhood" appears in frequent references to punishments which are said to fall on a whole community on account of general evils such as social corruption, civil disobedience, moral debasement, and lawlessness, which weak and corrupt kings allow to spread in the community. The idea of social "personhood" is found in early medical writings, particularly in the Caraka-saṃhitā named after the first-century exponent of the medical science called "Āyurveda." S. N. Dasgupta (A History of Indian Philosophy [1922-55], Vol. II, 409) explained Caraka's social pathology as a causal relationship of individual misdeeds, social ills, and disease epidemics.

> The misdeeds of the people can pollute the whole region and ultimately ruin it. When a country is ruined by civil strife, that also is due to the sins of the people, who are inflated with too much greed, anger, pride, and ignorance. Thus epidemics are caused by the conjoint sins of the people of a particular region.

Caraka's perception of the corporate personhood of societies is part of the cosmological understanding of his contemporaries in which individuals are perceived as microcosmic expressions or manifestations of the macrocosmic universe. But it is particularly with respect to the physical part which each individual plays in building up the karmic potentialities of the world that many of Caraka's medical prescriptions are relevant. Each individual act contributes a karmic potentiality to the natural world, even as each individual shares in the fruitions of those potentialities. On the one hand, the collective karmic potential unfolds the kind of world in which mankind as a whole receives its experience; and on the other hand, each human individual experiences that karmically conditioned world as a fruition of personally inherited karmas. But since it is the society to which he belongs which supplies the major perimeter of his experiential world, it is accordingly, the karmic collectivity of that social "world" that he faces in company with others. Hence the perceived relation between Karma, the world, the society and the individual, provides a distinctive Indian colour to Sir Walter Moberley's remark (Responsibility, London: Oxford University Press [1951], 35) that "any scheme of justice based exclusively on individual merit and demerit is wrecked on the fact of spiritual solidarity."

D. Forgiveness, Retribution, and Revenge

The penitential hymns of the Ṛgveda can be interpreted as intercessions for divine forgiveness. In this respect they have bearing upon the early Indian conception of Punishment inasmuch as divine forgiveness implies divine intervention against the just processes by which divine Law is affirmed or vindicated. Divine forgiveness also means that, instead of being morally indignant over human wrongdoing, the gods of justice behave toward the wrong-doer as though the wrongdoing did not exist or had never been done, and as though no punishment needed to be considered. Divine forgiveness in this light appears to be the opposite of divine justice. For, whereas divine justice is described in terms of "fetters" (*pāśa*) such as disease-afflictions by which the divine guardians of justice "bind" and thereby punish wrongdoers, divine forgiveness is presented as "loosening" and "removing" of the bonds and the restoration of the sinner to physical wholeness.[37]

Even the penitential hymns of the Ṛgveda portray the penitents as turning to Varuṇa for forgiveness not on account of grief over sin itself and recognition of just consequences, but with lamentation over the misfortunes which have come upon them.[38] This is also evident in the intercessions made to the Fathers (*pitṛs*) who are believed also to be able to punish and to remove the punishments of sins.[39] The invocations reflect a weak awareness of the guardian deities as ethical deities who ought to be righteously indignant over wrongs which violate their guardianship of the universal Order.[40] Instead, prayers for release from afflictions and protection from adversities suggest that the deities have arbitrary powers for "punishing" even the innocent with the guilty. The prayer of Ṛgveda 6.51.7 which reads "Let us not suffer for the sins of others, nor do the deed which you, O Vāsus, punish" suggests that the deities have a compulsion for retributing sins which is indifferent to the deserts of the innocent or of the guilty.

Such faulty indications could be present because, on the whole, the conception of forgiveness found in the Ṛgveda is weak and rudimentary compared with the strength of the Vedic conception of divine justice. Forgiveness appears hardly more than the foreshortening of punishments by the guardian deities for the sake of the intercessors. The penitents sometimes openly admit the gravity of their sins or acknowledge that their afflictions must be deserved, otherwise the deities would not have sent them. They seek the sinful cause of their afflictions in order that they might take remedial steps which will satisfy the deities as sacrificial or other compensations or atonements and thereby bring to an end the disease-bearing retributions. In other prayers, the request is made that the worshipper may be kept from falling into sin, either knowingly or unknowingly, since these would bring evil times upon him. But none of these intercessions add up to a doctrine of divine forgiveness which perceives God as removing sins and preventing their punishments. It is doubtful if the word for forgiveness (*kṣamā*) is even attributed to a Vedic deity, since the word denotes a human quality of forbearance by which the injuries inflicted wrongfully by others are borne with patience in the belief that such endurance is expiational in the sense that it destroys karmas. There is no respect in which the Vedic deities are represented as vicariously accepting and atoning for human wrongdoings.

In contrast to the self-purificatory act of forgiveness toward others, are the plain injunctions of the dharmasmṛtis that the sovereign and his agents must never pardon criminal offenders or deal less than just penalties. For, he who denies his vocation as a judge by not rewarding men in accordance with their just deserts makes himself a participant in their sins and brings their spiritual and karmic liabilities upon himself.[41] The ethical difference between a forgiving saint and a pardoning sovereign therefore is obvious. It is not the king who is injured by the crimes which his subjects commit, but the society of which he is the anointed guardian. Therefore, whenever he upholds the law upon which the social order depends, he is not yielding to vindictive or revengeful emotions, but is asserting the principle of Right or the sanctity of the social Order against persons and acts inimical to it. When he pardons criminals he puts that assertion into abeyance. This, he is not empowered to do.

Since forgiveness is not within the purview of the king's judicial office, but instrumenting Punishment is, it may be assumed that this instrumentation takes place through those functions which penologists have identified as retribution, deterrence, prevention, and reformation. Other functions have been added. D. W. Elliott (The Listener, London: British Broadcasting Corporation, January 1966) added with particular reference to "The Criminal Company"[42] certain other functions which he described as the "enforcement," "deprivative," and "legislative" functions of such punishment. Accordingly, a reason for punishing the owner (of a company) is "to make him bend his efforts to ensure that the law is complied with by those working for him." Another is that "fining a company relieves its owner of his ill-gotten gains, i.e. gains arising from the breaking of the law by the company's manager." A third reason is that "prosecution of a company is occasionally needed so that a court has a chance to make a ruling on whether the detailed provisions of the law are being observed."

But despite any present-day criticisms of the utility of punishment as a civil instrument, none of the above functions admits qualification into the commonsense perception of penalties as justicial acts which are distinct from and irreducible to actions intended for correcting or improving an individual's character, forcing compliance with the law, effecting social rehabilitation, or mitigating, compensating, or counteracting any wrongfully acquired gains. Nor can they be justified ethically as means of enforcement of judicial rulings or for enacting rulings on provisions of the law. Instead, penalties as justicial acts imply omissions or commissions which violate or transgress provisions of the law for which the offender may properly be considered to be responsible, answerable, accountable, or "guilty according to law," and therefore "deserving" of commensurate punishment.

The notion of ethical commensurality is not an assumption that the equation between a crime and the mode and degree of its punishment can be practically realized, but rather that ideal of just commensurality should be the right standard for the administration of punishments. This is reflected in numerous smṛti-statements in which the Hindu legislators embodied or affirmed the principle of "ethical commensurality" in their penal prescriptions.[43] The idea of justice is illustrated in the odd idea, for example, that a grain thief will be caused to expiate his past thefts in a future earthly existence in the bodily form of a rat, this being by nature a corn-thief.[44] The physical conditions of a rat's existence are deemed to function retributively. There are general equations of bodily conditions to moral deserts according to Manu (12.8-9):

> . . . (a man) obtains (the result of) a good or evil mental (act) in his mind, (that of) a verbal (act) in his speech, (that of) a bodily (act) in his body. In consequence of (many) sinful acts committed with his body, a man becomes (in the next birth) something inanimate; in consequence

(of sins) committed by speech, a bird or a beast; and in consequence of mental (sins he is reborn in) a low caste.[a]

This belief in "the ultimate retribution of deeds" (Manu 12.1),[b] that every act will receive its exact retribution in ethically appropriate physical, organic, and moral modes of being, guided the śāstrikas into recognizing the existence of ethically interrelated planes of being. Spiritual acts are normally retributed in spiritual bodies in one of the heavenly or hellish planes and moral acts on the earthly plane. In a Buddhist text,[45] the person who kills or sheds blood is said to be reborn in hell, but prior to this will be short-lived. Crimes of violence are said to produce bodily sickness, anger to produce physical repulsiveness, ambition to cause bodily weakness, miserliness to bring material poverty, pride and insolence to cause degraded rebirths, while disrespect for civic counsellors or state officers cause one to be reborn an imbecile in the next life.

The smṛti-writers generally held the belief in a principle of moral retribution as being operative in Nature; Nature itself follows the rule of "lex talionis," that is, of "life for life, eye for eye, tooth for tooth, hand for hand, foot for foot."[46] Śāstrikas even observed specific outworkings of the principle in individual and in public life. Manu (5.33), for example, asserted that a brāhmin who knows the law forbidding meat-eating and yet wilfully violates that law, will certainly be devoured by his animal victim in his next existence. Likewise (7.134), famine is only justice coming home to roost in that kingdom which permits learned brāhmins to pine with hunger. In each case:

---

[a]"Mānasam manasaivāyamupabhuṅkte śubhāśubham; vācā vācākṛtam karma kāryeṇaiva ca kāyikam. Śarīrajaiḥ karmadoṣairyāti sthāvaratām naraḥ; vācikaiḥ pakṣimṛgatām mānasairantyajātitām" (Manu 12.8-9; Chowkhamba 226, 661).

[b]". . . karmaṇām phalanirvṛttim . . ." (Manu 12.1; Chowkhamba 226; 659).

Where justice, wounded by injustice, approaches, and the judges do not extract the dart, there (they also) are wounded (by that dart of injustice . . .). Where Justice is destroyed by injustice, or truth by falsehood, while the judges look on, there they shall also be destroyed. "Justice being violated destroys; justice being preserved, preserves: therefore justice must not be violated, lest violated justice destroy us."[a]

The principle that justice must be vindicated is even to permit family vengeance in certain instances. As the Mahābhārata (3.11.34-5, in E. W. Hopkins, Religions, 375) states, "the unavenged shed tears which are wiped away by the avenger;" the brother of the slain victim declares therefore--"I shall satiate my brother with his murderer's blood, and thus, becoming free of debt in respect of my brother, I shall win the highest place in heaven." Almost as a comment upon this principle of family revenge, Haradatta explains the statement of Āpastamba (1.9.24.1; SBE II) as meaning that "he who is slain by anybody, becomes in dying, an enemy of his slayer (and thinks), 'O that I may slay him in another life' for the removal of this enmity!"

Although the principle of just revenge may have been allowed even for cases of accidental homicide, it appears also that the preferred prescription was the ritual slaughter of a determined number of domestic animals, in addition to monetary compensation to the bereaved family, as substitutions for the slayer's life. Manu, Yājñavalkya, and Āpastamba assessed the compensations at 1000 cows for the accidental slaying of a kṣatriya, 100 for that of vaiṣya, and 10 for a śūdra. No compensation appears to have been allowed for slaying a brāhmin, although where the slayer was a brāhmin, life-long penance or expiational suicide only were thought to suffice.[47]

[a]"Dharmo viddhastvadharmeṇa sabhām yatropatiṣṭhate; śalyam cāsya na kṛntanti viddhāstatra sabhāsadaḥ . . . . Yatra dharmo hyadharmeṇa satyam yatrānṛtena ca; hanyate prekṣamāṇānām hatāstatra sabhāsadaḥ. Dharma eva hato hanti dharmo rakṣati rakṣitaḥ; tasmāddharmo na hantavyo mā no dharmohatovadhīt" (Manu 8.12 and 14-15; Chowkhamba, 226; 377-378).

Slaying an enemy in self-defence appears also to have been treated as a form of lex talionis in the light of Āpastamba's statement (1.10.29.7) that "in a purāṇa (it has been declared) that he who slays an assailant does not sin, for (in that case) wrath meets wrath." But with respect to the legislation as a whole, it is evident that the śāstrikas felt a passion for justice which recognized no mitigative expediencies. Their insistence on justice was reiterated both positively and negatively, the latter in the form of grave warnings to judges and their counsellors of the dreadful consequences of losing sight of justice. Positively, they identified seven criteria through which the just administration of punishments could be ensured, these being: the gravity of the act; the social standing of the offender; his reputation as a citizen and person of moral character; his physical capacity for bearing corporal punishment or his economic capacity for bearing fines; the intentionality of his act, i.e. whether done deliberately or accidentally, in a rage or with calculated premeditation; the effect of the punishment upon his subsequent means of livelihood; and finally whether or not the offender confessed his guilt or tried to conceal it.

Since the śāstrikas perceived just retributions to be retributions of "acts," not inflictions on persons, they could not countenance any mitigation of the correct severity of punishment but only qualifications with regard to the forms in which that punishment might be administered. It was with respect to the forms of punishment that they were also able to admit humane considerations particularly with respect to different treatments of men and women. Yājñavalkya (2.278-9) prescribed, for example, death by drowning as a more fitting alternative for women guilty of grave crimes than the death by impalement on a stake which was prescribed for male offenders. Less obvious considerations however reflect the śāstrikas' understanding of just punishments where other than sexual distinctions are made. Kātyayana (956) considered looting the king's treasury more heinous than robbing of commoners and his prescription of penalties reflects this.[48] But branding with an iron followed by capital punishment prescribed for śūdras who adopt the insignia (*vipratvena*)[49] of a brāhmin in order to make a dishonest living is not easily justified. It suggests that the social interest did affect the calculations of the gravity of any act even though it was not the sole criterion, since it has been shown that even this offender's capacity for bearing corporal afflictions prior to capital punishment would have been considered in fixing the proper severity of the punishment.[50] In each instance of the administration of a punishment, the concern expressed by the jurisprudents was that there should be a just intention in the punishment, and that this intention should outweigh any expediencies borne of utilitarian considerations in either the social interest or in the interests of any parties. The intention that the punishment should be just is not, however, commensurate with indifference to humane considerations since, as Manu (9.262) decrees that corporal punishment of offenders has to be "according to their crimes," and fines also must be according to their means.[51] This humanity is to be found within the judges themselves who were expected to embody justice and not merely to profess it. When expressing the views of many authorities, Kauṭilya (Arthaśāstra 5) stated that when judges are inwardly just and formally scrupulous in administering justice, many benefits accrue both to themselves and to their society. The wicked are prevented from evil, the weak and the unstable are deterred, the people confidently pursue their lawful occupations, and the people, the judges, the king, and his kingdom, mutually prosper. Conversely, where greedy and partial judges sell justice for material gains, they bring evils upon themselves and distresses to their families; calamities befall the kingdom, and eventually everything perishes.

E. Form and Function in Punishment

The major attention given by the śāstrikas to legislation on punishments is because they perceived its indispensability for social control. Had there been a recognition of this functional utility in a system of rewards, they would have probably developed a system of reward-legislation also. But the śāstrikas perceived more in punishment than its purely social function since they perceived the social order or society itself as a materialization of the larger Order upon whose protection the well-being and survival of all creatures depends. For this reason, a transcendental perspective was never out of mind in their juridical legislations.

While recognizing the cosmical and societal functions of punishment, the Hindu jurisprudents also recognized practical functions of specific forms of punishments beyond the primary assertion of the law and the administration of justice. They recognized the deterrent and the preventative effects of capital punishment, and the effects of banishment, bodily dismemberments, forfeitures of property, and exactions of compensations in discouraging crimes. They perceived the usefulness of jail-terms for inducing penitence even while recognizing the reformative and rehabilitative value of penances in contrast to the social value of penalties. Yet it cannot be said that the Hindu jurisprudents used this distinction to work out utilitarian criteria in the administration of punishments. They simply admitted recognition of the reformative value of certain kinds of punishments such as public rebuke and admonition for very young or for first offenders and even for conscience-stricken brāhmins. They recognized the deterrent value of severe corporal punishments when these are publicly administered in public places and in the presence of the general public. Their recognition of the fearfulness of such public deterrence did not, however, lead them to formulate those severities in excess of the boundaries of retributive justice. On the whole, they might be said to have looked only a little beyond the principle of justice itself as the ground for punishments to humane considerations which might also be in the public interest while combining their retributive view of justice which served the interests of the society with a utilitarian view of punishment which could permit greater attention to the reformation and social rehabilitation of the offenders.

It appears instead, that the only persons who are specifically mentioned in the dharmasmṛtis as benefiting from the imposition of punishments are the king and the judges.[52] Those who are punished on the other hand "benefit" others inasmuch as they dissuade others from committing crimes on the principle enunciated by Manu (7.15) that through fear of him [i.e. *Daṇḍa*, Punishment] all created beings, both immovable and movable, conduce to the enjoyment (of others) and do not swerve from the path of rectitude.[a] But the degree and the form of a punishment may be intended in cases other than the supreme penalty to deter the offender from repeating his crime. For this reason the Daṇḍaviveka (Bhattacharya; 41) quoting Halāyudha (Kane, History of the Dharmaśāstra [1975], Vol. I, Pt. II, 633) on the matter of "first offenders" explains that:

> the punishment prescribed for specific offences (i.e. as laid down by Manu and other authorities) should not in all cases be meted out to the first offender, but this concession will only apply when it is understood that the infliction of the punishment will restrain the criminal from the further commission of the crime. Those criminals, who do not, however, desist from the repetition of the crime even after the imposition of the lenient forms of punishment are to be drastically deterred by the king, who will then devise such appropriate punishments for them as will incapacitate them to repeat the offences in future. [Emphases are added.]

The curbing of criminal propensities appears to have been emphasized to a degree which drew dangerously close to violation of the principle of justice.[53] For as the author of the Mitākṣarā--a commentary on the Yājñavalkya-smṛti--explained:

> When the curbing of the criminal propensity of a wrong-doer is not (completely) affected by the imposition of the prescribed pecuniary punishment, he should be awarded a higher punishment, while a poor person should be penalized with the imposition of a fine fit enough to put him into difficulty or to curb his arrogance.[54]

---

[a]"Tasya sarvāṇi bhūtāni sthāvarāṇi carāṇi ca; bhayādbhogāya kalpante svadharmānna calanti ca" (Manu 7.15; Chowkhamba 226; 320).

But the context indicates that it is the repeated criminality of the incorrigible offender which has to be subdued, but the judgement of incorrigibility is not to be based on mere opinion nor on unsure testimony. Although seemingly a judge would not justifiably "punish the evil character" of a recidivist criminal rather than punishing his repeated criminal acts, a pragmatic attitude toward the instrumentation of justice appears as the Mitākṣarā continues:

> If it is foreseen in the very beginning of a trial that owing to the waywardness of the criminal, the fine going to be imposed upon him will not be enought to restrain him from the further commission of the offence, he should be fined in the very beginning as much amount as is considered proper to restrain him.

The text concludes this point with the interpretative ruling that:

> If the settled view [i.e., based upon the directives of the chief jurisprudents] is that the first offender will be awarded the prescribed punishment and an older [i.e., second or repeated] offender a punishment commensurate with the requirements of his correction, then, if the first offender is unable even to pay the prescribed fine, he should be punished leniently (or he may perform physical labour as a means of earning his expiation).

But it appears that, even when relating the forms of punishment to the several functions of retribution, deterrence, prevention, and reformation, the over-all perspective of Hindu penology is retributional or expiational. The retribution of crimes and ensuring the expiation of wrongdoing for the safeguarding of the society and the correction of wrongdoers, are perceived as the primary roles of kings and judges beyond any other service they might render for the good of their societies and toward that larger Order whose guardianship they hold.

PART III. RETRIBUTION IN HUMAN EXPERIENCE

The utilitarian view that punishments can serve positive functions which are over and above their strictly retributive character did not have a large place in the thinking of the authorities on dharmaśāstra as judged by early Indian literature, either when writing about punishment per se, or prescribing forms of punishment to be administered by the judges and the king's agents. Moreover, the manifold forms of retribution which mankind experienced through divine and karmic sources could only partially be complemented by the forms of judicial penalties which the śāstrikas devised and/or regulated. Even while they recognized a scale of retributions from serried gradations of simple admonition and verbal rebuke to those of fines and corporal punishments, and approved a complementary range of penances as retributional alternatives to penalties, they did not go beyond specifying the forms to enunciating any rules concerning the forms of penalties which would meet the spiritual, moral and social requirements of retributive justice. The different forms of punishments which they prescribed and any conditions which they legislated for their instrumentation reflect their comprehension of the nature of punishment itself as a retributing principle whose manifested forms are the multivarious implements of divine, karmic, and judicial retributions.

For the purpose of identifying and analyzing the several forms, and to discuss the place which self-punishment has in Hindu penology and to its ethical character as a mode in which the offender himself affirms the principle of retributive justice, the forms of punishment are conveniently distinguished as involuntary or penal forms and voluntary or penitential forms of punishments.

Chapter 4. Spacial Conditions of Retribution

A penal system in which each criminal would be punished in the very place in which his crime was committed would hardly be feasible. But there is rationality in the idea that sins as spiritual acts against God or in violation of His laws are properly retributed in a spiritual sphere or plane of existence, while moral wrongs which have harmed fellow-beings are appropriately retributed on the earthly plane.

The notion of "appropriate spheres of punishment" appears to have been accepted by dharmaśāstrikas and used to buttress their penal prescriptions. They recognized that civil misdemeanours ought to be punished by civil instruments, and religious faults by religious procedures, not only on account of there being appropriate forms of penalty for these kinds of faults, but also on account of a belief that retributions are only fully effected where there are environmental and personal conditions which support an exact compensation.

The study of the spatial conditions envisaged by the śāstrikas as determining the effectiveness of retributions would include the extra-terrestrial spheres, namely heavens and hells, Nature itself or the natural universe as the sphere of karmic operations which includes also the human psychophysical organism itself as a place in which karmic fruitions are experienced, and the social sphere in which penalties are judicially administered for the suppression of crimes and the protection of the social order, and retributions are self-inflicted for moral purification and restoration in social communion.

A. The Twenty-one Hells

The śāstrikas declare that where sins and crimes are not expiated in this life they will be expiated in the next life, either in another earthly body, or in a hellish body. The imagery of royal punishments administered by Yama in the hells, and royal punishments inflicted in the king's prisons, is very close in Hindu jurisprudential writing. The quantity of references to internal retributions suggests that an extensive doctrine of Hell had been developed at a very early time. The Viṣṇu-dharmasūtra (43.1-45) names twenty-one hells, the kinds of torments their inmates suffer, and the kinds of sins which they are caused to expiate as they transmigrate between the hells. Although Manu (4.88-90) and Yājñavalkya (3.222-224) provide shorter lists of hells and appear to have treated the subject in lesser detail, this may be because they knew the list of the Viṣṇu-dharmasūtra and the doctrine of hell in the text for which Julius Jolly (The Institutes of Viṣṇu, SBE VII, Introduction, pp. xiiff.) argued the greatest antiquity.

Comparison of the different smṛti sources of the theory reveals some striking contrasts in their presentations on Hell. Viṣṇu says that "sinners who have not performed the penances prescribed for their crimes" are thrown into the hells. Manu makes punishment by the king (9.236) or rebirth with "disgraceful marks" (11.54) the consequences of such omissions. The Viṣṇusmṛti (43.23-32) presents sinners as transmigrating "in succession" (*paryāyeṇa*) through all the hells during a period whose length is proportionate to the gravity of their unexpiated sins. Manu presents the householder as falling into one or other of the hells according to his sin (e.g. 4.81, 165, 197) but one who deals with a king who acts contrary to the Dharmaśāstra, falls "in succession" into all twenty-one hells (4.87).[a] For good measure, Viṣṇu (43.34-44) adds a descriptive compilation of the "terrible pangs" prior to the "further pangs" (43.45) which sinners must undergo "in their migration through animal bodies." The point of the presentation, however, is explicated in the concluding exhortation (55.33): "Therefore must penance be performed by all means."[b]

Despite the early sophistication of the doctrine of Hell in the Viṣṇusmṛti and the status of this smṛti as an

---

[a] "Yo rājñaḥ pratigṛhṇāti lubdhasyocchāstravartttinaḥ; sa paryāyeṇa yātīmānnarakānekaṃviśatim" (Manu 4.87; Chowkhamba 226; 199).

[b] "Tasmāt sarvaṃ prayatnena prāyaścittaṃ samācaret" (Viṣṇusaṃhitā 45.33; Manmatha Nath Dutt, The Dharma Śāstra, Vol. II, Calcutta [1909]; 605).

early and authoritative text, there is uncertainty among Indian historians concerning how ancient the doctrine is, whether the early Āryan immigrants had such a doctrine, or whether and when they might have acquired it from non-Āryan Indian sources. A doctrine of Hell is not explicit in early Vedic literature, despite allusions to it in the Ṛgveda.[1] *Narakaloka* is mentioned in the Atharvaveda (12.4.[3].49; 9.2.[1].18) but could be translated simply as "the abode of Naraka," the mythical demon-king of Prāgjyotiśa slain by Kṛṣṇa, or mean simply "the Underworld," the abode of infernal creatures. References to conditions of the after-life in the later hymns of the Ṛgveda (e.g. 10.51.3), the Taittirīya-saṃhitā (e.g. 3.3.8), the Maitrāyaṇi-saṃhitā (e.g. 1.8.6) and the story of Bhṛgu in the Śatapatha-brāhmaṇa (11.6.1.1-13, SBE XLIV) paved the way for the enlargements of the doctrine of Hell in later dharmaśāstra-literature.

According to the legend of Bhṛgu, he is said to be Varuṇa's son who descended into Hell and received there a vision of the terrible afflictions imposed upon the wicked by Lord Yama's agents. The vision included a description of the terrible form of the King of Hell. He is black with yellow eyes. He holds a rod or staff. Two women are at his side, one fair, the other called *atikalyānī* or "beyond beauty," meaning either superlatively lovely or grossly grotesque. In the later epic and purāṇic literature, this interest in the post-mundane experiences of the wicked is more prominent. In the earlier epic and purāṇic literature, notably in Book VII of the Rāmāyaṇa and portions of the Mahābhārata, the conditions of Hell are vividly portrayed. S. Bhattacharji (The Indian Theogony [1970], 67) explains this by the opinion that the non-heroic matter in which the Hell imagery is prominent is quite late and due to Buddhist influence even though it appeared textually in the post-buddhistic period when Brāhmanism had recovered its social supremacy in India. This influence transformed Yama's benevolent personality into the sinister characters of the ruler of Hell as a place of retributive torment and suffering.

Her argument assumes, however, that brāhmaṇical

doctrines developed in an evolutionary historical framework, whereas the evidence more easily supports the observation that elemental retributional ideas which were treated in a rudimentary manner in one class of texts such as the brāhmaṇas would appropriately be treated more fully in contemporary dharmaśāstra sources especially in literature rich in mythological and descriptive data. W. Kern (Manual of Indian Buddhism, Strassbourg [1896]) is of the opinion that the personification of Yama and the depiction of his awesome personality and the representation of Hell as a place of damnation developed between 200 B.C. and A.D. 300 simultaneously with Brāhmanism, Buddhism, and Jainism.[2] Moreover, whereas in the Jaiminīya Brāhmaṇa (1.42-44 and 15.234-238) only three hells and three heavens are mentioned, in time these were increased to the twenty-one hells of the Viṣṇu Dharmasūtra. However, it was through Yama's mythical associations with the god of fire (Agni) that the epic hells of the Mahābhārata and the Purāṇas and the Jain and Buddhist texts acquired fiery territorial depictions as places of punishment.[3] References, moreover, are found to "*Yamapaṭṭikās*" or scrolls of Yama on which are inscribed the terrible torments for specific offences which are meted to the inmates of hell and which are displayed in order to incite dread and fear of punishment in sinners, to lead them to repent of their sins and to return them to the path of religion. The *paṭṭikās* can be purchased on city streets and in the villages of India today. But in the post-Buddhistic, neo-Brāhmaṇic period in which the epics and the earliest purāṇas were written, these served as powerful a purpose in gaining and holding control over the minds of the peasant masses as did the medieval Christian doctrine of hell-fire and portrayals of the Devil and his torturing angels.

E. W. Hopkins (The Religions of India [1895], 204ff.) admitted to being confused by the diverse views presented in the Indian scriptures regarding the fate of men after death. No less diverse are the modes and forms of their retribution. The Śatapatha Brāhmaṇa portrays the belief that the dead, on leaving this world, pass between two fires (*agniśikhā*) ranged on either side of his path.[4] These "scorch him who deserves to be scorched, and allow him to pass who deserves to pass" along one of two paths, the *pitṛyāna* or way of the fathers and the *devayāna* or the way of the gods (equivalent to heaven). In the Varṇaparvan section of the Mahābhārata (3.200.46 and 58), a pilgrim's path of eighty-six thousand leagues is described which passes also through the river called *Puṣpodaka*. The path and the river are rough or smooth and sweet or bitter according to the deserts of the travellers to Yama's abode. This belief is further illustrated by the Mahābhārata story of Naciketas' journey into Hell (Mbh.13.71) which follows closely the story in the Śatapatha Brāhmaṇa of Bhṛgu's descent to Hell. The opening chapter (*valli*) of the Kaṭha Upaniṣad also treats the visit of Naciketas to Yama's abode where he learns of the life hereafter. This could be a later version of a tradition which is found in the Taittirīya Brāhmaṇa (3.11.8.1-6).

The doctrine of Hell reflected in the Brāhmaṇas is in contrast to rather than in relation to their teaching on transmigration. There rebirth is perceived to be a return to earthly forms of bodily existence as a reward for a life of righteousness. It is one of three possible planes of retribution. Earthly rebirth is the reward of the righteous for it is said that they will enjoy the fruits of their acts here on earth after experiencing a new birth. Alternatively they may pass "into the next world" which is somewhere in the direction of the sun. The wicked, on the other hand, will die and pass into Hell.

The picture from the brāhmaṇas is not entirely clear, though Hopkins (The Religions of India [1895]; 207, footnote 1) attempted to unravel it by the explanation that according to the brāhmaṇas:

> . . . all are born again in the next world, where they are rewarded or punished according as they are good or bad; whereas in the Ṛgveda the good rejoice in heaven, and the bad are annihilated. This general view is to be modified, however, by such side-theories as those just mentioned, that the good (or wise) may be reborn on earth, or be united with gods, or become sunlight or stars.

But in the brāhmaṇas death rather than rebirth is presented as punitive and closely connected with Hell.[5] The Śatapatha

Brāhmaṇa (2.3.3.8) presents the idea of "repeated death" (*punarmṛtyu*). It is the punishment of those who, remaining on the dark side of the sun (which is itself regarded as a kind of death-existence), never acquire the divine status of immortality. Repeated death is, of course, equated with repeated rebirths in the world of darkness or Hell. Earthly rebirth, on the other hand, is the reward of those who know the divine mysteries.

A rudimentary theory of Karma is also present in the belief expressed in 6.2.2.27 that a man is born into the world which is made by him, that is, by former actions in a previous life. The "world" referred to, however, is not this earthly world but a supra-terrestrial sphere in which dwell the spirits of the dead. The idea that the saints take their physical bodies into the supramundane worlds is also suggested, though there is no elaboration of a supplementary doctrine of "retribution bodies."

The doctrine is not central in the Upanishads which depict the path of the afterlife more abstractly and less pictorially. Two planes of being are distinguished, namely mundane and supramundane existence analogized respectively as "darkness" and "light." The mundane world however is a triple universe of heaven, earth, and hells. The realm of light, on the other hand, is beyond all these and is *Brahmaloka*, the "world of no return," the abode of Brahman. This brāhmaṇic doctrine of Hell receives a richer formulation in the dharmasmṛti literature and the glossy pictorial presentations of the epic and paurāṇic literature. There, punishments and rewards are explicitly related to heaven, earth, and hell. Gautama, probably the earliest authority on dharmaśāstra,[6] warned that Heaven (13.7) is men's reward if they speak the truth; in the contrary case, Hell. He likened Hell (*naraka*) to a moral-spiritual state. Hell means "to be deprived after death of the rewards of meritorious deeds" (21.4-6), and even to be "deprived of the right to follow the lawful occupations of twice-born men, some call Hell." *Asiddhi*, or deprivation of success or happiness is similar to *asvargyam* or "loss of heaven."[7] Gautama (13.17) thought that Hell could be the punishment for a theft of land. Āpastamba considered

Hell to be a condition which is followed by rebirth into a debased earthly form.[8]

Offences or transgressions specifically mentioned as sending a soul to Hell are apparently religious or ritual transgressions; only secondarily are crimes mentioned as causing incarceration in Hell whenever a transgressor manages to avoid the judicial penalties. The contrast between civil and moral offences and spiritual acts or "sins" and their consequences can be seen in Vasiṣṭha's Dharmasūtra (6.1-7) where destruction is said to be the penalty of one who lives without observing good custom, but Hell (11.34) is the portion of ascetics who refuse to eat the sacrificial meat when requested to do so at a feast to the Manes. But Manu (5.35) says that the fate of the sinner who commits this offence is to suffer as many rebirths as the hairs on the body of the sacrificial animal. Another contrast with Vasiṣṭha appears in the doom which Manu (5.38) envisages for anyone who slays a beast unlawfully. Perjury, on the other hand, is both a religious and a civil transgression for which Āpastamba (2.11.29.9-10) envisaged both retribution in Hell and judicial penalties.

The religious character of the acts for which men will throw themselves into Hell is shown in the Manusmṛti and include disclosing to śūdras the secret rites and laws of the twice-born, accepting bribes for perjury or for averting the processes of justice, threatening or striking a brāhmin, refusing gifts to priests, and committal of any of the five great sins. These severally result in different severities of hellish retributions. The Mahābhārata also closely agrees with Manu in identifying acts of a religious or ritual character which cause violators to be cast into Hell and thereafter to be reborn in different degraded states and conditions of earthly existence.[9] These offences include refusing sacrificial meat, striking a priest, marrying persons of a lower caste, or committing any of the five great sins. Furthermore, since many sins have both religious and social implications, double retributions are envisaged for them. But the judicial penalties and religious penances are not always alternative modes of expiation but could be concurrent or consecutive punishments treating respectively the civil and the religious dimension of each transgression. For this reason it is said that persons who commit the five great sins live many years in the hells and afterwards obtain vile births.[10] In this case, E. W. Hopkins' (The Religions of India [1895], 261) opinion that such statements reflect a notion of "double retribution" or at least an incoherent parallelism of conflicting retributional theories, should be received with caution. He says:

> . . . throughout the whole legal literature one will find this same antithesis of views in regard to the fate of good and bad, although it is seldom that annihilation is predicted of the latter. Usually hell or rebirth are their fate--two views which no one can really reconcile. They are put side by side; exactly as in a priestly discussion in India and Europe it still remains an unsettled question as to when the soul becomes immortal.[11]

If instead it is recognized that from early times retributable acts were perceived as complex unities comprised of spiritual, moral, and social dimensions each having its proper mode of expiation in correspondingly appropriate spheres of retribution, then we have a demonstration of concurrent or consecutive retributions of different phases or dimensions of any act and not the evidence of the same act being punished twice or more times repeatedly.

The references to hells in the literature indicate no single ethical criterion by which the hell-causing character of acts can be ascertained. E. W. Hopkins (The Religions of India [1895], 336) speaks for the early Indian literature in general in the remark that, "Buddha, like the Brahmans, taught hell for the bad, and rebirth for them that were not perfected." In the Buddhist Kokāliyasūtta, where a list of hells is given with an estimation of the duration of penalties suffered in them, it is simply taught in the manner of the Hindu codes that "he who lies goes to hell," and so forth. But this is probably because the Buddhists took over the brāhmaṇic doctrine of hells, since even the names of brāhmaṇic hells are found there, "and several of those in Manu's list" also.

To what extent does the brāhmaṇic doctrine of Hell presuppose the idea of a retributing Deity? The role of

Yama as the ruler of Hell is widely depicted but his functions in the administration of hellish retributions is ambiguous. On the one hand, he appears to be little more than the general overseer of Hell who is not personally involved in or a participant in the afflictions which are meted out to the wicked inmates. Manu, on the other hand, mentions Yama in several places (12.17 and 12.21-22) as subjecting the hellish inmates to tortures. The Mahābhārata (1.74.27ff.), however, portrays these as testings by Yama according to the pattern of judicial inquiries which utilize the instruments of "trial by ordeal." Yama tests his subjects in order to ascertain the state of their consciences with respect to their degrees of innocence or guilt and in order that he may apportion their proper courses in the underworld. Otherwise, as in the Bhāgavatapurāṇa, it is Yama's "attendants of Death" who seek out the wicked and drag them off to Hell just as soon as their retributive sojourn on earth has been completed. Their function is explained in the Purāṇa by the exemplary instance of the fallen saint Ajāmila:

> Many years of his life passed in this evil way. Now he is ready to die in his sins. He will be compelled to expiate his evil deeds, and we are here to take him to the King of Death, who will punish him justly. The suffering which he undergoes will in turn purify him.[12]

The "attendants of Death" who speak in this Purāṇa remind one of "Yama's dogs" in the Ṛgveda and the Atharvaveda who likewise search out and carry into the underworld those who have reached their appointed hour of death.[13] On the other hand, the story of Ajāmila also introduces a sensitive refinement in an otherwise crude doctrine since it presents suffering in Hell as a purifying purgatorial prelude to a felicitous restoration. In a sense, the inmates of Hell purify themselves by instruments which their former acts manufactured. In the Jain doctrinal texts, the hellish agents are said to be those very victims whom the sinner formerly had wronged during his earthly life. The inmates of Hell are even both punishers and punished "as they avenge their evil actions upon each other,"[14] and even "remind by (similar) punishment (their victims) of all the sins they had committed in a former life."[15]

The purgatorial view of Hell rules out, of course, a doctrine of everlasting damnation; and on the whole such a doctrine is not found in early Indian writings. On the other hand, Madhvācārya (1199-1278) believed that his doctrine of eternal damnation was one taught by the ancient authorities. In addition to their teaching on Karma, they also taught, so he believed, that Hell is the eternal abode of beings such as *rākṣasas* and *piśācas* whose demonic natures are entirely composed of evil.[16] In addition, there are those human beings who during many lives turn themselves into totally reprobate sinners. These who become "the worst men" predestine themselves to be hurled by the Will of God into the demonic place of no return among the eternally damned.

Madhva's doctrine of divine predestination to everlasting damnation is supported on somewhat surprising grounds. For whereas Rāmānuja (died c. 1137 A.D.) had argued that the manifest differences of the psychophysical inheritance, social status, and life experience of individuals, are causal effects of Karma identifiable with "the Lord's Will," Madhva taught that the differences in men's fates arise from inherent features of individuals themselves. God does not direct their lives in accordance with the karmas; rather, each life-monad has intrinsic qualities ingrained by its constituent karmas, and these qualities determine the course of its earthly life. The Lord provides only the general conditions within which the monad's self-direction is made possible. These conditions constitute a kind of "moral occasionalism" of God through which each monad is enabled to individualize and particularize the general Will of God for the world into an individual programme commensurate with its constituent karmas. The Will of God is identifiable as a general "Karma of God." There is also, however, a "general Ignorance (*avidyā*) also allowed by God. Each monad individualizes the general Karma and Avidyā through decisions, choices and actions which determine his life-programme and its destiny. In this way, it is possible for individuals whose circumstances are individualized outworkings of the general predetermining Will of God, to work out that divine Will in a manner leading either to eternal salvation or toward eternal damnation. The wicked accordingly, predestine themselves to a perpetual recurrence of hellish and degraded earthly migrations. Each deepens and intensifies the earlier moral conditions toward the acquirement of a reprobate character which is so habitually conditioned toward evil that everlastingly repeated migrations through Hell's serried chambers becomes their self-chosen but now ultimate and irrevocable fate. Clearly, however, Madhva did not perceive such a reprobate character being easily acquired but rather being the outcome of a long self-willed retrogression toward which, presumably, very few individuals could sustainedly dedicate themselves.

B. This Earthly Purgatory

The retributive character of human conditions of earthly existence has already been indicated by references to Vedic conceptions of rewards and punishments and the upanishadic theory of Karma. Whereas in the Ṛgveda earthly conditions which foreshorten life and deprive individuals of favourable fortunes sufficiently demonstrate the principle of punishment, in the upanishads, life itself and the whole gamut of human experience acquires through the principle of Karma the character of a retributive process. Even the natural world in which the human predicament is experienced is perceived as a moral process, as though Nature itself operated through a principle of moral causation to connect deeds to consequences and bodily psycho-physical conditions to life-experiences.

Sophisticated formulations of the theory of natural retribution or moral causation are found in the theological writers from Nimbārka around the twelfth century A.D. which they believed to be derived from an ancient theory whose seeds are traceable in the earliest brāhmanas if not in the Vedas.[17] A foundation-statement in the Śatapatha Brāhmaṇa (6.2.2.27) asserts that an individual is born into whatever world he creates out of the acts of his previous existences. Here, however, the "world" referred to is a supernatural one.[18] In the Aitareya Āraṇyaka (2.1.1.5) is the statement that "sinners are born again on earth." The statement, however, does not comprise a theoretical development of the doctrine of transmigration since it arises in a context where a theory of hellish retributions is implied. The upanishadic literature reflects a conception of the universe in two distinct planes providing different conditions of experience. These "perishable" and "imperishable" worlds are respectively distinguished as "light" and "darkness"; but they are not identified as Heaven and Hell, since Hell is rarely mentioned in the upanishads. The distinction, instead is between being in reality or in unreality, the conditions of finitude having the nature of unreality and darkness, while enlightenment or transcendental knowledge is that liberated state of being in which finitude is transcended and there is eternal release from the burdensome round of transmigrations.

While earthly existence itself is represented in the upanishads as a retributive process, it is indicated that the wicked only experience it as a "living hell." This punitive connection between life-experience and moral deserts is represented in more concrete imagery in the Dharmaśāstra literature as the experience of transmigration in despicable and degraded natural bodies. Here also, the image of life itself as a purgatorial or punitive state is expressed in the earliest of the extant dharmasūtras, namely Gautama (21.4-6), in the definition that: "to be an outcast means to be deprived of the right to follow the lawful occupations of twice born men, and to be deprived after death of the rewards of meritorious deeds; some call (this condition) hell." In this connection, E. W. Hopkins (The Religions of India [1895]; 253ff.) makes the point that the word *asiddhi* in the Gautama statement has the sense of "deprivation of success or happiness" which in turn, is regularly associated in dharmaśāstra texts, as in Gautama-dharmasūtra 21.4-6 and 20, with transmigration (*saṃsāra*), or else is connected with the word for hell (*naraka*). This suggests that a reciprocal identification between earthly and hellish existence early formulation. Thus, whereas Manu (11.207) declares that one who abusively threatens a brāhmin "shall remain in hell during a hundred years," Gautama (21.20) says, "for one hundred years, lack of heaven (*asvargya*)," a phrase which could mean hell or rebirth in a degraded earthly form. The combination of both meanings is clearly made by Gautama in 11.29-30, and even more explicitly in a passage from Āpastamba (2.5.11. 10-11).

The composer of an early section of the Mahābhārata (1.90.6ff.) seems to have bridged the distance between the spheres of retribution in writing of the "hellish conditions" which arise even from earthly transmigrations, and stating that "the wicked are cast into degraded and miserable earthly conditions; that is hell." The idea that the natural world itself is either heaven or hell is part of a wider belief that our world is somehow of our own making and its members severally experience it as a world of happiness or suffering in accordance with their individual karmic inheritance. The converse of this doctrine is the belief that we self-project our hellish or heavenly experience. This idea appears even as early as the Ṛgveda in a passage (4.5.5, Griffith's trans.) which says that "those who regard not Varuṇa's commandments and the clear steadfast laws of sapient Mitra . . . who are full of sin . . . they have engendered this abysmal station" (a phrase which the commentator Sāyaṇa interprets as "the place of Hell," *naraksthāna*). More explicitly, the Śatapatha Brāhmaṇa (6.2.2.27) states that "a man is born into the world made (by him)." The idea is colourfully depicted in the description of the pilgrimage of the dead through the underworld in the Mahābhārata (3.200.46 and 58) which is found to be pleasant or painful as an effect of the earthly deeds of the pilgrims. Hell can be a psychical illusion of Hell effected by an evil imagination corrupted by past deeds or created by burning covetous desires, as the Buddhist philosopher Vasubandhu (fourth century A.D.) perceived:

> Sinners, owing to their sins, fancy that they see the infernal ministers, and the thought arises in them: "This is hell; this is the place of hell; this is the time of hell . . . this is the infernal minister . . . ." As a consequence of their bad karma, they fancy that they see and experience the various infernal tortures.[19]

There is, in other words, a sense in which "the individual becomes his own hell,"[20] or the idea of self-projected hells is simply a representation in mythical language of the view that life and experience become what we make of them and are reflections of our very being and character. By an illusionary (*māyavic*) projection, men perceive Hell as a place somewhere located in space. Furthermore, through a kind of psychical introjection, they "make fuel of themselves" in the Hell of *saṃsāra*.[21]

C. Retribution Bodies

The theory that physical bodies are provided with sense-organs atuned for the kinds of experiences which retribute former deeds is a feature of the general theory of Karma. Such "retribution-bodies" are deemed necessary inasmuch as without them neither heavenly or hellish or earthly retributive experience is possible. Manu (12.1) refers to hellish retribution-bodies in a chapter which treats of transmigration and "the ultimate retribution for deeds" (*karmaṇāṃ phalanirvṛtti*), and in a manner which suggests that the notion of retribution-bodies was already widely accepted and needed neither warrant nor explanation. The statement however explains that the retribution-body is formed from "five elements." It is "produced after death (in the case of) wicked men;" and it is "by means of that body" that they suffer the torments imposed by Yama (Manu 12.16-17).[a] Conversely, the soul of one who "chiefly practices virtue" or vice "only to a small degree" becomes "clothed with those very elements" which cause him to experience "bliss in heaven" (12.20).[b] Individual souls, however, repeatedly enter "those very five elements, each in due proportion" (12.22), and it is "these transitions of

---

[a]"pañcabhya eva mātrābhyaḥ pretya duṣkritināṃ nṛṇāṃ; śarīram yātanārthīyamanyadutpadyate dhrūvam. Tenānubhūya tāḥ yāmīḥ śarīreneha yātanāḥ; tāsveva bhūtamātrāsu pralīyante vibhāgaśaḥ" (Manu 12.16-17, Chowkhamba 226; 663).

[b]"Yadyācarati dharmaṃ sa prāyaśo 'dharmamalpaśaḥ; taireva cāvṛto bhūtaiḥ svarge sukhamupāśnute" (Manu 12.20, Chowkhamba 226; 664).

the individual soul" which "depend on merit and demerit" (12.23).[a]

The strong interest in moral retribution in the dharmaśāstra literature makes its doubtful if the theory of retribution-bodies presented in Manu is a post-Vedic development. It is true that the idea is not apparent in the Ṛgveda whose theory of the afterlife is that only the righteous attain immortality in future earthly existence whereas the wicked suffer for a time in Yama's abode or wander forlornly as earth-spirits for a time prior to their annihilation. The theory is found in the Śatapatha Brāhmaṇa and appears to reflect an assumption that souls are incapable of disembodied experience since experience is through sense-organs of physical or of supernatural bodies. The Śatapatha Brāhmaṇa (11.6.1.1-13) describes the supramundane trial which takes place immediately following death. Rewards and punishments are meted according to the individual's merits, and these are experienced in supramundane bodies whose organs of sensation are specifically attuned to the kinds of experiences which his merits and demerits warrant. But the idea that supramundane retribution requires the sense-organs and perceptions of a supernatural body suggests the parallel idea that earthly bodies are also retribution-bodies whose sense-organs are attuned to experiences corresponding with an individual's inherited karmas.[22] It is not difficult to imagine even intermediate bodily states which early writers would have recognized. S. Radhakrishnan (Indian Philosophy, London: Allen & Unwin, 2nd ed. [1929], Vol. I, 445ff.) indicates that a distinction was primarily made between gods, demons, and hellish beings among the intermediate embodiments and human beings. The former beings "are apparitional and their birth-consciousness can make for itself a new body out of unorganized matter." The birth-consciousness of human beings as well as of animals and ghosts or souls of deceased persons "presuppose

---

[a] "Yāmīstā yātanāḥ prāpya sa jīvo vītakalmaṣaḥ; tānyeva pañca bhūtāni punarapyeti bhāgaśaḥ. Etā dṛṣṭvā 'asya jīvasya gatiḥ svenaiva cetasā; dharmato 'dharmataścaiva dharme dadyātsadā manaḥ" (Manu 12.22-23; Chowkhamba 226; 664).

physical circumstances." If, however, such physical circumstances are not realizable immediately at the moment of death, then: "the dying consciousness cannot continue at once into the birth consciousness" of a new earthly being. Instead, it enters an "intermediary existence in a short-lived *gandharva* form."

This state, like that of "discarnate spirits," is abandoned at the earliest opportunity when the *gandharva* creates, "with the help of conceptual elements, the proper embryo." That embryo has qualitative potentialities which are realized as pleasant and unpleasant experiences and circumstances after its earthly embodiment.

The point of this embodiment is, however, that this experience cannot occur outside of a body whose number and kind of sense-organs decide the forms of those retributive conditions and experiences through which its tale of inherited karmas will be expiated. That no actualization of karmas is possible without the instrumentality of a body appears to be the point of the statement of the Chāndogya Upaniṣad (8.2.1):

> O Maghavan, verily, this body (*śarīra*) is mortal. It has been appropriated by Death (*mṛtyu*). (But) it is the standing-ground of that deathless, bodiless Self (*Ātman*). Verily he who is incorporate has been appropriated by pleasure and pain. Verily, there is no freedom from pleasure and pain for one while he is incorporate. Verily, while one is bodiless, pleasure and pain do not touch him.[a]

The statement clearly implies more than a theory of the body as the prison of the soul, since bodily incarceration is necessary for the experience of pleasure and pain and is not merely circumstantial to it. It is probable that the upanishadic doctrine of physical integument rationalized the

---

[a]"Maghavan, martyaṃ vā idaṁ śarīramāttaṃ mṛtyunā tadasyāmṛtasyāśarīrasyātmano 'dhiṣṭhānamātto vai saśarīraḥ priyāpriyābhyāṃ na vai saśarīrasya sataḥ priyāpriyayorapahatirasti aśarīraṃ vāva santaṃ na priyāpriye spṛśataḥ" (Chāndogya Upaniṣad 8.12.1, Daśopanishads, Vol. II [1936], 219).

extension of the theory of supramundane transmigration to embrace earthly conditions of retribution. But it may be an oversimplification to assume a developmental step between the brāhmanic doctrine of supramundane transmigration to a "triple-plane" doctrine of heavenly, hellish, and earthly embodiment. Professor Deussen (The Philosophy of the Upanishads, Edinburgh and New York, T. & T. Clark [1908], 328ff.) contrived a highly plausible theory of historic development through a masterly synthesis of relevant texts which unfortunately seems to have been too strongly influenced by an evolutionary view of brāhmaṇic intellectual development. The literary evidence shows no more than different largely contemporaneous sophistications of the doctrine in different types of literature. At the most it can only be argued that independent development occurred in some sources, and a synthesis of Vedic ideas of fate and destiny with ideas and doctrines concerning supramundane and mundane transmigrations in others. Tentative reconstructions of a developmental theory lead naturally toward the important contention of Professor Deussen that the syncretistic amalgamation of independent but related ideas and doctrines created in effect a theory of "double-retribution" by which "the entire conception of (just) recompense is destroyed." The combination of a statement of the Chāndogya Upaniṣad (5.10.5ff.) with one from the Bṛhadāraṇyaka Upaniṣad (6.2), suggests that the retribution of any act may be in either the lunar world, or in one of the hells, or on the earth after rebirth in an earthly body. But the suggestion that an act could be expiated first in a hellish and then in an earthly body, however, implies that a sinner would be punished twice for the same act. Deussen is of the opinion that while attempts were made to overcome the logical difficulties of a "two-way" and a "three-way" theory of the afterlife, no attempt was made to overcome their ethical incongruities. This means either that the difficulty was not noticed or that the problem did not exist. Śaṅkarācārya could be credited with the ethical "reconciliation" in his treatise on the Brahmasūtra 2.1.4-18 where, after recognizing the Vedic-Upanishadic synthesis, he distinguished between ritual offences which are acts of a religious character and are retributed in the afterworld and moral acts whose retributions make requisite an earthly transmigration.[23] But it does not appear that Śaṅkara was consciously trying to resolve an ethical problem so much as distinguishing the respective spheres in which spiritual or religious acts and moral acts are appropriately expiated. The retribution of ritual transgressions in the afterworld is recognized in the brāhmaṇas, as Deussen (The Philosophy of the Upanishads [1908], 324) admits. For:

> . . . the chief aim of the Brāhmaṇas is to prescribe acts of ritual, and to offer for their accomplishment a manifold reward, and at the same time sufferings and punishment for their omission. While they defer rewards as well as punishments partly to the other world . . . the idea of recompense is formulated, involving the necessity of setting before the departed different degrees of compensation in the other world proportionate to their knowledge and actions.

Deussen's references to the "other world" and his admission that acts may be partly expiated in the other world and partly in this world suggests the problem of "double retribution" is his own rather than of the ancient authorities, since Professor F. Max Müller purports to be following the authoritative interpretation of the Chāndogya text (5.10.8; SBE I, 83) in his note that "besides the good sacrificial works, the fruits of which are consumed in the moon, there are other works which have to be enjoyed or expiated, as the case may be, in a new [earthly] existence."

The problem of the just retribution of acts is the problem of the spheres as well as the forms in which that retribution would be justly appropriate. Hence what seems to E. W. Hopkins (The Religions of India [1895], 380ff.) to be an early attempt in the Mahābhārata to arrange incongruous beliefs about rebirth and Hell on a sort of sliding-scale is rather a recognition of where and how any act might be properly retributed such that:

> . . . one that does good gets in the next life a good birth; one that does ill gets an ill birth . . . . By good acts one attains to the state of the gods; by 'mixed' acts, to the state of a man; by acts due to confusion of mind, to the state of animals and plants; by sinful acts one goes to hell.

It would follow that if acts are perceived to be composite unities, their total retribution would not be fulfilled solely in a hellish or in an earthly body. Whatever the place of retribution, a residue of merit or demerit would require a subsequent place and set of expiational conditions. It is on account of such a "remainder" that an appearance of "double retribution" arises. But as Āpastamba (2.1.2.3) explains in a context which does not suggest that he is presenting a new idea, it is "by virtue of a remainder of merit" that a righteous man, having enjoyed heavenly experiences, returns to earthly conditions for the experiencing of the "remainder." Conversely the wicked experience different phases of the expiation of their deeds, as Āpastamba (2.1.2.6-7) further explains:

> . . . after having undergone a long punishment in the next world, a person who has stolen (the gold of a brāhmin) or has killed a (brāhmin) is born again, in case he was a brāhmin as a *caṇḍāla* (low born, outcaste), in case he was a *kṣatriya* as a *paulkaśa* (that is, of a mixed-caste pedigree), in case he was a *vaiśya* as *vaina* (rope-dancer or equilibrist?). In the same manner other (sinners) who have become outcast in consequence of their sinful actions are born again, on account of (these) sins, losing their caste, in the wombs (of various animals).

Given the belief that no act is likely to be totally expiable in any one plane of experience, there is no ethical incongruity in Āpastamba's assertion (2.11.29.8-9) that "if (the court witness) is found to be speaking an untruth, the king shall punish him. Besides, in that case, after death, hell (will be his punishment)." This would only mean that any judicial penalty would not be ethically sufficient to expiate the moral and the spiritual dimensions of his act of perjury. For these penances would be required under threat of future retribution in Hell.

D. Society and Community

The recognition by the dharmaśāstrikas of the social sphere as the plane of <u>penal</u> sanctions does not contradict their recognition of society as being also a plane of <u>karmic</u> retributions. As explained already, the theory of Karma included not only the assumption that an individual's personal experiences are predetermined and conditioned by his past acts but that his physical being and his social status are also karmically conditioned. The manifest social inequalities and the fluctuating fortunes of individuals and communities could lend rational and experiential support to the belief that the social order itself is a retributive one through which the members experience severally and corporately the fruitions of acts of past generations.

Not only karmas, however, but even public acts by rulers could generate for individuals a socially retributional environment. The disgraceful branding with the *yoni*-symbol of an adulterous brāhmin, for example, was not only prescribed as a judicial penalty but also was perceived as a public defilement of the brāhmin's caste purity or a declaration of its defacement whereby he had effected his own spiritual "banishment" prior to any civil banishment or formal excommunication.[24] Removal of the offender from the society and his community would deprive him both of the means of expressing and preserving his brāhmanic identity and his soul's security. The banishment could be seen as a propulsion into Hell where demonic beings would lay upon him sicknesses and other afflictions from which he might not survive. The deterrent effect of the contemplation of such spiritual and physical terrors of banishment might have caused some brāhmins to prefer the penitential expedients of self-immolation or other violent self-destruction to the world of "outer darkness."

Yet in a much wider sense than the impressions and experiences received by individuals through banishment and excommunication was society perceived to be a retributional environment. Plagues, drought, famines, earthquakes, and other natural disasters, communalistic violence, crime-waves, civil strifes, economic disasters, and foreign invasions were all perceived as public outworkings of the karmas of the society generated by the deeds or misdeeds of past generations. The thought that social conduct could be detrimental to future members of the society is implicit in Manu's strong warnings (8.22) of the miseries and ills which certainly erupt in the future of any society which loses its moral and religious standards, or which allows brāhmins to fall negligent of their daily duties, or kings to abandon their public responsibilities for the prevention of crimes and the suppression of criminals. The plight of such an "unjust society" is that of a world in which the "law of the fishes" operates as Kauṭilya (Arthaśāstra 4.9) explains, the strong swallow up the weak and bring about the destruction of everything.

Imprisonment may have been perceived as an alternative to banishment for some brāhmins. Like banishment, imprisonment removed an individual from the society and, by depriving him of his religious as well as civil liberties, exposed him to the baneful outworkings of neglected caste rituals and other obligations. Yet like banishment for which no term-amercements are prescribed, no list of prison-terms appear to have been devised by the dharmaśāstrikas. This suggests that they did not think of imprisonment itself as "a punishment" or "form of retribution" but only as a place in which certain forms of punishment could be conveniently or properly administered. Thus when the Manusmṛti (8.310) states, "Let him (i.e. the king) carefully restrain the wicked by three methods--by imprisonments, by putting in fetters, and by various (kinds) of corporal punishments,"[a] it is not clear whether there are three punishments or one, corporal punishment (*vadha*) being the penalty, and the prison and the fetters facilitating administration of the corporal punishments. In this matter the Daṇḍaviveka[25] explains Bṛhaspati's fourfold definition of Punishment--admonition, reproof, fines, and corporal punishments--as entailing three kinds of corporal punishment, viz., torture, mutilation of limbs, and the death-sentence.[26] Torture subsequently consists of four kinds--beating or whipping, restraint, putting in fetters, and harassment. "Restraint" he defines as "curbing a man's activities by imprisonment and so forth." "Putting in fetters" is explained as intended for the purpose of "obstructing the

---

[a]"Adhārmikaṃ tribhirnyāyairnnigṛhṇīyātprayatnataḥ; nirodhanena bandhena vividhena badena ca" (Manu 8.310, Chowkhamba 226 [1953]).

operation of his free will." Harassment "may be effected in many ways." The Daṇḍaviveka adds such penalties as the shaving of the culprit's head, mounting him on an ass, imprinting on his body, or branding it with, the name of, or a symbol for, his crime, and causing him to publish his crime as he proceeds from town to town beating a drum and confessing his offence aloud, and so on.

From Bṛhaspati's explanation as followed by the Daṇḍaviveka, imprisonment appears to be a particular form of punishment. But a statement of Kātyāyana (967) according to Bhattacharya (Daṇḍaviveka, pp. 53-54) suggests a different function for imprisonment. For he decrees that "a brāhmaṇa culprit, worthy of the death-sentence or of having his limbs mutilated should be placed in solitary confinement, where being imprisoned (*nirodhanena*), he will not be able to perform his (religious) duties." In the same context (968ff.), he specifically cites criminal dismemberment of a person as the reason for confining a brāhmin where he would "be restrained from the performance of his daily avocation (i.e. religious duties) by imprisonment." On this the Daṇḍaviveka (pp. 53-4) clarifies Kātyāyana's statement as referring particularly to *vipra* brāhmins, that is, brāhmins "bent upon practising religious duties," and who therefore are not refractory, recalcitrant, or reprobate. "The proper punishment for a pious brāhmin consists however, in restraining him from the proper performance of his religious acts." Presumably, if this restraint could be effected appropriately without recourse to his imprisonment, the punishment would materialize in the baneful consequences of his failure to perform religious duties.

Kātyāyana (479) also ruled that impoverished brāhmins who could not pay the fines imposed upon them (for example, for theft), "should be compelled to perform the king's menial services, and those (physically) unable to do so, should be put in prison." Here too the Daṇḍaviveka qualifies as well as elucidates the regulation by explaining that in such cases of inability of a brāhmin offender, if he be possessed of a good conduct and Vedic studies [emphasis added], he should be bound up with fetters or with ropes in solitary confinement and be compelled to undergo expiatory rites "for this purpose of his correction," failing which he should be banished from the territory.[27] On the other hand, "if a brāhmaṇa, either of the superior or inferior type, sent to exile, returns to his home territory, uncorrected, and indulges in bad acts as before, he should then (in that extreme case) be kept imprisoned either up till the end of his life or so long as no correction occurs in his conduct."[28]

Without working out a "penology of imprisonment" in which different jail-terms would be matched with different types and degrees of criminality, the Hindu jurisprudents clearly stated the circumstances and the conditions under which imprisonment should be managed. In addition to references already quoted, Kâtyāyana (670) prescribed that "that wicked person, who does not obey the laws, promulgated by the king, and thereby sets at naught the king's orders, is to be imprisoned (*grāhyaḥ*) and punished" [emphasis added].[29] Manu orders (9.288), "Let him (i.e. the king) place all prisons near a high road, where the suffering and disfigured offenders can be seen." Following Julius Jolly's quotation (*Hindu Law and Custom* [1928], 282) of "Nandāchārya's" rendering of the word "all" in this statement, the order reads "Let the king set places where the treatment is severe [emphasis added] near a high road . . . ." Kauṭilya (2.5) advises on the construction of jails to accommodate men and women separately, and advises (2.36) on conditions and circumstances under which prisoners may be released.

But aside from the smṛti references, the Bṛhat-Saṃhitā (47.8) is cited by Kane (*History of the Dharma-śāstra* [1973], Vol. III, 406ff.) concerning imprisoned persons marked for execution for crimes against the king's person of harem. Kane's citations also indicate the usual grounds for indefinite extensions of imprisonment as being inability to pay fines or to bear corporal punishments due to bodily infirmities. Persons imprisoned for inability to pay fines could earn their release by performing a prescribed amount of daily labour or by submitting to an equivalent corporal punishment. Charitable persons could be permitted to pay the fine on the debtor's behalf by a certain date, on which the prisoner would be released. Less favoured debtors would have to wait upon the king's pleasure or take their chances on declarations of general releases of prisoners on the king's birthday, on his coronation, or on his victorious conquest of a new territory.

But none of these conditions indicates the framing of "jail sentences" or "jail terms" formalized by penal prescriptions. Even Kane's quotation of the Bṛhaspati text (SBE XXXIII, p. 362), in Caṇḍeśvara's Vivādratnākara (Bibliotheca Indica series, p. 331), is unspecific regarding the term of a jail sentence. For the statement "when a man of good character and a diligent reader of the Veda has committed theft he shall be kept in prison for a long time and shall be caused to perform penance after having been compelled to restore the goods" is translatable as "until such time as he shall become desirous of doing penance and making atonement." There is, moreover, an ambiguity here, to which Kane (History of the Dharmaśāstra [1953]; IV, 69, note 166) draws attention in a footnote. "It is possible that this verse means that a learned brāhmaṇa who has been well conducted but fell a victim to the temptation of theft should not be jailed for a long time because jail torments his mind and therefore he should be made to restore stolen property and given penance."

In any case, a penological interpretation of the references to indefinite periods of imprisonment would need to be in line with the śāstrika perception of punishments as penal acts which negate criminal acts by some kind of justicial correspondence. Even karmic retributive experiences have boundaries determined by the specificality of the acts which they retribute. Hence the circumstance of imprisonment may be recognized as an occasion through which karmic expiations become operative without the assumption that a "jail sentence" has been formulated as a specific judicial prescription for the retribution of a named criminal offence. On the basis of the--albeit limited--evidence, it appears that the smṛti-writers who did not work out a penology of imprisonment shared a common spirit with the Biblical jurists of the Jewish Testament which, as Deitrich Bonhoeffer once observed (Letters and Papers from Prison, NY: Macmillan [1972], 134), never punishes anyone by depriving him of his freedom.[30]

Chapter 5. Penal Instruments of Retribution

The different forms in which the principle of punishment is represented by the sāstrikas can be distinguished as penalties and as penances. The former comprise both divine afflictions as well as judicial penalties, and the connections of these with penal curses and oaths, the outworkings of ordeals as instruments of judicial inquiry, catastrophic happenings such as earthquakes, famines, and natural disasters of all kinds, insofar as these are retributively interpretable, and such social evils as civil strife, economic misfortunes, political disturbances, enemy invasions, and other such civil calamities as can be attributed to the misdeeds of mankind. The penances comprise all self-inflicted punishments under civil and/or religious constraints, and the voluntary elements and features of sacrificial offerings, ascetical disciplines or yogic practices, including expiational suicide or the expiational element in ritual suicide and substitutional practices.

A. Divine Afflictions

The belief that physical diseases and human misfortunes are inherently retributive appears in the earliest brāhmaṇic literature long before the doctrine of Karma became the dominant theory of moral retribution. Four moral causes of sickness and disease were distinguished: sinful acts or "untruths," evil sorceries worked by one's enemies, demonic possession, and the anger of the gods. Each of these causes however, could be neutralized or counteracted by magical, ritual, or penitential prescriptions.

An apparent incongruity with this belief is the theory of Fate (*vidhi*, *daivam*, and their correlates) which explains life's afflictions not in terms of immoral acts of wilful beings but as experiences of the unquestionable but arbitrary attitudes and actions of dieties beyond moral accountability. It is possible that the idea of Fate reflects the feelings of the early thinkers, while the idea of moral causation reflected a conscious effort at making sense of human experience.

Fates, however, are not necessarily divine instrumentations according to the meaning of such words as *niyati* and *kāla*--which have the sense of fate, luck, fortune, or destiny--and *yadṛcchā*, which has the sense of accidence or chance. But all fates, from any source or cause, can be warded off by magic, neutralized by charms, or assuaged by appeasing rituals.

The belief that seemingly adventitious misfortunes are not really 'adventitious' since they have determining moral causes, is strongly represented in the early literature where misfortune and adversity are frequently indicated as being signs of divine displeasure at, and divine acts against sins or caused effects of sins. Fates, moreover, are not perceived merely as idle and arbitrary acts of God but as divinely gracious attention-drawing indicators of spiritual maladies which need to be investigated and brought to light as hidden or forgotten sins of the present or of past lives which must be expiated in order to restore that personal and communal wholeness and order in which the wellbeing of the divinities themselves is involved.

The connection of diseases with sins is specifically recognized in the Vedas in the connection of sexual vices with venereal diseases which cause infertility and deformed offspring. Although the representation of this connection is not sophisticated, its prominence for the Vedic sacerdotal specialists of the Atharvaveda is evident in the large volume of charms and other magical and ritual prophylactics in which the fourth Veda is worded. The volume of magical and ritualized treatment of evils is also evidence of popular recognition of the connections of sin and disease even with respect to vulnerability to the curses of one's enemies. The Atharvaveda is possibly an indicator of the size of a popular science ritually administered by priests which afforded in ancient times less expensive remedies for infirmities, diseases, and other afflictions than were available from the medical herbalists of the Āyurveda. On the other hand, the visibly unpleasant character of the ritual prescriptions for neutralizing malific influences of such sins as marital infidelity and gluttony, suggests that they might have been intentionally devised to excite such feelings as would quicken the conscience over the deeds they are intended to antidote. This unpleasant feature of the purificatory charms could even have been intended as a retributive feature designed to compensate, deter, and prevent future commissions of sinful acts. While this may not be their entire explanation, the Vedic charms can be interpreted as mechanistic functions serving as a form of punishment, even if this feature of them is neither central nor explicit.

The substantial identity of man with nature in the Indian cosmology added significances to the relation of sin and disease. Just as natural disasters reflect "dis-ease" in the natural world so also sicknesses, disasters, and material misfortunes reflect dis-ease in the microcosm of the individual, that is, disturbance of a biological order upon which physical and mental wellbeing depends. Since disease is a manifestation of conditions contrary to an order of some kind, it is perceived as having a moral source in the actions which cause diseases and cause the disturbance of the balance to be manifested. There are, in this light, no merely natural causes of sicknesses and adversities. Nature itself acts upon individuals according to their merits and demerits. Sicknesses need, accordingly, both herbal or physical remedies and moral remedies. Even nightmares or evil-dreaming, the enmity of neighbours, the curses of enemies, the influences of demons, the forces of ill omens, the effects of sorcery, ritual errors, and the taints arising from the company of deformed persons, are perceived as spiritual-moral contagions and even as infectious inasmuch as they are communicable between individuals and classes, between successive generations, and even from gods to men, and needing to be antidoted or remedied by the ritual prescriptions of the Atharvaveda, much as natural diseases require the herbal antidotes and remedies of the Āyurveda.

The seemingly crude and naive methodology for removing sins found in the Atharvaveda, nonetheless reflects a sound principle that total wholeness or health has spiritual and moral bases as well as physical ones such that virtue and even material prosperity are interdependent. It is also probable that the priestly interpreters of the

Atharvaveda recognized the psychodynamics of their ritual and magical prescriptions as depending considerably upon psychospiritual conditions of their users for releasing the mechanisms of healing brought into play by the positive will and spiritual states of their users. Modern psychosomatic medicine may therefore, provide a modern rationality for what has been denigrated as crude superstition.

The ascription to Varuṇa of the divine agency of disease in Vedic times persisted into the classical period through the Mahābhārata and the Manusmṛti. Manu referred to diseases as "Varuṇa's fetters." It is important that men should not give false evidence in a court of law or are bound to give "true evidence," since "he who gives false evidence is firmly bound by Varuṇa's fetters, helpless during one hundred existences."[1] Vasiṣṭha (Vas.Dhs.6.6) perceived the relation of sin and disease in broader terms. "A man of bad conduct is blamed among men, evils befall him constantly, he is afflicted with disease and is short-lived." Such afflictions are only healed through virtue; for (6.7) "through good conduct a man gains spiritual merit; through good conduct he obtains acceptability . . . obviates the effects of evil marks . . . (and) lives a hundred years."

Yet closely associated with the idea of the divine origin of diseases as punishments for sins is the idea that either Karma, the malignant actions of demons, the operations of Fate, or the inscrutable will of the gods are the causes of misfortune and disease. E. W. Hopkins (The Religions of India [1895], 374) notes that in the Mahābhārata misfortune and disease are "invariably ascribed to the malignant action of the devil, although the Karma doctrine should suggest that it was the result of a former misdeed on the victim's part." He was of the opinion that the divine origin of disease-afflictions, understood in terms of Fate or the inscrutable will of the gods, may have been a firmly conceptualized belief long before the emergence of the theory of Karma, but managed to survive only as an alternative theory of disease rather than as a rival doctrine. A synthesis of the different theories led to the belief that man's life is dependent upon exterior powers at three levels, *daiva* or the inscrutable will of the gods, *haṭha* or cosmic force or chance, and Karma, or the ripened potentialities of the actions of a previous existence. E. W. Hopkins is of the opinion that *daiva* and *haṭha* may have been treated as synonymous in certain texts such as the Mahābhārata (3.183.86). He explains that fate was originally conceived as an act of the gods. In its simplest form, this theory of man's lot is "that a man owes what he gets, not to his anterior self, but to the gods."[2] Whatever the gods arrange, be it good or bad, kindly or malicious, is his appointed lot (*vidhi*); what the gods decree (*diṣṭa*) is his divinely appointed destiny (*daiva*). If the gods bestow a goodly share (*bhāga*) then this is his luck (*bhāgya*). But generally, when a person's fortune is thought to have a divine origin it is called "*daivam;*" otherwise it is *vidhi* or fate, or accident of Nature or chance (*haṭha*). Manu (11.47) appears to suggest that *daiva* or divine intervention could cause a man to sin; and that under the form of *kāla* or Time it determines the length of a man's life.[3] It is personified and worshipped.[4]

These references do not indicate whether or when the idea of Fate and the theory of Karma might have been assimilated or the doctrine of Fate interpreted in relation to Karma such that a person's fate or destiny might be said to be the effect of his karmas. In a text of Manu (11.47), a twice-born man is presented as performing penance on account of acts committed either before birth (i.e. in a previous earthly existence), or by fate.[a] Several commentators (such as Medhātithi, Nārāyaṇa, Kullūka, SBE XXV, 439) interpret *daivāt* in this text as meaning "by chance" or "by accident," in the sense of "through carelessness" in this life. One motive of their interpretation could be to overcome certain ethical and logical difficulties in the notion of pre-birth sins. Just as Manu (7.205) attempts the assimilation of *daiva* with Karma, also Yājñavalkya (1.348) explains *vidhi* (fate) or *diṣṭa* (that which is decreed) as

---

[a]"Prāyaścittīyatām prāpya daivātpūrvakṛtena vā; na saṃsargaṃ vrajetsadbhiḥ prāyaścitte 'kṛte dvijaḥ" (Manu 11.47, Chowkhamba 226; 605).

being the result of a man's actions" performed in a previous body." As Manu says (SBE XXV): "all undertakings (in) this (world) depend both on the ordering of fate and on human exertion; but among these two, (the ways of) fate are unfathomable; in the case of man's effort, action is possible."[a]

Whatever assimilation between the idea of Fate and the theory of Karma might have been effected, this could not have been a total absorption since the idea of Fate was retained with independent characteristics as an alternative theory of human experience throughout the literary history of India even in spite of apparent attempts of some writers to get rid of the idea of Fate either by denying its influence in human lives or by calling the idea a mere fiction and deception. The unknown author (c.1300 A.D.) of the Yoga-Vasiṣṭha (2.8.16) regarded the word *daivam* as a mere name, a consolatory word which is merely a deceptive substitute for those real root inclinations (*vāsanā*) in undisciplined sense-organs which through the activity of the mind, lead to actions. The idea of Fate is emphatically rejected by the narrator of the story of the girl Kṛṣṇa in the Mahābhārata (4.20.7-29) who, though renowned for her virtue, had been afflicted by a disease or misfortune which she attributes to Fate or to the effects of a forgotten "fault against the gods" which she had committed when she was still a child. The narrator apparently rejects her plea of innocence, by insisting that on account of the misfortune, she could not in fact have been innocent since she must have deserved the misfortune which the divine Ordainer (*Dhātṛ*) had inflicted upon her.[5] Her misfortune, accordingly, could not have been the outworking of Fate as if it had no moral antecedents. For, the narrator argues in Mbh.12.291.11-14 that "not without seed is anything produced; not without the act does any receive the reward. I recognize no Fate. One's own nature predetermines one's condition; it is Karma that decides."

---

[a]"Sarvaṃ karmedamāyattaṃ vidhāne daivamānuṣe; tayordaivamacintyantu mānuṣe vidyate kriyā" (Manu 7.205, Chowkhamba 226; 369).

Abandonment of the notion of Fate could seem more reasonable than its assimilation to the theory of Karma if the two theories are contradictory. The theory of Fate explains human experience in terms of divine interventions which are inscrutably unrelated to any moral deserts. The theory of Karma on the other hand is the interpretation of that experience through moral deserts. The experience of the processes of Karma could lead to an amendment of life; but the experience of the operations of Fate can at best lead only to passive resignation or "fatalism." Where Fate is perceived religiously as the inscrutable but arbitrary Will of God, "fatalism" takes the form of resignation to God's Will. Moreover, when that Will is perceived to be benevolent and gracious, then *prapatti* or absolute, unconditional, voluntary self-surrender to the divine Will as envisaged by the Alvars and as theologized by Rāmānuja and his disciples from the twelfth century becomes a recognizably legitimate and valuable response. For persons who feel themselves to be subject to powers over which they have no control, or to beings from whom they can claim no rights or protections, can at the best throw themselves hopefully upon the divine mercy and grace in order that those divine powers may act favourably apart from any moral or spiritual deserts.

But theistic notions of divine grace and favour are likewise contrary to the theory of Karma, and indeed, the idea of Grace appears very much like a theologized version of the older theory of Fate translated as the inscrutable Will of (an albeit benevolent) God. Nicol Macnicol (Indian Theism, London: Oxford University Press [1915], 81) was of the opinion that the doctrine of divine grace was a belated attempt to overcome problems in the doctrine of Fate. "The doctrines of grace and of reprobation, the exercise by the Supreme Lord of His *māyā* in order to save men or to bewilder and destroy them are really means by which the antinomy of the free moral activity of God and the fatal power of the "deed" is sought to be reconciled." Yet statements in the Mahābhārata (e.g., 3.30.20ff.) and the Bhagavadgītā (e.g., 7.15 and 25) suggest that there may have been a long-standing debate on the conflicting theories of Fate, Karma, and the Will of God. The Mahābhārata passage (3.20.20ff.) particularly, brings out sharply the dilemma of an all-powerful and supposedly good God who pitilessly permits sorrow and suffering in the world. In lay terms spoken by a thoughtful queen, it is said:

> Verily is it an old story (*itihāsa*) that 'the worlds stand under the Lord's Will.' Following the seed, God gives good or ill in the case of all beings . . . . Like a wooden doll, moving its limbs in the hands of man, so do all creatures move in the Creator's hands . . . . As a bull is led by the nose, so man follows the Will of the Creator; he is never a creature of free will. Every man goes to heaven or to hell, as he is sent by the Lord's Will. God Himself, occupied with noble or with wicked acts, moves about among all created things . . . . The blessed God . . . plays with his creatures just as a boy plays with toys, putting them together and destroying them as he chooses.

God's irresistible power leads the reciter to reflect upon the kind of God who behaves as He does.

> Not like a father is God to His creatures; He acts in anger. When I see the good distressed, the ignoble happy, I blame the Creator who permits this inequality. What reward does God get that he sends happiness to this sinful man (thy oppressor?). If it be true that only the individual that does the act is pursued by the fruit of the act, then the Lord who has done this act is defiled by this base act of his. If, on the other hand, the act that one has done, does not pursue and overtake the one that has done it, then the only agency on earth is brute force . . . and I grieve for them that are without it.[6]

The logic of her argument is difficult to counter, which the king admits even as he takes refuge in a plea of orthodoxy. "The argument is good, clear and smooth; but it is heterodox. The world may seem as you suppose but the scriptures declare its order to be otherwise." Nevertheless, elsewhere in the Mahābhārata (5.175.32, E. W. Hopkins' trans.), a woman cries out in defiance of Fate, "Fie on the Creator for this bad luck" but for many "Time and Fate and what will be these are the only Lord," an opinion to which even the wise king assents. On the other hand fatalism must always contend with faith; hope repeatedly rises up even in the face of Fate; and faith transmutes the very blind forces which condition human experience into processes operative of a benevolent and gracious divine Plan.[7]

Closely related to divine disease-afflictions are what may be called "moral diseases." The chief exponents of Āyurvedic medicine, namely Caraka, Cakrāpani, and Suśruta discussed the karmic sources of physical disease.[8] On the other hand, they did not attribute diseases solely to karmic causes, that is to actions performed in a previous earthly existence. They recognized hereditary factors in disease as well as in physiological deformities and mental retardation. Much physical sickness (*vikāra*) is admitted as being due to lack of psychophysical equilibrium through unsuitable dietary and climatic conditions, excessive, deficient, or harmful administration of material objects, or the misuse of intelligence (*prajñāparādha*). When through "the misuse of intelligence" transgressions are committed, these survive as causationally efficient potentialities for disease and sickness which must surely take effect after a lapse of time. One important ethical distinction, therefore, is between bodily afflictions which have a recent causal origin, and those whose origins lie in acts of a previous earthly life. These latter effects only are moral or karmic diseases inasmuch as they come to fruition through *adharma*, a word which has more than the simple negative meaning of "absence of merit" but refers also to a negative power or potentiality which expresses itself as ethically commensurate sicknesses, diseases, and adversities. The disease-effects of *adharma* therefore are moral retributions instrumented through Karma.

The relation of sin and disease in Indian medicine is even more explicit in statements using the term "*mala*" which can be translated both as "impurities," "polluting agents," "waste products" and as "sin." The materialistic interpretations of this word are most commonly used by the medical writers to provide an explanatory cause of physical disease. Therefore *kiṭṭa*, meaning waste-products or "secretions" of the human physical body, may become "*mala*" just as soon as they accumulate in sufficient quantity as to cause bodily disease. But there are also secretions of the mind and the soul which may be harmful to the body. Therefore *mala* describes moral and spiritual impurities also, such as sins, and pertains indeed to any harmful discord of psychic and physical energies arising from conflicts between the physical cravings generated by sense-perceptions and the spiritual-moral imperatives of the will. In this case, physical health is integrally dependent upon spiritual health which in turn is a wholeness which comprises a harmonization of interior spiritual, moral and psychic powers. For this reason, Caraka (1.12.13; S. N. Dasgupta, A History of Indian Philosophy [1922-55], Vol. II, 327) says through the sage Ātreya, that:

> Just as it is necessary that religious duties (*dharma*), wealth (*artha*) and desires (*kāma*) should be equally attended to,[9] for just as the three seasons of winter, summer and rains all go in a definite order, so all the three (constituents of the body which make for health)[10] when they are in their natural state of equilibrium, contribute to the efficiency of all the sense-organs, the strength, colour and health of the body, and endow a man with long life. But when they are disturbed, they produce opposite results and ultimately break the whole balance of the system and destroy it.

Kumārila, commenting upon the Kauṣika-sūtra which belongs to the Atharvaveda, distinguished two types of diseases, namely, those which are caused by an unwholesome diet and those caused by sins and transgressions.[11] He explained the former as being amenable to Āyurvedic treatments and the latter to Atharvavedic formulas. It is doubtful however that the leading authorities on Āyurveda, made the distinction so strongly, but rather perceived herbal remedies and ritual remedies as affordable alternative and supplementary treatments for diseases. Caraka (6.1.3) positively regarded penances (*prāyaścitta*) as a medicine (*bheṣaja*). This means, as Cakrāpani explained, that just as penances remove spiritual diseases or sins or diseases brought about through sinful acts, so medicines remove diseases. Accordingly *prāyaścitta* is a *bheṣaja*.[12]

Caraka also recognized factors of social morbidity which are explained by S. N. Dasgupta (A History of Indian Philosophy [1922-55], Vol. II, 409):

> When the chief persons of a country, city or locality transgress the righteous course and lead the people in an unrighteous manner, the people also in their conduct continue to grow vicious and sinful . . . . The gods forsake that place, there is no proper rain, the air, water and the

country as a whole become polluted and epidemics break out. Thus the misdeeds of the people can . . . pollute the whole region and utterly ruin it.

This statement would suggest that in such a corrupt society the good would perish with the evil and the virtuous along with the wicked. But Caraka was of the opinion that whenever natural disasters such as epidemics break out or political and economic evils befall the society, the virtuous are protected by their virtue. When epidemic diseases break out, they are able to protect themselves through the virtuous efficacy of medicines, whereas the nonrighteous would not benefit from them without first resorting to the appropriate penances for expiating their deeds.

A less developed outline of Caraka's theory of social morbidity is found in the dharmaśāstra literature, although it appears that whereas Caraka attributes the productivity or nonproductivity of the land to the virtuous and evil actions of the citizens, Manu (8.22) attributes the public wellbeing to the character of the inhabitants. The distinction, however, may not be a sharp one, and accordingly, "the kingdom where śūdras are very numerous, which is infested by atheists, and destitute of twice-born (inhabitants) soon entirely perishes, afflicted by famine and disease."[a]

In any society, the worst evil envisaged by the Śāstrikas is adultery, since this brings about a confusion of the castes and thereby destroys the divinely created structure of the brāhmaṇic society. This breakdown in turn effects cosmical and natural repercussions in the form of natural disasters. For when the castes become confused by adulterers, their offspring cannot be properly qualified sacrificiers; without the sacrifices the harmony of the cosmos which they serve cannot be sustained. Consequently, disharmony arises; and when this is caused to happen, no rain falls, the crops perish, the land goes foul, epidemics break out, famine becomes rife, and everything perishes.

---

[a]"Yadrāṣṭram śūdrabhūyiṣṭhaṃ nāstikākrāntamadvijam; vinaśyatyāśu tatkṛtsnaṃ durbhikṣavyādhipīḍitam" (Manu 8.22; Chowkhamba 226; 380).

Manu (11.48) also believed that physical diseases are the consequences of transgressions in this life, though others result from "former sins."[a] Deformities, sicknesses, and other defects of the body and mind are signs and symptoms of inherited sins.[13] Diseased fingernails signify a former gold-thief; blackened teeth signify a former spirit-drinker. A sufferer from tuberculosis was formerly the slayer of a brāhmin; the victim of a skin disease, one who previously violated his guru's bed.[14] As was the sin, so is the sickness. Yet the sicknesses do not comprise the totality of the effects. For, says Manu (11.53), "in consequence of the remnant of (the guilt of former) crimes, [there] are born idiots, dumb, blind, deaf and deformed men, who are (all) despised by the virtuous."[b] The sickness and the deformities are apparently final outworkings of moral retribution since the gold-stealer (Manu 11.49) may have received capital punishment in his previous life,[15] or any of several kinds of corporal punishments.[16] These could only have expiated the civil or criminal element of his sin, leaving a remainder comprising a spiritual element which would be expiated in one of the hells, and a moral element for which rebirth in an earthly body and expiatory earthly experience would be needed. The threat of such future moral experience is always present, in Manu's judgement (11.54), as long as sinners do not resort to religious penances. They should submit to penances while they can since the pain of these is certainly less terrible than the penalties which must surely work out in the next life from fructifying karmas. "Penances must always be performed for the sake of purification, because those whose sins have not been expiated,

---

[a]"Iha duścaritaiḥ kecitkecitpūrvakṛtaistathā; prāpnuvanti durātmāno narā rūpaviparyayam" (Manu 11.48; Chowkhamba, 226; 605).

[b]"Evam karmaviśeṣeṇa jāyante sadvigarhitāḥ; jaḍamūkāndhabadhirā vikṛtākṛtayastathā" (Manu 11.53; Chowkhamba, 226; 606).

are born (again) with disgraceful marks."[a]

The ideas of Divine punishment, Fate, Karma, and demonic influences as explanatory causes of disease imply a diversity if not a confusion of theories concerning the origins of suffering especially of the forms which are manifested as disease-afflictions. On the one hand, the diversity of theories may have afforded also a diversity of remedies. But it is possible that different conditions effected afflictions from different causes. Thus, certain bodily afflictions such as epidemic diseases, and social disasters such as famine, anarchy, civil war, and plague, come immediately upon the society's degradation to such a low moral level as to cause the gods to forsake the evil land which is infested with wicked persons.[17] And the anger of these gods also falls immediately upon such persons who are then smitten with diseases and have no resistence to the adversities which the social calamities bring to them. On the other hand, there are tribulations which befall mortals as mortals through the fruition of their inherited karmas. There are also biological constituents in that karmic heritage which account for the circumstances in which some are "born (as) idiots, dumb, blind, deaf, and deformed."[18] Yet in the end the magnitude of the dilemma of human suffering could never be sufficiently explained by any combination of plausible theories, a point most poignantly expressed in the Bhāgavata Purāṇa:

> You are curious to know the cause of my suffering but what it is I do not know. There are many different opinions about the true cause of pain and suffering in this world. Some say we ourselves cause our own unhappiness and suffering; others say the stars or planetary conditions are the cause--or, peradventure, fate; again others say Karma is the only cause. Still others think that God sends us either happiness or misery. I am at a loss to know which of these views is correct.[19]

---

[a]"Caritavyamato nityaṃ prāyaścittaṃ viśudvaye; nindyairhi lakṣaṇairyuktā jāyante 'niṣkṛtainasaḥ" (Manu 11.54; Chowkhamba 226; 606).

B. Judicial Penalties

Arguments concerning whether or not an ethical conception rather than a utilitarian view of Punishment guided formulations of penal sanctions in early Indian dharmaśāstra literature would be less abstract if there was certain evidence that the texts reflect an historic juridical system of penal sanctions and not merely a theoretical model contrived upon the triple formula of ideal king, ideal polity and ideal state which is portrayed in the Kauṭilīya Arthaśāstra. Several grounds for doubt that smṛti-regulations were actively implemented in Indian courts of law have been put forth by scholars. One argument is that since the duties of the king as the supreme judge in the brāhmanical society are not treated in the dharmasūtras, and these are the earliest dharmaśāstra texts, this can only be because there were no royal or civil courts in brāhmaṇical states in India in ancient times but only religious regional and local tribunals administered by brāhmin pandits expert in providing judicial services for local communities and regions. The extensive works of a largely juridical character known as "dharmasmṛtis"--which emerged later as a secondary and even a subordinate category of writing with respect to the largely unwritten tradition of ancient *samiti* or tribunal regulations, rulings, and precedents which developed out of and were guided by "approved conduct" (*sadācāra*)--reflect the emergence of the king in the role of judge and punisher, first as the sanctioner of the *samiti* rulings, next as the decider of grave crimes, and finally as the upholder of juridical regulations compiled in the texts of different schools of ancient and medieval law throughout India. The sūtras and the smṛtis reflect two distinct legal jurisdictions serving parallel functions among which the rulings of local and regional *samitis* had precedence over rulings of royal courts. If this is so, then any inferences about the workings of ancient courts which might be drawn from the smṛti-literature alone would be of doubtful historicity.

Another cause for doubt arises over the historical

relation of law to custom in ancient India. Kātyāyana (37) (in Derrett's translation: The Classical Law of India, Berkeley: University of California Press [1973], 176) defined custom (*caritra*) as "all that a person practices, whether or not it conforms to *dharma* (*dharmyaṃ vādharmyaṃ eva ca*) simply because that is the constant usage of the country." It appears that both Manu and Āpastamba recognized the importance of "custom" as a guide of proper conduct, while Āpastamba particularly recognized "approved conduct" (*sadācāra*) as a source of judicial reference and defined this as those customs which are approved "by those who know dharma" or which are practiced by learned and upright persons (*śiṣṭas*), who themselves are embodiments of, as well as standards of, *dharma*. It appears that custom (*caritra*) was given precedence over law (*dharma*), though it is doubtful that Āpastamba (1.1.1.2) implies the subjection of *dharma* to *caritra*. The relation of *dharma* to *caritra* was never explicitly defined, and indeed there is evidence of disagreements about their relationship among jurists of different law-schools of ancient and medieval India. Robert Lingat (The Classical Law of India [1973]; 176-206) wrote extensively on this topic and attributed certain "obvious contradictions" in Manu's regulations on customs as being due to the enormous power and authority of "customs too deeply rooted for their prohibition to be efficacious." Lingat also drew attention to cases of *dharma* being in direct conflict with custom, that is, regulations worded in a manner intended to delimit to the extreme point prior to abolition certain outmoded and even obnoxious customs. It is doubtful, however, from Lingat's discussion, that the regulation of conduct through either law or custom was merely academic, since ancient custom presented a factor of conduct and morality to which juridical law had to be adjusted wherever the juridical law had to be positively implemented.

A third doubt arises in connection with a peculiar theory of the Manusmṛti (1.84-86) concerning certain regulations which are no longer appropriate for the present age, the *Kaliyuga*. Such regulations could not be sanctioned by a court. The theory of appropriate ages (*yugas*) conveniently enabled jurisprudents from Bṛhaspati onwards to adopt a principle of professional consensus for adapting ancient customs to present conditions. Lists of practices formulated and approved in the smṛtis but deemed worthy of prohibition in the Kaliyuga were developed. J. D. M. Derrett (Essays in Classical and Modern Hindu Law [1977], 142) refers to at least thirty such regulations which ninth- and tenth-century jurists deemed inappropriate for the present age and which were accepted as obsolete "with some alacrity" by jurists "all over India" on the principle that "any rule which met the determined opposition of any section of the public, was to be ignored and was not to be enforced." Clearly, without such lists as sources of reference, it could be difficult to regard any smṛti-regulation as reflecting real historic practice in ancient India.

Doubts concerning whether or not the smṛti regulations were intended to be prescriptive or merely tentatively indicative for the suppression of crimes are raised by Derrett (Essays in Classical and Modern Hindu Law [1977], 27ff.)[20] on the ground that certain extraneous considerations not anticipated by the smṛti-writers were sometimes allowed to limit or to provide new interpretations and applications of smṛti rulings. Political and economic exigencies, for example, could not merely either weaken or intensify smṛti rulings but might even overrule them as if they were temporarily redundant. Under such circumstances, the king had to decide, probably on the advice of his counsellors, when such expediencies were operative and how far they affected the gravity and the punishment of acts forbidden by the smṛtis. But, if it is true that the smṛti rulings did not have the permanent force of legal statutes, but could be subjected to non-judicial expediencies, then it is impossible to regard any smṛti ruling as reflecting historical juridical practice in ancient India.

The nagging doubt over the congruity or non-congruity of ecclesiastical and civil law in the long and ongoing debate of Julius Jolly and others on whether Hindu law developed out of, or through the convergence of, two subsequent historical systems of law may have been cogent in the context of jurisprudential discussions of the problem of adapting traditional sacred law to modern case-law or "lawyer's law" as Khare defined it (R. S. Khare, "Indigenous Culture and Lawyer's Law in India", Comparative Studies in Society and History, Cambridge: The University Press, [1972], 74) in British India. The problem of a dual legal-tradition would not be intrinsic to the traditional Indian conception of law which permits a distinction between the religious and the civil instruments of its administration without a bifurcation of its unity. In this light, the "lawyer's law" which Khare defines as "a public, institutionalized mechanism for maintaining public order, facilitating cooperative action, legitimizing power, authority and influence, and defining and reinforcing rights and responsibilities" and comprized in "state law and its various branches like criminal, civil, administrative, and 'common' law (p. 74)," is an expression of the larger "system" of "sacred law, expressed in a body of codified rules, as well as regional or local customs," coming from *sruti* and *smṛti* sources and comprised under the general title of *dharmaśāstra*.

This comprehensive law is sacred not only because it integrates religiously the totality of human individual and social values, but also because its ultimate function is religious, namely the vindication of divine Dharma or of the principle of Order which the guardian-deities are believed to articulate as "divine ordinances" and to protect through divine sanctions. The law is "sacred" because, in Khare's words, it integrates itself with the sacred Order and is 'born' out of dharma, serves "the contextual and microscopic aspects of dharma," and "links up with the 'basic principle of the universe'."

This means that the distinction between 'religious' and 'civil' law is contextual and not essential. Hence, the largest concession that may be made to Jolly's arguments for two distinct historic traditions is that, insofar as public order appears as the major concern of certain exponents of traditional Indian law, these make prominent state law and its respective branches of criminal, civil, administrative and 'customary' law in their prescriptions.

The historical question of which prescriptions and to

what extent their prescriptions might have been implemented in Hindu courts from ancient to modern times is one for historians to decide, although it is doubtful if the jurisprudents intended their prescriptions to be merely academic. The literary sources of those prescriptions, however, is a rich minefield of the religious and philosophical assumptions and presuppositions which moulded their conception of the nature and meaning of punishment in relation to their ideas of law and sanction. Since, on the other hand, the manuals in which those prescriptions are to be found are not "lawbooks" in the modern sense, the conceptions of law and punishment formulated in them are broader in perspective than would be expected of definitions intended solely for a 'state-law' system. This does not mean, however, that the religious, moral, and judicial connotations of the terms are confused by the Hindu jurisprudents, because different kinds of religious, moral and judicial enunciations are sufficiently distinguishable from each other as to have enabled the British administration in India to construct an Indian 'state-law' system from the comprehensive textual sources.

Manu (8.129) and Bṛhaspati (9.12-13 and 29.2) distinguish four kinds of punitive treatment of criminals: admonition (*vāg-daṇḍa*), reproof (*dhigdaṇḍa*), fines (*dhanadaṇḍa*), and corporal punishments (*vadhadaṇḍa*). Furthermore, ten kinds of corporal punishment were indicated (Manu 9.125) and subsequently divided into three degrees of severity, the first degree being torture or physical chastisement, the middle degree being dismemberment of limbs or organs, and the highest degree of severity being capital punishment. Nārada and Saṅkha consequently declared that corporal punishments fully range from prison confinements to the death sentence.[21]

The recognition of degrees of severity and the definition of "punishment units" which could be implemented individually or in groupings enabled the jurisprudents to prescribe penalties corresponding with types and degrees of guilt, and to allow for extenuatory mitigative considerations as follows:

(a) considerations due to caste or professional standing;[22]

(b) considerations due to the thing involved (i. e.

destroyed, stolen, or damaged);[23]

(c) considerations due to the utility of the object;[24]

(d) considerations due to the mental condition of the the offender;[25]

(e) considerations due to the moral circumstances of the act (poverty, need, etc.);[26]

(f) considerations related to the frequency of the act (first offence, etc.);[27]

and (g) considerations of the capacity of the offender for bearing punishments (age, wealth, health, ...)[28]

The calculation of the units also enabled the jurisprudents to formulate punitive programmes for each of six categories of crimes identified in the Daṇḍaviveka as homicide (*tatkāri* = *hatyā*), theft (*steya*), molestation (*abhimarṣana*), abuse or defamation (*vāk-pāruṣya*), assault (*daṇḍa-pāruṣya*), and "miscellaneous" (*prakīrṇaka*), and to prescribe proportionate penalties for degrees of guiltiness in numerous specific cases.

Their categorization of lowest, middle, and highest amercements of fines affords a distinctive example of their calculations. (A table of amercements of fines as calculated by five major jurisprudential authorities is provided as an addendum to the endnotes belonging to this chapter.) For instance, the first amercement prescribed by Kātyāyana (960) for an unsuccessful attempt at theft was interpreted as meaning one quarter of the prescribed penalty in the first instance of the attempted crime, and half the prescribed punishment in the case of several abortive attempts. A successful attempt, on the other hand, was to receive the full penalty prescribed only after consideration of the moral circumstance and material capacity of the thief for the punishment. As Kātyāyana states: "the prescribed punishment shall be inflicted (in full) on the criminal who has committed it to its fullness (*paryāpta*)[29] unless he be a first offender," in which case the prescribed penalty for the specific offence will apply (according to Halayudha's commentary on Yājn̂avalkya's directive) "only when it is understood that the infliction of punishment will restrain the criminal from further crimes." Recidivists, on the other hand, are to be severely deterred by the king who may even devise beyond the penalties prescribed by law such treatments as would dissuade or incapacitate future repetitions.[30]

The manifold and varied prescriptions for the suppression of crimes do not, however, manifest a clear distinction between acts which are thought to warrant corporal punishments only or to warrant fines only, or to be amenable to treatment either by corporal punishments or by fines. According to the Manusmṛti (8.129-130), fines apparently stand in relation to corporal punishments as do lower to higher severities, as in the statement of "admonition in the first instance (of an offence), reproof in the second, fines in the third, and corporal punishment as the last resort," with the understanding that when a person is not successfully checked by corporal punishments, then all four kinds can be applied cumulatively. Bṛhaspati, who openly acknowledges the leading authority of Manu (Bṛhas.Dhs.27.3, SBE XXXIII), follows Manu in distinguishing four severities of punishment applicable to differing degrees of guilt. He says (27.5):

> (Let him inflict) a (gentle) admonition, when the offence is very light; (harsh) reproof, for a crime in the first degree; a fine, for a crime in the (second or) middlemost degree, and arrest, in the case of high treason.

Yet in the same section on "miscellaneous" regulations, Bṛhaspati also distinguishes the categories of persons for which each of these forms of punishment can be deemed appropriate: gentle admonition for elders, domestic priests, and gentry; fines for litigants found guilty; corporal punishments for "perpetrators of heavy crimes,", with the extra provision that fines and corporal punishments may only be administered by the king. A further qualification admitted by Bṛhaspati (27.11-12) in this connection is that a brāhmin who is guilty of a capital crime may be subjected to a fine or banishment, but not to capital punishment. Apart from this option, however, accorded only to guilty members of the 'twice-born' caste, the apportionment of penalties is made

---

[a] "Vadhenāpi yadā tvetānnigrahītum naśaknuyāt; tadaiṣu sarvamapyetaṃ prayuñjīta catuṣṭayam" (Manu 8.130; Chowkhamba, 226; 408).

in the matter of fines on a clear distinguishing of first-, second-, and third-degree crimes and corresponding first, middle, and highest pecuniary amercements. This is demonstrated by the treatment of the crime of assault (*pāruṣya*) in the Bṛhaspati-dharmasūtra (SBE XXXIII, 355ff.). Assault could be either physical as in bodily assault or verbal abuse. Each of these is distinguishable into types having differing degrees of gravity. Verbal assault, for instance, is distinguishable into defamation of one's country, village, sub-caste, guild, family, or the like in the lowest degree, scornful or contemptuous utterance against a man's sister or mother, or false accusation of a minor sin, being defamation of the middling sort. Laying of a false charge of a grave sin, or malicious public exposure of a man's faults, is defamation in the highest degree. If two persons fall into an altercation, their guilt is equal when they are of equal caste. But the member of a lower caste doubles his guilt through verbally assaulting a superior. The latter, on the other hand, is only half as guilty in the matter of degree of guilt if he defames an inferior. Hence, by combining Bṛhaspati's distinctions of verbal assault as calculated "by persons learned in the law" (Bṛhas.Dhs.20.5-15, SBE XXXIII), the following table of amercements of fines is presented:

The highest amercement will be one hundred *paṇas* (copper pieces).
The middle amercement will be fifty *paṇas*.
The lowest amercement will be twelve and one-half *paṇas*.

Two persons of equal caste abusing one another will deserve fines each of thirteen and one-half *paṇas*.
A brāhmin who abuses a kṣatriya deserves a fine of fifty *paṇas*.
A brāhmin who abuses a vaiśya deserves a fine of "half of fifty" *paṇas*.
A brāhmin who abuses a śūdra deserves a fine of twelve and one-half *paṇas* (provided that such abuse is unwarranted).

Conversely:
A vaiśya who reviles a kṣatriya deserves a fine of one-hundred *paṇas*.
A kṣatriya who reviles a vaiśya deserves half of the above fine.
A śūdra "shall be compelled to pay the first fine for abusing a vaiśya (i. e. twenty *paṇas*), the middling fine of fifty *paṇas* for abusing a kṣatriya, and the highest fine, i.e., one-hundred *paṇas* for abusing a brāhmin, although Manu makes the penalty to be corporal punishment for this.

It is apparent that the śāstrikas recognized an equivalential relation between fines and corporal punishment while permitting a limited commutation to fines with respect to a specified category of crimes and of criminals. The commutations mentioned in the texts afford a convenient measure of gradations of criminality recognized as bearing upon the just administration of penalties. Bṛhaspati (27.12, SBE XXXIII, 388), permitted, for example, the death sentence to be changed to a fine of one hundred *survaṇas* (these being gold coins), amputation of a limb to fifty gold coins, amputation of a thumb and index finger to a quarter of the full amount, and so on. Kātyāyana (964) (in Bhattacharya, Daṇḍaviveka, 52) also permitted the commutation of banishment to a fine of twenty-five gold coins. Such commutations, however, are expressly reserved for brāhmins who are able to afford such large fines.

Impoverished brāhmins could avoid the shame of public capital punishment or corporal mutilation by opting for a penance-unto-death, or alternatively, provided they are of noble and upright families, and are dutifully observant of their religious duties, they may forfeit their estates and be banished from the king's territories.

In this light, the equivalence system, while not being apparantly a complete programme of calculations of criminal gravities and punitive severities, did at least admit an explicit and reasonable flexibility into the administration of justice which could allow fair consideration of relevent extenuating factors. The possibility that a full scheme may have existed is supported by the large number of specific directives in the texts which make possible a plausible construction. For, if the prescribed penalty for a crime in a major regulatory text indicates the highest severity due for an act whose doer can plead no extenuating circumstances by way of mitigative excuses, then it is possible to set in order each of the lesser forms of the five major crimes, their lesser penalties and their pecuniary equivalents. Such an over-all scheme would then display the full scope of the śāstrika understanding of the relation of justice to the treatment of crimes according to degrees of guilt and in the measure of the monetary equivalents for the prescribed corpo-

measure of the monetary equivalents for the prescribed corporal punishments. Using the Bṛhaspati-dharmasūtra, which is such a major early source of penal legislation, the following scheme of gradations and pecuniary equivalents becomes apparant.

Grave crime	Penalty prescribed	Pecuniary equiv.
1. murder	capital punishment	100 *survanas*
2. physical assault (not fatal)	corporal mutilation	100 gold coins
3. molestation	dismemberment	50 gold coins
4. theft.	corporal punishment.	25 gold coins.

(The fine of fifty gold coins (*survanas*) for molestation is equivalent to one thousand and sixty-eight copper pieces or *paṇas*.)

Since these equivalences are applicable to the fullest severity of a crime and its punishment, it is to be expected that portions of these would be calculated for proportionate degrees of guilt. The theft of articles of different material value and the penalties for these are illustrative of this distinction which is made by jurisprudents and their interpreters.[31]

Theft	Corporal Penalty	Money Equivalent
1. large theft of base metals	death/mutilation	100 gold pieces (*survaṇas*)
2. gold (any amount)	death/mutilation	100 gold pieces
3. principal jewels	death/mutilation	100 gold pieces
4. inferior jewels	mutilation	50 gold pieces
5. small theft of base metals (less than 100 *panas*)	mutilation	25 gold pieces
6. copper theft (less than 50 *paṇas*.	mutilation	11 by 50 *paṇas*
7. metals (less than 25 *paṇas* in value).	mutilation	10 by 25 *paṇas*.

Here also, as in the earlier table, the equivalences stated only assume culpabilities unmitigated by extenuative conditions. However, in several places it appears that fines are assumed to be the proper mode of punishment whenever an offence deserving corporal punishment was attempted but proved unsuccessful and therefore did not cause actual bodily harm. If an unsuccessful bodily assault is reasonably interpretable as an injury to the society, then punishment by a fine would seem appropriate. Yājñavalkya (2.216) may have had this in mind when stating that fines of ten and twenty *paṇas* must be imposed on persons who raise an arm or a leg respectively, in an attempted bodily assault, a fine of the "middle amercement" being required whenever the assault is attempted with an instrument or weapon, with the understanding that these penalties "hold good among all the *varṇas* beginning with the Brāhmaṇas."[32]

But aside from such special considerations, it appears that the śastrikas generally prescribed corporal punishments for immoral acts hurting persons and other living beings and fines for crimes involving damage to or destruction of property. Since, however, many criminal acts cause both moral and material damages, both kinds of penalties are frequently ordained concurrently. For grave sins (*mahāpātaka*) and violent crimes (*sāhasas*) dual penalties are warranted as Manu (9.236) decrees: "corporal punishment and fines according to the law."[a] But since there are offences whose moral and social damages are not distinct, one or other form of punishment is appropriate. As Manu says (8.191), "he who does not return a deposit, and he who demands what he never bailed shall both be punished like thieves, or be compelled to pay a fine equal (to the value of the object retained or claimed)."[b] On the other hand (8.193), "that man who by false pretences may possess himself of another's property, shall be publicly punished by various (modes of) corporal (or capital) punishment, together with his accomplices."[c] Manu (8.198) also ordained that a relative who, without permission, sells a kinsman's property, is not to be punished as a thief, that is as a moral transgressor, but as a civil

---

[a]". . . śarīraṃ dhanasaṃyuktaṃ daṇḍa dharmyaṃ prakalpayet" (Manu 9.236; Chowkhamba, 226; 540).

[b]"Yo nikṣepaṃ nārpayati yaścānikṣipya yācate; tāvubhau cauravacchāsyau dāpyau vā tatsamaṃ damam" (Manu 8.191; Chowkhamba, 226; 423).

[c]"Upadhābhiśca yaḥ kaścitparadravyaṃ harennaraḥ; sasahāyaḥ sa hantavyaḥ prakāśaṃ vividhairvadhaiḥ" (Manu 8.193; Chowkhamba, 226; 424).

offender for whom corporal punishment has been prescribed by law as the proper penalty.

Offences for which Manu specifically indicates fines as the proper penalty include: wrongful sale of property (8.198), failure in honouring legal contracts with respect to work (8.216-7) or of any other kind of public agreement (8.228), coercive dealings in business transactions (8.223), false pretences in order to contract the marriage of a minor aged female (8.224); and malicious public defamation of a person's character (8.225). The purpose of such penalty is, as Manu explains (8.228), to correct the offender and to keep him on the road of rectitude "in accordance with the rules given above."[a]

Such corporal punishments as are perceived to be proper for the correction of grave crimes are manifestly of a deterrent kind where the deterrence is directed to witnesses of such punishments as well as to the offenders themselves. In order that the effect of public deterrence will be maximized, the punishment must be administered in a public place (Manu 9.288). To this end, places of confinement (*bandhana*) must be set up in such places where the criminals can be seen and their punishment observed. Incarceration in the prison is not itself the punishment, but the place where the punishment prescribed by law is to be administered. This merely locative purpose of the prison explains the absence of positive legislation on 'terms of imprisonment' which could serve as measures of criminality. The references to imprisonment (*nirodha*) in the context of punishments, as found in Manu 8.310 and 375 for example, are directive rather than prescriptive.[b]

The restraining function of amputations of limbs and organs as corporal punishments for non-capital crimes is

---

[a] ". . . tamanena vidhānena dharmye pathi niveśayet" (Manu 8.228; Chowkhamba, 226; 433).

[b] "Adhārmikaṃ tribhirnyāyairnnagṛhṇīyāt prayatnataḥ; nirodhanena bandhena vividhena badhena ca" (Manu 8.310; Chowkhamba, 226; 445).

understood in the statement of Manu (8.334) that "with whatever limb a thief in any way commits (an offence) against men, even of that shall (the king) deprive him in order to prevent (a repetition of the crime)."[a] The deterrent purpose is expressed by Manu (8.368) in the matter of private hurts caused by one individual against another. "A man (of) equal (caste) who defiles a willing maiden shall not suffer the amputation of his fingers, but shall pay a fine of two (times five) hundred (*paṇas*) in order to deter him from a repetition (of the offence)" [emphasis added].[b] For a grave crime such as adultery (*saṃgrahaṇa*), the punishment is intentionally deterrent according to Manu's directive that "men who commit adultery with the wives of others, shall the king cause to be marked by punishments which cause terror, and afterwards banish" [emphasis added].[c] The reason for this is provided. "A man who is not a brāhmin ought to suffer death [i. e. capital punishment] for adultery; for the wives of all the four castes even must always be carefully guarded."[d] For, as Manu, in this context, has already explained, "by (adultery) is caused a mixture of the castes (*varṇa*) among men; then (follows) sin, which cuts up even the roots and causes the destruction of everything."[e]

---

[a] "Yena yena yathāṅgena stenonṛṣu viceṣṭate; tattadeva harettasvapratyādeśāya pārthivaḥ" (Manu 8.334; Chowkhamba, 226; 458).

[b] "Sakāmām dūṣayaṃstulyo lāṅgulicchedamāpnuyāt; dviśatantu damaṃ dāpyaḥ prasaṅgavinivṛttaye" (Manu 8.367; Chowkhamba, 226; 466).

[c] " Paradārābhimarṣeṣu pravṛttānrin mahīpatiḥ; udvejanakaraiḍaṇḍaiścihbayitvā pravāsayet" (Manu 8.352; Chowkhamba, 226; 462).

[d] "Abrāhmaṇaḥ saṃgrahaṇe prāṇāntaṃ daṇḍamarhati; caturṇāmapi varṇānām dārā rakṣyatamāḥ sadā" (Manu 8.359; Chowkhamba, 226; 464).

[e] "Tatsamuttho hi lokasya jāyate varṇasaṅkaraḥ; yena mūlaharo 'dharmaḥ sarvanaśāya kalpate"(Manu 8.353; Chowkhamba, 226; 462).

One would not be correct in drawing the inference from the dreadfulness of corporal punishments prescribed by the ancient jurists, that they were disposed toward the instrumentation of cruel and unusual punishments out of zeal for the repression of criminals and the suppression of crimes. For while they recognized the deterrent efficiency of certain punishments, they recognized also that even mild penalties are deterrent in certain cases. Therefore, in their prescriptions of the range of penalties which might be imposed for a named crime, they usually proceeded from the milder to the harsher penalties and appear to have understood that the lightest penalty which would serve the ends of justice while deterring future repetitions of the offence was always to be preferred. On the other hand, the harshest forms of physical punishment are necessary to restrain habitual criminals and to cure recidivism. Hence, when pronouncing sentences in accordance with the lawful prescriptions, judges could decide humanely, without any disregard for justice, which prescriptions might best serve both the assertion of the law, the society's lawful interest, and the offender's moral good. For such an enlightened approach to the administration of justice, they were to be guided by the principle enunciated in the Manusmṛti (8.24) of "knowing what is expedient or inexpedient, what is pure justice or injustice" whenever they would "examine the causes of suitors according to the order of their castes."[a]

It appears, on the whole, that the ancient jurists worked out their jurisprudence primarily in the interest of justice, and consequently and secondarily in the public interest and the moral good of the offender. Furthermore, despite the obvious practical difficulties of determining the ethical relation of 'amounts' and 'forms' of punishment to degrees of gravity of guilt, they assumed the responsibility for determining as reasonably as possible a relation between the degree of guilt and the severity of punishment which would justly support the law and would not be indifferent to the demands of true justice. In this connection, they clear-

[a]"Arthānarthāvubhau buddhvā dharmādharmau ca kevalau; varṇakrameṇa sarvāṇi paśyetkāryāṇi kāryiṇām" (Manu 8.24).

ly distinguished penalties as such from compensations to injured parties and any other pecuniary demands that might serve the public interest.

If this is so, then there is an ethical problem affecting the just administration of penalties arising from the apparently excessive weight placed on caste considerations in the ascertainment of guilt and the fixing of penalties, particularly since such considerations appear to be discriminatively favourable to brāhmins over members of the lower castes. Hindu jurisprudence in general, accordingly appears as a highly developed scheme for safeguarding the privileges of, and engrandizing a minority of, the citizens even at the expence of the majority of the citizens who are not brāhmins. Statements which appear to allow judges to "bend the law" in kindly consideration of brāhmins suggests that the Hindu judicial system was not dedicated to justice in the social interest but to the maintenance and protection of the social order itself on the foundations of its caste-structure. The qualifying influence of caste considerations upon the administration of justice appears to be indicated, for example, by the penalties which are prescribed for the crime of murder.[33]

Offender/Caste		Crime	Penalty
1. kṣatriya	(who slays a)	brāhmin,	capital punishment/forfeiture of property.
2. kṣatriya	(who slays a)	lower caste person,	corporal punishments/fines
3. brāhmin	(who slays a)	ksatriya,	1000 cows and a bull.
4. brāhmin	(who slays a)	vaiśya or śūdra,	110 cows and a bull.
5. śūdra	(who slays a)	woman, cow,	corporal punishment/fines.
6. śūdra	(who slays a)	menstruating woman,	capital punishment with forfeiture of property.

Caste distinctions which are recognized in penal prescriptions include Yājñavalkya's ordinance that perjurors should be fined twice the total cost of the lawsuit, unless they are brāhmins who should be banished.[a]

---

[a]"Sa dāpyo'ṣṭaguṇam daṇḍam brāhmaṇam tu vivāsayet" (Yājñ. Dhs.2.82; Bombay: Nirnaya Sagar Press, [1949], 189).

When interpreting Kātyāyana, the Kṛtyasāgara prescribes fines of 50, 100, and 500 copper pieces (*paṇas*) respectively according to the degree of perjury, but adds that while in accordance with Manu 8.102-111 and 123, brāhmins are only to be exiled, members of the remaining three lower castes should be both fined and exiled.

The question of whether and to what extent discriminatory administration of justice might effect a violation of the principle of justice itself, appears in connection with the numerous references in which the caste of offenders is taken into consideration in calculations of guilt and prescribing of penalties. Yet to be fair to the śāstrikas, it is apparent that a primary distinction is the practical one of the deterrent utility of corporal punishments for low-caste criminals and their impropriety for high-caste persons. A secondary consideration is the accessibility of twice-born persons to ritualized expiational modes of punishment which are inadmissible to low-caste persons. A third distinction appears in the degree of shame which could be felt by a conscience-stricken brāhmin who soils the good name of his family and excludes himself from his social group, and the absence of such influences upon the consciences of low-caste persons. Hence whatever we might think of the justicial implications of caste-discrimination, it has at least a rationale which is not tantamount to a violation of the impartial administration of justice which is a prominent concern of the śāstrikas. The prescriptive distinctions arise rather out of a concern for an ethical equalization between penalties and guilt in the light of the real influence that caste relations have upon degrees of culpability, but without a presupposition that higher-caste persons are always more or less guilty of their wrongdoings than low-born ones. This can be seen by comparing references in the smṛtis to crimes and punishments in which caste-distinctions are explicitly recognized as bearing upon the fair administration of justice.

In the Manusmṛti (8.268), for example, defamation of a brāhmin by a śūdra incurs the śūdra's corporal punishment. In the opposite case of a brāhmin abusing a śūdra, the brāhmin is merely to be fined twelve copper-pieces. Gautama

(12.13) makes the śūdra's corporal punishment to be dismemberment of his tongue; but Haradatta on the basis of Manu 8.268 considers a brāhmin's abuse of a śūdra not to be a civil offence or crime.[34] But any injury, insult, or offensive act by a śūdra against a brāhmin is a criminal offence subject to the prescribed penalties of physical dismemberments or mutilations.

It is not true, on the other hand, that the severities of the law were solely loaded against lower caste persons. Moral offences, for example, when committed by brāhmins, are consistently treated as more grave and warranting of severer penalties than if committed by śūdras. Gautama (12.17), for example, directed that where a learned man breaks the law "the punishment shall be very much increased." This is presumably because the brāhmin either knew that his act was against the law, or that morally he should have known better. On the other hand, Gautama would have appreciated that curses or abusive words against a high-born person constitute a larger offence than the reverse, and the greater guilt in the śūdra's abuse warrants the severer penalty.

An informative example in which caste considerations establish degrees of guilt is found in the dharmasūtra of Gautama (12.15-16) on the crime of theft. Judging by the measures of the fines prescribed, it appears a brāhmin's guilt is measured at eight times more than a similar act of theft committed by a śūdra, while the fines imposed on a Kṣatriya and a Vaiśya caste offender are fixed at four times and two times the lowest fine respectively. Manu (8.337-388) more severely fixed the fine of a brāhmin thief at sixty-four times, a hundred times, or "twice four-and-sixty-fold" the fine which should be imposed upon one who is "altogether ignorant of the law." In Manu also (8.352-3), the higher a man's caste status the more responsible he is expected to be by being better equipped to distinguish between right and wrong, and between what is lawful and unlawful. Similarly, the king (Manu 8.336) and the judges--who above all should be visible exemplars of the law--become many times more guilty and deserving of larger fines than lay-persons.

The two types of crimes in which caste considerations appear to be the most important are adultery and bodily assault. Since these crimes could easily cross caste boundaries, the jurisprudents clearly bore these in mind when propounding principles for just penalties. The penalty for adultery by a śūdra with a brāhmin woman is capital punishment. A brāhmin who commits adultery with a brāhmin or with a person of a lower caste is subjected to appropriate amercements or fines. Bodily assault and accidental homicide across caste boundaries similarly involves penalties and degrees of compensation respective to the castes of the parties.[35] Murder of a brāhmin always entails the death penalty. But if the slayer is a brāhmin, and since the king is forbidden to impose the capital sentence upon a brāhmin, he must be subjected by a religious or caste assembly (*pariṣad*) to a capital penance, that is, one which will result in forfeiture of life.[36] Not all the jurisprudents, however, appear to have agreed on the exemption of brāhmin offenders from civil punishments.[37] On the other hand, none ostensibly permit brāhmins to "get away with murder;" rather, by permitting resort to capital penance they afforded brāhmins honourable and just means for removing the stigma of caste-excommunication (*bahiṣkāra*) from themselves and their families, preventing retributive incarcerations in the hells, and preventing the scandal of public capital punishment even while undergoing retributive justice for their crimes.[38]

From a different perspective, the brāhmin's self-destruction through the performance of a capital penance was perceived as a kind of self-excommunication or social banishment which the sinner took upon himself even in order that no public stigma might befall innocent relatives. As far as his family and community were concerned, the act of self-exclusion which turned him into a "dead person" at the same time removed from them the taint of his sin. This "dying to his kith and kin" might even have been sacralized through an impressively public symbolic death-ritual.[39] When the transgressor is the eldest son and heir, then, following Manu 11.187ff., his name and titles and privileges could be formally transferred to a younger brother in the course of the ceremony, after which all further mention of the offender ceased from the lips of family members. More frequently, however, excommunication from the community was probably recognized as a merely temporary isolation pending the purifications to be effected by the requisite penances and atonement rituals in which the excommunication itself could be formally reversed and the "excommunicate" restored to his community. Only when, however, the sinner's offence was grave enough to warrant a life-time excommunication could an act of penitential self-annihilation remove its stigma and effect his spiritual restoration to the community of his forebears, make possible his reinstatement in the family and community records, while assuring himself and his family that he would not become in his next earthly life a despicable being through birth from a "shameful womb." Similar benefits were apparently thought to follow even when he submitted readily to a public expiation through capital punishment, in lieu of the privilege of opting for capital penance. Such a belief in the spiritual efficacy of capital punishment is found, for example, in the Manusmṛti (8.318) as well as in the Vasiṣṭha Dharmasūtra (19.45).

The following crimes are specifically mentioned as incurring a death-sentence:

(a) Adultery of a low-caste person with one of a higher caste (cf. Manu 8.359 with Manu 8.371-372).

(b) Murder of any person (Manu 8.349; cf. Viṣ.Dhs.5.1-3).

(c) Gold-theft (including kidnap) (Manu 8.323; cf. footnote of SBE XXV).

(d) Rape of a brāhmin woman (Manu 8.374-379).

(e) Forging of royal edicts, spying, treachery against the State (Manu 9.323).

(f) Dacoity or professional burglary or thuggery (Manu 9.270-271, and 278).

(g) Theft from the king's treasury, insurrection or treachery (Manu 9.274, 278 and 280).

(h) Sabotage (Manu 9.279).

(i) Theft from the royal storehouses, armouries, temples (Manu 9.280).

(j) Debasement of coinage (Manu 9.292).

(k) Acts of sacrilege against holy idols (according to

Nārāyaṇa's comment on Manu 9.285).

(l) Murderous incantations (according to Medhātithi and Kullūka; see footnote to Manu 9.290 in SBE XXV).

Although the political gravity of these capital crimes is manifest, their number also is manifestly small and they are not crimes in which ordinary citizens, as distinct from professional criminals, might engage. This suggests that the jurists did not promote general use of harsh penalties. There is even evidence of humane considerations in their advice on the administrations of penalties, such as the adverse effects of the death-penalty on family dependents. For, although Vasiṣṭha ruled that the death-sentence should be used to punish the gravest or violent crimes (*sāhasas*), yet this might be withheld when the offender voluntarily confesses his guilt to a brāhmin and submits to such approved penances as would expiate his misdeed.[40]

C. Curses, Oaths, and Ordeals

The devising of charms, incantations, and magic to ward off the evil influences of enemies, of malicious deities and harmful spirits, and of curses and imprecations for avenging injuries and punishing wrongs, belong to the earliest traditions of the Vedic Aryans. References to them appear in the Ṛgveda, and by the end of the Vedic period incantational ritual and verbal magic had become a sophisticated public craft. Charms and incantations moreover, had become alternatives to prayer and sacrifice, since ritually intoned expressions were apparently assumed to serve the same provisions and protections effected by many prayers of the Ṛgveda.

Much of the curse-ritual of the Vedas however, is protective rather than vindictive, since its aim is more usually concerned with averting evil influences than with bringing harm or hurt to others. In this respect it serves a similar function to the prayers for deliverance from evils or for protection from misfortunes which are found in the Ṛgveda, yet with the distinction that the curses remove evil by coercive rather than supplicatory means. Nevertheless the exigencies covered by the protective curses in the

Atharvaveda appear to include preventatives not only for the malicious acts of vindictive relatives or neighbours, but also for the bodily and the material effects and consequences of immoral and sinful acts.

Curses (*śāpa*) are apparently divine potencies which, either automatically or as stimuli, provoke the justiciary deities to move against evil-minded persons who have willed harm to the worshipper. This power of curses for arousing the justiciary deities suggests that they were not perceived merely as magical devices. As justiciary instruments, they could work against evildoers in the manner of divine punishments. This ethical dimension is suggested, for example, in the following extract from the Atharvaveda (2.7) in E. W. Hopkins' translation (The Religions of India [1895], 155):

> The sin-hating, god-born plant, that frees from the curses as waters (wash out) the spot, has washed away all curses, the curse of my rival and of my sister; (that) which the Brahman in anger cursed, all this lies under my feet . . . . With this plant protect this (wife), protect my child, protect our property . . . . May the curse return to the curser . . . . We smite even the ribs of this foe with the evil mantra eye.[a]

Despite possible translational variations in this statement, the ethical features are apparent.[41] The potency of the magical plant stems from the "sin-hating god." The reference to the brāhmin's curse being "in anger" suggests its judgemental character. Though uttered by a brāhmin with

---

[a]"Aghadviṣṭā devajātā vīrucchapathayopanī; āpo malamiva prāṇaikṣīt sarvān macchapathām̐ adhi. Yaśca śāpatnaḥ śapatho jāmyāḥ śapathaśca yaḥ; brahmā yanmanyutaḥ śapāt sarvaṃ tanno adhaspadam . . . . Pari māṃ pari me prajāṃ pari ṇaḥ pāhi yad dhanam; arātirno mā tārīnmā nastāri-ṣurabhimātayaḥ. Śaptārametu śapatho yaḥ suhārt tena naḥ saha; cakṣurmantrasya durhārdaḥ pṛṣṭīrapi śṛṇīmasi" (AV 2.2.7.1-5, Bareilly: Saṃskriti Saṃsthāna [1962], Vol. I, p. 50).

righteous indignation, its outworkings are expected to be retributive inasmuch as they are deserved. Since the curses against which the petitioner seeks protection are evil curses of enemies, right is on the petitioner's side as he seeks the protection of the "sin-hating" gods.

Ethical features are discernible in numerous curse stories which are found in epic and purāṇic literature.[42] The stories frequently depict clearly the conditions under which the moral principles addressed become operative. The well-known story of the curse of Valmīkī in the opening chapter of the Rāmāyaṇa is a striking example. In C. Rajagopalachari's translation (Rāmāyaṇa, Bombay: Bharatiya Vidya Bhavan [1958], 15ff.) the incident of Valmīkī's curse reads:

> As he was walking along the river bank, he saw in a nearby tree two loving *krauncа* birds sporting and singing in their joy of life. Suddenly the male bird fell down, hit by a hunter's arrows. The female bird seeing her lover rolling on the ground lamented in piteous fashion. Observing this, Valmīkī burst into a curse: "O hunter, as you have killed one of these love-intoxicated birds, you will wander homeless all your long years.

The prominent ethical features of this curse include its opening with an account of a wrong done, a declaration of the hunter's guilt, and the declaration of the penalty. The role of Valmīkī as the righteous judge carries the certitude that his pronouncement of punishment will come to pass unless the hunter seeks penitential expiation. Behind the curse is the belief that the justiciary deities will ensure its exact outworkings.

Another feature of curses is discernible in the statement of the Bṛhadāraṇyaka Upaniṣad (6.4.12) that "whomsoever a (curse-ritual-knowing) brāhmin curses . . . departs from this world impotent and devoid of merit." The suggestion here is that curses have a merit-negating power which exposes the one who is cursed to conditions having a negative and painful character even including premature death. The statement also suggests that curse-ritual functioned like *mantras* though in reverse, for whereas *mantras* when formally enunciated could encapsulate and introject magical power, curses could drain it away. Even formal rituals could be turned into curse-bearing devices simply by the reciting of *mantras* incorrectly or portions of a ritual in reverse or through intentional fumblings of powerful utterances.[43] The question is whether their power lay in such devices themselves or in the victim's belief in their power. As Manu (3.57-58) says that "where the female relations live in grief, the family soon wholly perishes . . The houses on which female relations, not being duly honoured, pronounce a curse, perish completely, as if destroyed by magic."[a]

On the whole, curses are distinguishable from magical imprecations (*abhicārāḥ*), which the śāstrikas roundly condemn, and which belong rather to the field of witchcraft (*kṛtya*) than to ethics. Concerning these Manu (9.290) decreed that "for all incantations intended to destroy life, for magic rites with roots (practiced by persons) nonrelated (to the one against whom they are directed), and for various kinds of sorcery, a fine of two-hundred *paṇas* shall be inflicted."[b] Manu clearly sets such practices within the purview of crimes even though it appears that resort to them might be permitted under certain conditions, as G. Bühler explains:

> According to the commentators the *abhicāras* comprise all incantations and sacrifices, taught either in the Veda or in secular works, which are intended to destroy life. The magic rites, performed with roots, are those which are intended to bring a person into one's power. These are permitted, if practised against a husband or a relative (so Nārāyaṇa understands). The *kṛtyā* (sorceries) are such spells as produce diseases, or cause the failure of an adversary's undertakings. If the *abhicāras* are successful, the punishment is that of murder.[44]

---

[a] "Śocanti jāmayo yatra vinśyatyāśu tatkulam; . . . jāmayo yāni gehāni śapantyapratipūjitāḥ; tāni kṛtyāhatāniva vinaśyanti samantataḥ" (Manu 3.57-58; Chowkhamba 226; 113-114).

[b] "Abhicāreṣu sarveṣu kartavyo dviśato damaḥ; mūlakarmaṇi cānāptaiḥ kṛtyāsu vividhāsu ca" (Manu 9.290; Chowkhamba 226; 552).

No such strictures stand against the recitation of curses. For curses are penal sentences based upon righteous judgements. Hence in Manu (9.313-316) the king is warned not to provoke brāhmins into cursing him, because by doing so, they could instantly "destroy him together with his army and his vehicles." The commentators Medhātithi and Nārada explain that brāhmins are angered by "deprivation of property" or by "threatening them insolently or shamefully." Kullūka explains that the king's destruction would be "by magic rites and curses" which may be a reference to the Mokṣadharma section of the Mahābhārata (12.343.55; 57ff., and 1.108.14) which contains stories of curses such as of the moon becoming a consuming fire through the curse of Dakṣa, and a "*Vadavamukha*" who turned the ocean into salt in order to punish King Dakṣa's disobedience.

According to the Manusmṛti, the using of curses as retributional instruments appear to be allowed solely for brāhmins, for which reason Manu (11.31-32) says that "a brāhmin who knows the law need not bring any (offence) to the notice of the king; by his own power alone he can punish those men who injure him. His own power is greater than the power of the king; the brāhmin, therefore, may punish his foes by his own power alone."[a]

In the light of the argument presented so far that curses are penal instruments comprising justicial pronouncements of the wrong which has been done, and the penalty which it deserves, it is misfounded to regard them merely as a-moral magical devices applied to non-moral ends and bearing no relation to the moral deserts of a wrongdoer. Already it has been noted that moral indignation might precede a curse pronouncement. Also some texts indicate that the retributive power of a curse is dependent on a demeritorious condition in the recipient. Should no guilt be present, no

---

[a]"Na brāhmaṇovedayata kiñcidrājani dharmavit; svavīryyeṇaiva tāñśiṣyānmānavānapakāriṇaḥ. Svavīryyādrājavīryyācca svavīryaṃ balavattaram; tasmātsvenaiva vīryyeṇa nigṛhṇīyādarīndvijaḥ" (Manu 11.31-32; Chowkhamba 226; 601).

conditions through which ripened Karmas can fructify as experiences, the curse-powers become neutralized or reverted upon the head of the curser. In the Rāmāyaṇa-epic,[45] the "divine arrows" of the enraged king Viśvāmitra fail to overcome the ṛṣi/seer Vasiṣṭha. The divine-magical power inherent in the spoken utterance is acknowledged for it renders incandescent the sacred rod which Vasiṣṭha carries both as the symbol of his office and of the vows of purity, and so forth, upon which his holy life is based.[46]

Like curses (*śāpa*), oaths (*śapatha*) are penal sentences or formal declarations of punishment. But whereas curses are retrospective inasmuch as they pronounce judgement upon acts which have already been committed, oaths are anticipatory and therefore also conditional. "Because thou hast done this . . .;" such is the formal introduction to a curse. "If thou doest this, then shall . . .;" such is the formal introduction of an oath.[47]

The close association of oaths (*śapatha*) with ordeals (*divya*) as penal implements in ancient Indian law and custom is affirmed both by Edward Westermark (Early Beliefs and Their Social Influence, London [1932], 84) and A. E. Crawley ("Oath: Introductory and Primitive", ERE IX; 433). Crawley particularly regarded oaths as the primary constituent of an ordeal, and the majority of ordeals as being in fact "concrete oaths taken by the accused party" on the assumption of a divine imprecation falling immediately upon the guilty. Drawing on several authorities, Shivaji Singh (Evolution of the Smṛti Law, Varanasi: Bhāratiyā Vidyā Prakāśana [1972], 104) suggests that it is because of this close connection between "oath" and "ordeal" that the word *śapatha* is used in the older smṛtis for either designation as in the statement of Manu (8.115) that, "he whom a blazing fire burns not, whom the water forces not to come up, who meets with no speedy misfortune, must be held innocent (on the strength of) his *Śapatha*."[a] On the other hand, the

[a] "Yamiddho na dahatyagnirāpo nonmajjayanti ca; na cārttimṛcchati kṣipraṃ sa jñeyaḥ śapathe śuciḥ" (Manu 8.115; Chowkhamba 226; 405).

Saṅkhalikhita uses the word *śapatha* with reference to divine means of proof such as the "poison" and the "fire" ordeals, whereas in later texts such as the Nāradīyasmṛti (4.247-252) and the Mitākṣarā (on the Yājñavalkyasmṛti 2.96) the word *śapatha* is restricted to oaths, the popular word *divya* being utilized for ordeals.

The penal dimensions of a typical oath are apparent in the coronation-oath of the king as found in the Aitareya Brāhmaṇa (8.4.15.20; HOS XXV). "I swear that thou mayst take from me whatever good works I do to the day of my death, together with my life and my children, if ever I should do thee harm," or, as Martin Haug (Ait.Brāhmaṇa) renders this, "Whatever pious works . . . etc. . . together with the position, they good deeds, thy life, thy children, I would wrest from thee, shouldest thou do me harm." The belief is also implicit that the oath will become effective as a curse at the moment the king causes harm to a brāhmin. A typical formulation of an oath, accordingly, might be, "If I have told you a lie, then let this (evil) now happen to me." It is probable that this verbal form of oaths was used as an investigative instrument in courts of law.[48]

Oaths, like curses, moreover, were believed to carry their own potentiality for fulfilling the terms of their formulations, although the immediacy of their outworkings could be enhanced by such intensifying ritual acts as holding holy water or sacred *kuśa*-grass during the enunciation of the oath. Manu ordained, for example (8.113-115), that a man should swear his oath on that which is most sacred to him and which he would fear most to lose. Hence, a judge should cause a brāhmin to swear by his veracity (*satyena*), a kṣatriya by his chariot (*vāhana*), his steed, and his weapons, a vaiśya by his merchandise such as his kine, grain, and gold (*gobījakāñca*), and a śūdra by the demerit of all grave offences (*sarvaistu pātaka*).[a] Alternatively, these might vindicate themselves through either

---

[a]"Satyena śāpayedvipraṃ kṣatriyaṃ vāhanāyudhaiḥ; gobījakāñcanairvaiśyaṃ śūdraṃ sarvaistu pātakaiḥ" (Manu 8.113; Chowkhamba 226; 404).

the "fire ordeal," the "water ordeal," or the "evil-touch ordeal."[a]

The wording of certain oaths employed in court-trials suggests that their effects might be manifest immediately. Nevertheless, Manu (8.108) advised that, for the sake of justice, a waiting period of seven days should be observed, and in the absence of any signs of an accused person's guilt, the case against him should be dismissed. On the other hand, any oath having an explicit time-period for the manifestation of its effects, could not be used to effect a judgement before that time. Nevertheless, a murderer who falsely swears his innocence could become immediately struck dead by the power of his oath or by the direct action of the supervisory deities of court-hearings.

In contrast to the magical, protective, prophylactic, or therapeutic functions of oaths which are found in the Atharvaveda, their penal functions are explicit in those oaths which are found in the dharmaśāstra literature as implements of "trials by ordeal. The magical imprecation which is to be enunciated by the court chaplain before the sacred Ghee [clarified butter] in the "heated gold ordeal" (*tapta-māṣa-divya*)[b] has a manifestly retributive tone. The oath pronounced by the litigant in the "ordeal by Dharma"[c], on the other hand, is a typical self-vindicating one which plainly

---

[a]"Agniṃ vāhārayedenamapsu cainaṃ nimajjayet; putrādārasya vāpyenaṃ śirāṃsi sparśayetpṛthak" (Manu 8.114, Chowkhamba 226; 404).

[b]"O Ghee! thou art the holiest thing in sacrifices, thou are nectar; burn him (the *śodhya*) if he is a sinner; be cool as ice if he be innocent" (Kane, History of the Dharmaśāstra, Vol. III [1973], 375). (*Śodhya* = an accused person, one who has to clear himself of a charge laid against him, Apte's Sanskrit Dictionary.)

[c]"The *śodhya* should repeat the words 'if I am free from guilt may (the image of picture) of Dharma come to my hands.' Saying this he should take out one ball from the vessel. If he takes out Dharma he is innocent. This resembles the drawing of lots" (Kane, History of the Dharmaśāstra [1973], Vol. III, 375).

brings oaths and ordeals closer to the forms of expiatory devices. Indeed, the ordeal is recommended for persons "who desire to undergo this ordeal as an expiation for sins" (Kane, History of the Dharmaśāstra [1973], Vol. III, 375).

The self-directed oaths enunciated by litigants during "trials by ordeal" carry retributive implications in the sense of: "if I am guilty then let such and such an injury come to me." On the other hand, there are clear indications in the early dharmasmṛtis that ordeals were not intended as instruments for proving guilt but rather as appeals of innocence. This is partly due to their optionality for litigants who invoke this means for resolving disputed matters. In this light, they only became retributive instruments if a participant knowingly--or even more particularly unknowingly--is de facto guilty of a charge laid against him.

Kane's essay on ordeals (History of the Dharmaśāstra [1973], Vol. III, 361-378) draws extensively on two digests --the Vyavahāramayūkha of Nīlakaṇṭha (1615-1645 A.D.) and the Vyavahāraprakāśa, which is part of the Vīramitrodaya of Mitramiśra (1615-1645 A.D.)--which he claims contain "the most elaborate treatment of ordeals." Kane's citations from these works show that, both in kind and degree, ordeals were made to be appropriate to the charges for which divine proofs had to be sought in the absence of human proof. The ordeals of "balance" (*tulā* or *dhaṭa*), "fire," "poison," and "water," were specifically devised for investigating charges involving claims of a thousand *paṇas* (copper pieces) or more, charges of treason, or charges involving any of the five "great sins" (*mahāpātaka*). But Kane (History of the Dharmaśāstra [1973], Vol. III, 365) perceives "a spirit of tolerance, kindness, and concern for the weaknesses of mankind" in the explicit directions relating to the extenuating factors and conditions which must be considered before staging a "trial by ordeal." These concern the caste, age, sex, health, and pecuniary circumstances of one who is to be tested, as well as the season or climate. These may be perceived, on the other hand, simply as factors to be taken into consideration for ensuring the efficiency of these investigative instruments.

Ordeals apparently could not be staged at any place which the judges or the litigants considered convenient. Instead, according to the Pitāmahasmṛti (known only through quotations in other sources), ordeals are to be administered by the king and the judge in a public place in the presence of the judicial authorities and of the general public. According to the Kātyāyanasmṛti (434-437 in Kane's reconstruction and English translation), ordeals must take place in a temple ground whenever grave sins are in question, or "near the royal gate" in treasonable cases, or in a public place such as at crossroads where sexual offences must be examined, or otherwise "in a hall of justice."

Among the liturgical provisions of an ordeal is the invocation of the divine guardians of justice by a "writ of subpoena" enunciated in the form of powerful mantras. The deities summonsed to appear in the orderly assembly include Dharma--the presiding deity of ordeals--then Indra, Yama, Varuṇa, Kubera, and Agni, and scores of lesser divinities as prescribed in the Mitākṣarā on the Yājn̂valkyasmṛti (2.97 and 99). Their summons indicates a strong belief that justice is a divine concern, and that divine powers are watchfully "on the scene" whenever justice itself is "in the balance."

The summoning of the justiciary deities to such trials carries the assurance that no deity who is summoned will fail to be in attendance. But although this suggests a high degree of moral readiness on their part to serve the cause of justice, it seems that their presence is because their own survival and well-being are consciously invested in the safety of the social order which is a pillar of that larger Order to which they belong. The pragmatical concern suggests, of course, that justice is not an essential attribute of the deities on account of which they are properly considered to be ethical beings. But if they are essentially amoral they merely appear on the side of stabilizing justice in order to protect that Order within which the survival and well-being of all creatures--heavenly and earthly--subsist.

That the instrument of "trial by ordeal" is extremely

ancient is evident from early literary references such as, for example, a fire ordeal in the *Pañcaviṃśa-* or *Tāṇḍya-Brāhmaṇa* (14.6.6) which is referred to in Manu (8.116) and the "heated-axe ordeal" in the Chāndogya Upaniṣad (6.16.1). Lasting confidence in the efficiency is evident in the survival of the practice well into the modern eighteenth century, even despite voiced misgivings which Medhātithi in a comment on Manu 8.115 was hard put to assuage. Numerous epigraphic and other references referred to or cited by Kane (History of the Dharmaśāstra [1973], III, 376-378) show that during this long period no other means were sought for treating doubtful cases where documentary, testimentary, or other material evidence were in want, and which could be perceived as being as proficient as "trial by ordeal." One cannot agree, therefore, with Julian Morgenstern in perceiving the eventual discontinuance of the practice as a belated perception by peoples of ancient cultures of its superstitious and irrational character.[49] Its disuse in modern India is the expected result of the inadmissability of judicial instruments which carry philosophical and theological presuppositions which are inappropriate to a modern secular judicial system, and no longer have the psychological effectiveness of standards and norms whose "true explanation," Derrett remarks, "has long been forgotten."[50]

Given the considerable information on ordeals made available through the Vyavahāramayūkha and Vyavahāraprakāśa, it is reasonable to assume that jurists who supported the continuous use of such a highly developed system of investigative instruments were not unmindful of the principles as well as the usages of ordeals, and recognized psychological as well as metaphysical grounds through which the operations of an ordeal might be explained. We might argue even that not only did they transmit through their schools of law a long juridical tradition, but also bore in that oral transmission the principles as well as the procedures of ordeals. Moreover, their continued use, according to J. D. M. Derrett's sources, even as late as 1783 or 1855 (JOAS 98.1.1978; 102), may be considered as evidence of their proven reliability during this long course of Indian judicial experience.[51]

Derrett however has not denigrated the rationality of ordeals as such but has only questioned whether or not the reasons were remembered by the users of ordeals, or "got lost" behind the practices until their rediscovery through scholarly analysis. Derrett shows how the rational sense which is observable in the "ordeal-by-balance" (*dhaṭa*) supports the probable rationality of all ordeals. One may ask, however, if a rationality which a modern Western scholar is able to discover at this distance in time from the ancient Indian practice of law would not have been more readily discernible by the early Indian jurists!

The inherent rationality of ordeals demonstrated by Derrett is supported also by a rich documentation of the modern discussion of the ritual of "trial by ordeal" in ancient societies, beginning with A. F. Stenzler's essay (1855) and concluding with an article on the subject entitled "Gottesurteil" in the Brockhaus Enzyklopädie 7 (1969). Derrett's essay, moreover, is in laudable contrast to the regrettably "supercilious manner" in which ordeals have been treated by modern writers in Hasting's Encyclopedia of Religion and Ethics (9, 1917; 505-533) and by E. W. Hopkins (The Religions of India [1895]; 275-279). His argument, richly supported by a background of ancient and modern Indian references to ordeals, is that here, as in other matters of ancient belief and practice, "a piece of apparent nonsense will yield to careful investigation, and such facts . . . be brought to light" whereby its panditry "is not at all discredited" but "can well be the reverse."

To what extent therefore, in addition to the rational sense of ancient ordeals, can their metaphysical and ethical presuppositions be ascertained from the literature? Since references to the "heated-axe ordeal" in Chāndogya Upaniṣad (6.16) and to the "water ordeal" in the Mahābhārata (3.134.26-27) indicate that the practice is extremely ancient, it is difficult to defend E. W. Hopkins' contention (The Religions of India [1895], 275) that apart from these two ordeals, the rite of "trial by ordeal" presented in the Manusmṛti is quite late. For although the Manusmṛti (8.114) mentions only two ordeals, the Nāradīyasmṛti (4.251) declares that Manu indicated five kinds of ordeals. The Saṅkhalikhita[52] mentions four, the Viṣṇu Dharmasūtra (9.10-11) and the Yājñavalkya-smṛti (2.95) each have five, the Nārada smṛti (1.247-252; 4.337 and 343) describes seven, and Bṛhaspati (10.1-5) with Pitāmaha (according to Aparārka) quoted in the Mitākṣarā (on Yājñavalkya 2.95) mention nine. One might fairly conclude that the relative amounts of space given in the texts to ordeals indicate early recognition of their utilitarian efficiency as divine means of proof (*pramāṇa*), as reliable sources of information whenever documentary (*likhita*), testamentary (*sākṣi*), or other material (*bhukti*) evidences were not available, and as retributions for hidden crimes which had escaped the king's surveillance.[53]

The numerical progression of ordeals could imply an evolution of this investigative instrument, particularly if the suppositions of Julius Jolly (Hindu Law and Custom [1928], 47) and P. V. Kane (History of the Dharmaśāstra [1930], Vol. I, 202) are accepted that the higher the number of ordeals the later the text. On the other hand, if the texts are seen as reflecting regional variations in compilations of juridical regulations prior to the codification of smṛti material in the digests, then their contentions, and Shivaji Singh's contention (Evolution of the Smṛti Law [1972], 92-103), that humane considerations in later smṛtis reflect an ethical evolution in the theory and practice of ordeals, are historically doubtful. Even if it could be proved that ordeals developed from being forms of enquiry, proof, judgement, and penalty into mere forms of inquiry, it would still require proof that humane considerations came later and were not part of the judicial considerations to which the formal implementation of ordeals were subjected.[54]

In any case the status of ordeals in the ancient Indian penal system is evident in their setting within a distinct body of regulations under the title of law in the Yājñavalkyasmṛti and the Nārada Smṛti as being trustworthy instruments for the examination of witnesses, as proxies where witnesses could not be found, and as devices for the effecting of punishments upon guilty persons. Moreover, they were not seen as devices which could be utilized for any matter of concern to the courts, but only with respect to specific concerns for which other more appropriate, more convenient, and less elaborate implements were not available. The Manusmṛti (8.113-116) explicitly limited their use to the ascertaining of the guilt of grave crimes and for authenticating oaths; Medhātithi, Govinda, and Kullūka likewise limited their proper use to removing doubts in grave criminal matters. And as with curses and oaths, their effectiveness rested upon their guilt or the innocence of a litigant, with his virtue serving as a positive force and his criminality acting as a negative influence upon the outcome. Bṛhaspati (10.3) is consistent with other śāstrikas in ordering this recourse only when an offence happened so long ago, or so secretly, that no witnesses are available, when witnesses are perjured, when (10.17 followed by Nār.Dhs.1.235-348) uncertainty arises over documentary or oral evidence, "and when ratiocination fails." Specific circumstances which Bṛhaspati declares (10.1-2) as properly justifying a trial by ordeal even when there are witnesses are cases of forgery of gems, pearl or coral, withholding of a deposit, physical violence (a ruffian), an adulterer, and generally in charges relating to grave crimes or the misappropriation of security deposits.

Theft particularly falls within the category of those grave crimes for which Bṛhaspati (10.17) ordains the use of ordeals. Allowing for considerations of the physical stamina and the moral character of the accused, he presents the following ordeals:

property worth 1000 *paṇas* -- the ordeal by poison
property worth 750 *paṇas* -- the ordeal by fire
property worth 400 *paṇas* -- the ordeal by hot gold
property worth 300 *paṇas* -- the ordeal by rice grains
property worth 150 *paṇas* -- the ordeal by sacred libation
property worth 100 *paṇas* -- the ordeal by Dharma.

All these ordeals, however, are applicable only to low-caste persons. Middling and high-caste suspects are to be treated as if doubly and four-times suspect, that is, as if they were suspect of stealing twice or four times as much as lower-caste persons. A brāhmin accused of stealing one-hundred paṇas worth of property could be tested by the "ordeal by hot gold," and so forth, on the assumption that the degree of probable guilt would be proportionate to his education and social position, higher-caste persons bearing greater responsibility for their actions than lower-caste ones. A law-breaker of the brāhmin caste in particular, who by upbringing and education ought to have known better, would be subjected to a severer ordeal whose outworking would accord with the measure of his culpability while causing him to experience, in Bṛhaspati's words, "purgation through ordeal."

On the other hand, such confidence as Bṛhaspati felt in the reliability of ordeals may not have been shared by all leading jurisprudents, according to his reply to critics of the method (10.16) that even the normal method of inquiry through witnesses "is apt to become invalid" either through partiality, malice, or greed, whereas "an ordeal properly administered never loses its validity." If it is improperly administered, that is, "against the rule," either with respect to its administrators or its ordained procedures, then, "as a means of proving what ought to be proved" it is invalid.[55]

In the Nārada Smṛti, two important considerations reveal the concern of the smṛti-writers for justice by not placing the accused under any physical, psychological, or other disadvantage. "Trials by ordeal" are intended, says Nārada, to prove the innocence of a litigant. His willing participation accordingly is essential for its just operations. For this reason, the text states (1.253; SBE XXXIII) that "(these ordeals) have been ordained here by Nārada for the purpose of <u>proving the innocence</u> of criminals who are defendants in a lawsuit, (and) in order that right may be discerned from wrong." Furthermore (1.256 and 313-315), climatic factors, bodily infirmity, spiritual duties and obligations (vows, ascetics), and so forth, must be considered as grounds for withholding a trial by ordeal in any particular case "if the dictates of justice are listened to." And "where no one declares himself ready to <u>undergo punishment</u> an ordeal cannot take place."[56] It follows from this that in Nārada's view (1.313ff.) ordeals are not compulsory, one must not be compelled to undergo them.[57]

The Kātyāyanasmṛti (458) has a statement to the effect that Fate is the supervisory deity of "trials by ordeal," and that in accordance with a man's guilt he inflicts different kinds of physical disease. "The diseases brought on men by Fate are tuberculosis, diarrhoea, boils, pain in the palate and bones, eye-disease, seizure (by evil spirits), headache, and fracture of the arms."

Yet concerns were bound to arise sooner or later over the reliability of trials by ordeal when a person "proved" guilty through an ordeal was found on new evidence to have been de facto innocent. Referring to such cases Medhātithi, commenting on a statement of Manu (8.115) (as per Bühler's footnote, SBE XXV, 274), explained that notwithstanding such mistakes, the value of ordeals is not entirely negatived, particularly since such failures are infrequent. For even though perception and rational inference can prove faulty, we do not abandon them for this reason. Witnesses sometimes give false testimony, yet we do not dispense with witnesses. So, just as we must rely on imperfect sources of information even as we must rely on evidence submitted by uncertain witnesses, so we must rely on ordeals. If however, in any particular case, the outworking of an ordeal should lead to a mistaken judgement, this is not because the accused was innocent. He was indeed guilty, but of a crime in a previous life. Justice, through the instrument of Karma, has translated the ordeal into an occasion for a just recompense.[58]

In every case, however, the ordeal itself was believed to contain a potentiality which equates consequences with deserts, or more commonly the potentiality was believed to lie in the powers of the deities who instrument that equation. Less frequently, where the structure of an ordeal could permit only an ascertainment of the guilt or the innocence of an accused person without any retributional effects, any deserved punishment would have to be meted through penal instruments. Even here, however, an ordeal would declare the judgement of that God (Dharma) who is the Overseer and Guarantor of its just operations.[59]

But what if a suspect was guilty in some partial sense,

that is to say, not entirely responsible for a criminal action? How then would an ordeal indicate the degree of his guilt? The ordeal might certainly indicate the fact of his guilt, but not the degree of it, unless the jurists were ready to consider that one who is badly burned in a "fire ordeal" is more guilty than one who is lightly burned! This distinction, however, is not apparent in the texts. If in fact trial by ordeal was generally resorted to in matters of grave criminality, then its negative outcome could be expected to manifest itself only with extreme severity. The possibility of extenuating circumstances mitigating the degree of guilt could not be allowed for within the process of a trial by ordeal but only in deciding which ordeal would be appropriate in the light of such circumstances. Nevertheless, it appears to have been generally believed that the outcome of any ordeal would be strictly just so that there could not be an undeserved or unjust result.[60]

Chapter 6. Modes of Self-Retribution

"Voluntary punishment," or the idea that a person may punish himself, fits uneasily into a view of punishment as a purely hetero-personal function. But modern developments in penal reform include exploration of the feasibility of involving offenders in "personal reparations" for their crimes as a voluntary alternative to judicial punishments. An advisory council report dated August 1970 on the subject of "Reparation by the Offender" stemmed from a request of the British Home Secretary in 1966 for advice on "how the principle of personal reparation might be given a more prominent place in the [English] penal system." In an article on the subject of Penal Reform,[1] Tom Hadden (New Society Journal [1971], 952ff.) admits that any penal measure will be more successful in reforming the offender when he recognizes the punishment as being fair and just in his circumstances. This factor of "acceptance," therefore, "is at least as important as the nature of the punishment or treatment itself." He adds, "In simple terms, some offenders accept their punishment, whatever it may be, and reform themselves; others do not and drift on into a long criminal career."[2]

The inculcation of a positive attitude toward punishment, however, could hardly succeed without a prior penological distinction between punishments which could help offenders to reform themselves and others which might have adverse effects and even lead to recidivism. Consideration of the rehabilitative forms would reasonably include evaluation of new and ancient modes of self-punishment which imply that an offender has admitted his fault, has accepted the justice of its recompense, and recognizes the value of paying for his misdeeds as a precondition of his full restoration to the society.

If penitential theory had religious presuppositions in ancient India, penitential practices were not essentially religious inasmuch as they were adopted as means for removing guilt, which is a moral rehabilitative function. In this light, Sir Henry Maine may have misjudged the rationality of the ancient Indian juridical system when he considered penances as a religious intrusion upon the civil functions of laws through the survival of a common substratum of outmoded habit lying beneath Hinduism and Christianity and inherited from a common prehistoric Indo-European culture. The character of his misjudgement, however, is perceptible from the textual sources themselves in which the general notion of *prāyaścitta* or formal penance and its specific formulations in relation to civil and religious laws are indicated.

Less obviously than penances, yet not unimportantly, ascetical practice in general has perceptible retributional elements which have bearings upon the Indian conception of Punishment. These retributional elements clearly arise in connection with a sense of guilt due to having fallen short of, strayed from, transgressed or violated, or erred with respect to a standard of Right by wrongful acts committed ignorantly or unknowingly, through carelessness, or on account of a misdirected moral will, but which can be removed through purgative expiational processes arising from a voluntary self-infliction of pain.

A. Punitive Asceticism

The functions of asceticism as a voluntary self-punishment is discernible in the rich attestation to ascetical practice in early Indian literature. The general nature of asceticism itself has been insightfully defined by Oscar Hardman (The Ideals of Asceticism, London: S.P.C.K. [1924], 9) as:

> . . . a voluntary activity in which the soul of man endeavours to effect its release, or to prepare for and to find satisfying self-expression in its relations with others. Resting on a multiform religious or ethical foundation, it comprises diverse types of moral and spiritual enterprise; but, though wide in its scope, it is legitimately known by the one name, which carries with it no more danger of confusion than such terms as prayer and sacrifice; for each type is readily distinguished by adjectival qualification, and is to be estimated on its own merits.

From the definition alone, it can be seen that ascetical practice is much wider than self-punishment and therefore cannot be equated with it. But the punitive element in ascetical practice is manifest enough to its analysis and ascertainment of its bearings on the Indian conception of Punishment. The penal and penitential elements may even be ascertained in ascetic practices which are not overtly penitential or self-punitive, nor generally considered to be such, including yogic methods and practices whose aim is some kind of "consciousness raising" toward the development of psychical and/or extra-physical powers. For the implicit assumption that the self-infliction of pain is requisite for the realization of those enhancements suggests an implicit acknowledgement of the essential function and power of self-punishment in all yogic self-realizational practices.

Ascetical practices which bear explicitly upon the conception of Punishment are those which J. C. Flugal (Man, Morals and Society, London: Duckworth [1945], 92) identified as "punitive asceticism." In these the moral element of "self-punishment" is "the sole or predominant factor," into which category "fall a great number of more or less institutionalized religious practices such as fasting and penance," which are symptomatic of a strong personalized sense of guilt and of a need for cleansing "characterized by all degrees of consciousness of the punitive purpose." Such practices range from simple self-discipline to extreme forms of self-punishment. Yet all meet one essential condition, as Flugal (op.cit., 92ff.) explains, namely, "the culprit willingly submits to the punishment and is himself a party to its execution."[3]

This self-punishment moreover is a public function which has had a prestigious status in different cultures as well as testifying to a deeply rooted psychological and religious intuition that self-punishment does "put the sinner right" with himself, with society, and with God before whom it is better to punish one's own self than to be punished by Him in the hereafter. Indian ascetical practice however is uniquely perceived as an intensification and shortening of an expiational process. Karmas which could require many life-times of incarceration in transmigrational bodies can be consumed within a single lifelong expiational programme with the certitude of final liberation when the programme of self-punishment has been accomplished. In this respect, Indian asceticism could even be defined as a programme of anticipatory karmic retribution through ascetical practice. The value and even the necessity of preferring this resort to the extended processes of hellish and earthly transmigrations, are frequently reiterated. As iterated in the Bhāgavata Purāṇa (5.2): "If a man commits sinful acts which he does not expiate in this life, he must pay the penalty in the next life; and great will be his suffering. Therefore, with self-controlled mind, a man should expiate his sins here on earth."[4] The nature of it, however, may be ascertained through examination of two important ascetical concepts: *tapas* and *yoga*. The sanskrit word *tapas* is that word which is most commonly translated as "austerity," "self-denial," or "asceticism." Since the word comes from the root *tap-* which has the meaning of "to be hot" or "to burn," the word suggests that Indian ascetical practice is perceived as a "burning away of dross," of that which clings to, weighs down, darkens the translucent quality of, the burdened soul. This fire-symbolism in Indian ascetical thought is in several respects ideal. For, it expresses the upward movement of fire which reflects man's upward strivings for liberation and the transcendalizing transmutation of gross matter into spiritual matter through the painful application of intense heat; and it also suggests the sacrificial fire-altar on which the ascetic immolates his gross nature and releases his spiritual self toward Brahman.[5]

The connotation of warmth and heat in the word is reflected in the Rgveda in both the literal and the metaphorical sense.[6] A penitential tone is evident in its use as the "sense of guilt" which burns the conscience of the penitent.[7] This "smiting of the breast" with an afflicted conscience is called *tapta*. But there are other *tapas* where the word has an objective connotation with respect to the divine inflictions which the gods cause to befall sinful men. The *tapas* of the gods take the forms of bodily diseases, material misfortunes, and social calamities such as drought, famine, civil strife, and war. In the Vedas, generally, there is accordingly, no ethical distinction between the *tapiṣṭhena* or thunderbolts of retribution which the guardian deities of order hurl upon sinful men, and the *tapas* or punishments which they send to men.[8]

Psychological dimensions of the word *tapas*, however, appear more explicitly in the brāhmaṇas where ascetical practices appear to be intended for the acquisition of superior physical and magical powers as well as for the attainment of material benefits or rewards. But whether or not the ethical notion of compensating wrong acts or expiating misdeeds is prominent there, it is implicit in the belief that through self-afflictions of various kinds one realizes the purified state from which flow physical, mental, and spiritual powers, as well as other benefits in this life and in the hereafter. Since, however, the practices are not based on calculated degrees of guilt, it is not possible strictly to call them "punishments" beyond the recognition of their intrinsic punitive elements.

Although in the Upanishad period prior to the sixth century B.C., lifelong asceticism--known as *saṃnyāsa*--had become the vocation of "*saṃnyāsins*," there is also evidence that earthly life itself had acquired the character of an ascetical ordeal by the same period.[9] Prior to the appearance of the earliest dharmasmṛtis at least, as reflected in the extant texts, all four vocations (*āśramas*) of studentship, the householder, the monastic, and the solitary ascetic had acquired an expiational character. In Manu (4.12-24), for example, each dutifully performed act of a brāhmin serves a purificatory function by removing sins and effecting progress toward the goal of final liberation. Manu (11.236) even subsumed all duties within the class of expiations by emphasizing the penitential character of caste-obligations. But whereas the *tapas* of a brāhmin is sacred study, that of a kṣatriya is the protection of the state, of a vaiśya the pursuit of trade and agriculture, and of a śūdra, service to others.[a]

---

[a]"Brāhmaṇasya tapo jñānam tapaḥ kṣatrasya rakṣaṇam; vaiśyasya tu tapo vārtā tapaḥ śūdrasya sevanam" (Manu 11.235; Chowkhamba 226; 652).

Not only vocational obligations but even the life-experiences of individuals could have an expiational purpose according to the Bṛhadāraṇyaka Upaniṣad (5.11) where the major tragedies of life--sickness, the funeral procession, and the funeral pyre[a]--are called "supreme austerities" which lead the soul toward liberation unlike the merely temporal benefits of the duties and penances prescribed in the smṛti texts.

It is possible that this upanishadic text is untypical of the upanishadic teaching in general which appears to emphasize voluntary penance or austerity as having the higher salvific benefit. Even virtue, when practiced according to the scriptural ordinances, is a *tapas* or self-purifying austerity. This assumption appears to be a recognition that the practice of virtue requires painstaking dutiful effort. Hence, the Mahānārāyaṇa Upaniṣad (8) could reflect the view of the upanishadic thinkers by its description of the virtues of everyday morality as "lower mortifications" or *tapas* and its interpretation of daily life as being properly a penitential diet comprising the subjugation of the senses, the eradication of pride, and purgation of the soul.

Moral acts, however, conceivably consume or expiate karmas, and do so, not as preventatives of karmic processes or operations, but as their anticipations. By self-inflictions for purificatory purposes, the fruitions of karmas are forced into the present life so that the full tale of karma-expiations is willingly experienced within the concentrated ordeal of a single penitential life. While accordingly, the conditions and experiences common to our ordinary lives are fruitional outworkings of karmas, those voluntary acts which are additional to the required obligations of one's caste and vocation are pure austerities which intensify and foreshorten the karmic process and hasten the day of one's final liberation. It is this expediting power of austerities which could explain their high status in the Manusmrti (11.238-40):

---

[a]"Etadvai paramaṃ tapo yat vyāhitastapyate . . . etadvai paramaṃ tapo yaṃ pretamaraṇyaṃ haranti . . . etadvai paramaṃ yaṃ pretamagnāvabhyādadhati paramaṃ haiva lokaṃ jayati ya evaṃ veda" (Bṛhad.5.11; Adyar [1936], 491-2).

> . . . medicines, good health, learning, and the various divine stations are attained by austerities alone; for austerity is the means of gaining them. Whatever is hard to be traversed . . . hard to be performed, all this may be accomplished by austerities (*tapas*); for austerity is difficult to surpass. Both those who have committed mortal sin (*mahāpātaka*), and all other offenders, are severally freed from their guilt by means of well-performed austerities . . . . Whatever sin men commit by thoughts, words, or deeds, that they speedily burn away by penance. . . The gods, discerning that the holy origin of this whole (world) is from austerity, have thus proclaimed the incomparable power of austerity.[a]

Moreover (12.104) "austerity and learning are the best means by which a Brāhmaṇa secures supreme bliss; by austerities he destroys guilt, by sacred learning he obtains the cessation of (births and) death."[10,b]

Like *tapas*, the punitive elements of the technique of *yoga* can be discerned to some extent by an analysis of the word itself, and by the comparison of its technical and non-technical uses. In the Ṛgveda, the word *yoga* simply means "yoking" in the literal sense of the yoking of animals. The heavenly bodies, perceived as celestial beasts, are said to be yoked by Ṛta to their preordained courses. Likewise the actions of the gods and of men are under the yoke of Ṛta which is that cosmic Order of which they are living elements.

Yoga or the yoking of the self, therefore, is a discipline which brings one's selfhood into harmony with the cosmic Order. But insofar as this self-discipline includes voluntary self-infliction of pain, Yoga-practice implies self-punishment. Although in the Kaṭha Upaniṣad (6.11) "Yoga" is explicitly defined as self-control: "The firm

---

[a]"Auṣadhānyagado vidyā daivī ca vividhā sthitiḥ; tapasyaiva prasiddhyanti tapasteṣām hi sādhanam. Yad duṣtaraṃ yad durāpaṃ yad durgaṃ yacca duṣkaram; sarvantu tapasā sādhyaṃ tapo ti duratikramam" (Manu 11.237-238; Chowkhamba 226; 652).

[b]"Tapo vidyā ca viprasya niḥ śreyasakaraṃ paraṃ; tapasā kilbiṣaṃ hanti vidyayā smṛtamaśnute" (Manu 12.104; Chowkhamba 226; 682).

holding back of the senses, that is called 'yoga,'"[a] S. N. Dasgupta is of the opinion that the practice acquired ascetical connotations long before the fourth century B.C. publication of Painini's Sanskrit Grammar, through an etymological identification of "yoga" with "a new fanciful verb-root," *yuj* having the sense of "concentration" as the practice of a new class of "persons who practice austerities." In Yoga Philosophy in Relation to Other Systems of Thought (Calcutta: The University Press [1930], 46) he explains that the different kinds of asceticism generally subsumed under the name of *brahmacarya* were already prevalent, but a definite system of mental disciplines under the name of "Yoga" were being practiced in ascetical communities or schools "whose adherents were called Yogins."

In the context of the history of the idea of punishment, Dasgupta's explanation does not explicate the development of yogic practices as forms of punishment in voluntary expiation of past sins. Admittedly, it cannot be said that the practices were consciously developed along retributional lines but since the yogic practice itself required painful effort intended to cancel the negativities of inherited karmas or past evil deeds, an implicit punitive element is recognizable and reflects the influence upon Yoga of early Indian ideas of punishment.

Āpastamba (1.8.23.3ff.) describes Yoga simply as a means for "the eradication of the faults" which tend to destroy creatures. This eradication is the means by which one "obtains salvation." Those "faults" are anger, pride, discontent, covetousness, injury to others, hypocrisy, deceit (lying), gluttony, calumny, envy, lust, secret hatred (malice), self-indulgence, and a distracted mind. Freedom from all of these together with peaceableness toward all creatures and constant contemplation enable one to enter "the universal Self" (*paramātman*). His description of yoga however, is found in a chapter on penances which are

---

[a] "Tām yogamiti manyante sthirāmindriyadhāraṇam" (Katha [vallyu] paniṣad 6.11, Daśopanishads, Adyar [1935], Vol. I, 120).

applicable to brāhmins and other caste-members of "all (the four) orders" also. Yoga is the supreme penance. Therefore, whatever other elements it may contain, or functions it may serve, Āpastamba's presentation of yoga imbues it with the character of a moral retribution in the form of penitential voluntary self-punishment.

Whereas in Jain usage, the fundamental meaning of the word *yoga* is "activity" with reference to activities of body, speech and mind, and this activity is perceived to cause "inflow of karma-matter" into or rather "onto" the soul, it does not have the psychical quality of its brāhmaṇic and buddhist uses. The yogic "inflow" (*āśrava*) moreover is distinguished into "good" meaning virtuous or meritorious karmas and bad or demitorious karmas.[11] *Tapas* or austerity accordingly is a special kind of *yoga* or "inflow" activity which does not generate karmas but effects a "purging away" (*nirjara*) of karmas.[12] In Jainism, therefore, the relation of asceticism and penance to the retributive principle of Karma is more explicit than in the contemporaneous traditions. In Hinduism and Buddhism, moreover, the contrast between yoga and Karma is not between two kinds of activity but between an avocation on the one hand and an experiential life-process on the other. Nevertheless, the yoga-practice is not unrelated to the dynamic principle of Karma inasmuch as the practice implies the principle and in effect, accelerates the process of karmic expiation by means of an intensification of yogic expiation.

But in order for yoga to fulfil this accelerative expiational intensification, it is agreed by the authorities that the practices must be performed dispassionately and without materialistic motives. Since only pure acts of this kind really purify the soul of karmas even the manner of performing the austerities is important. As the Bhagavadgītā (18.5-6) says:

> works of sacrifice, almsgiving, and austerity should not be abandoned, but surely should be done; sacrifice, almsgiving, and austerity purify thoughtful men. But . . . these should

be done with abandonment of attachment and (abandonment) of fruits" (i.e. anticipated or expected rewards).[a]

The extreme ascetical disciplines which are intended to purify the self and lead the mind toward the supreme bliss of liberation, may meanwhile plunge the ascetic into terrifying spectacles of Hell. It may be more than coincidental that the most vivid depictions of Hell appear in early Jain texts in which the extremest forms of asceticism are advocated. In a modern study of the physical and psychological effects of such austerities, Aldous Huxley (Heaven and Hell, London: Penguin Books [1959]), drawing upon a study by A. Keys (The Biology of Human Starvation, Wisconsin: University of Minnesota Press, 1950) concerning the 1955 reports of Dr. George Watson and his associates in Southern California on the role of vitamin deficiencies in mental disease, underscored this "hellish" dimension of ascetical experience. The hellish forms in which the visionary material is projected are presumably affected by one's religious beliefs, but from the point of view of punishment, ascetic practices can produce "hellish" rather than heavenly experience, as if self-punishment itself sometimes led the ascetic mentally to the very place of punishment itself where for a time he "sees" his tormenters and undergoes their punitive inflictions.

B. Penitential Punishment

The importance of penance in the thinking of Indian jurists of ancient times is evident in the extensive discussion of the subject by Kane (History of the Dharmaśāstra [1953], Vol. IV, 57-178 and in other volumes) in which he has comprised numerous and extensive references

---

[a]"Yajñadānatapaḥkarma na tyājyaṃ kāryam eva tat; yajño dānam tapaś cai 'va pāvanāni manīṣiṇām. Etānyapi tu karmāṇi saṅgam tyaktvā phalāni ca; kartavyānī'ti me . . ." (Bhagavadgītā 18.5-6; S. Radhakrishnan, The Bhagavadgītā, [1948]; 353).

from the dharmasmṛtis, their digests, and the commentaries. If the theory of penances is more fully articulated in the commentaries and the digests, the numerous early smṛti references show that a system of penances for dealing with sins and crimes was not a late development. Ten out of twenty chapters of the Gautama dharmasūtra, for example, are devoted to penances; the Vasiṣṭhadharmasūtra devotes nine out of thirty chapters to the subject, the Manusmṛti devotes to this subject 222 verses out of 266 verses of chapter eleven; and the Yājñavalkya-smṛti (3.205; 327) devotes to it 122 verses in a text totalling 1009 verses. Kane also illustrates the prominence of the subject in some of the ancient purāṇas particularly in reference to seven chapters (168-174) of the Agnipurāṇa, fifty-two chapters of the Garuḍapurāṇa, and four chapters of the Kurmapurāṇa.

Major commentaries which expound extensively on penances include the Mitākṣarā, the commentaries of Aparārka, Hemādri (which he nevertheless warns is of doubtful authenticity), Bhavadeva, Nāgojibhaṭṭa, and Śūlapāṇi (thirteenth century) whose Prayaścittaviveka is not only "the most elaborate treatment" of the subject but cites and quotes the major earlier authorities and sources on penance. Madhva's unique treatise on *vyavahāra*, the Parāśaramādhavīya (fourteenth century), contains a valuable exposition on penance. Its originality can be found in the manner in which the author has pegged his treatise onto a single verse of an important early smṛti text--the Parāśarasmṛti--which is mentioned both in the Kauṭilīya Arthaśāstra and in Mitramiśra's famous treatise on penance, the Prāyaścitta-prakāśa. However, Kane's warning (History of the Dharma-śāstra [1975], Vol. I, Pt. II, 828) should be noted, that "it is difficult to believe that all these [i.e. the numerous penances described in Śūlapāṇi's treatise] (or even large portions) were actually practised by the people in the author's days or even centuries before him." Yet it is surely more problematic to suppose that jurists would have referred at length to prescriptions for sins of omission and commission and confessions of guilt brought before their courtly pariṣads, which were not even available for use when required.

The nature of penance is partly ascertainable through the designatory words. Kane is of the opinion that the "two forms of the word" for penance--*prāyaścitti* and *prāyaścitta* appear "without distinction" in Vedic works. But in the Taittirīya Saṃhitā (as in TS 2.1.2.4; 2.1.4.1; 3.1.3.2-3; 5.1.9.3; and 5.3.12.1) *prāyaścitti* occurs in the sense of averting the effects of a mishap, such as accidental breakage of a cooking vessel, or neutralizing the malefic influences of an inauspicious event, such as an eclipse of the sun, or (as in 5.3.12.1) of removing the guilt of sins. By combining the several usage-meanings of *prāyaścitti* and *prāyaścitta* indicated by such early sources as Atharvaveda 14.1.30; Aitareya Brāhmaṇa 5.27; Kauṣitaki Brāhmaṇa 5.9 and 6.12; Śatapatha Brāhmaṇa 4.5.7.1; 7.1.4.9; 11.5.3.8; and 12.4.1.6, penances appear as formal procedures for diverting or warding off evil influences arising from any inauspicious event or happening which could cause unpleasant and/or harmful effects. In this respect they are like the charms defined in the Atharvaveda. They are summarily grouped by the Mīmāṃsā distinction into *kratvarta-prāyaścittas* and *puruṣārtha-prāyaścittas* according to whether the penances are for averting either ritual faults, and are prescribed in the Śrautasūtras, or treating transgressions, and prescribed in the smṛtis.[13]

Etymological considerations in the digests and commentaries bear out the punitive aspect of penances. *Prāyaścitta* is interpreted as a combination of *prāya* (perceived as a synonym for *tapas*) with *citta* in the sense of "firm resolve." *Prāyaścitta* accordingly means the firm resolve to perform austerities for the burning away of sins. *Prāya* is also interpreted as "sin," and *citta* as "purification," in Bālambhaṭṭi's comment on the Yājñavalkyasmṛti 3.206 (Kane, History of the Dharmaśāstra [1953], Vol. IV, 59), while Hemādri interprets *prāya* as meaning "destruction" and *citta* as "joining together" in the sense of mending or "putting right" to supply a definition of penance as "making good what is lost" by means of an "occasional" (*naimittika*) act of atonement or expiation of sin. Other derivations of meaning include that of Madhva's Parāśaramādhavīya which explains *prāyaścitta* as the means by which the *citta* or mind of a repentant sinner is made "generally" (*prayaśah*) free by the *pariṣad* (assembly of learned brāhmins).

The word *prāyaścitta* is also closely associated with *vrata* in the sense that penance is a form of *vrata*. *Vratas* are means, methods, or recourses for fulfilling such personal aims as material benefits, health, mental and magical powers, and divine favours. Penances and fastings are kinds of *vrata*,[14] but "any act of religious devotion or austerity" could be a *vrata*.[15] Penances, accordingly, have positive as well as negative functions inasmuch as they not only "remove sins" but also produce material and spiritual benefits.

An early smṛti distinction between intentional (*kāmata*) and unintentional (*akāmata*) acts may have prompted the considerable commentarial discussion which arose on whether or not penances compensate both kinds of sinful acts. Since, however, intentionality appears to have been perceived as affecting only the degree of guilt not the substance of it, the discussion really turned on which penances are proficient for intentional sins and which are not proficient, not on whether penances are efficient for compensating sins. Kane may have been aware of this distinction in his discussion of the problem since he cites Manu (11.45-6) and Yājñavalkya (3.226) as saying that only "unintentional" sins are destroyed by penance or by Vedic study, but misreads the ambiguity of Gautama (19.3-6) and Vasiṣṭha (22.2-5) who declare that penances should not be performed for deliberate misdeeds whose expiation is only possible through suffering their consequences; but penances should be performed for "removal of the effects of sins."

On the question of whether penances could be effective for removing guilt caused by deliberate acts Kane appears also to be confused by contradictory citations, since in the second half of Manu 11.45 it is said that some teachers declare "on the evidence of revealed texts (*śruti*) that penance may be performed for an intentional act." Gautama (19.7-10), for example, quotes Vedic texts which prescribe penances for intentional offences; and the Aitareya Brāhmaṇa (7.28) is also cited in agreement with this opinion by some commentators (according to Bühler, The Laws of Manu, SBE on Manu 11.45, note 45). Manu doesn't appear to hold the onesided view which Kane attributed to him, since in the following verse (11.46) Manu adds that a sin which is unintentionally committed is expiated by one kind of penance, namely, the recitation of Vedic texts (while fasting?) but "that which (men) in their folly commit intentionally, by various (special) penances."[a] But the confusion could be resolved by the observation of what penances are perceived to remove or not to remove. Kane interprets Yājñavalkya 3.226 (latter half) as meaning that penances do not remove or destroy deliberate sins but remove only those spiritual taints which exclude the sinner from social intercourse. This is consistent with Manu 11.47 which states that persons liable to undergo penance should avoid social connections with untainted (here *siddha*) men. But both Manu and Yājñavalkya appear to be of the opinion, as Kane (History of the Dharmaśāstra [1973], Vol. IV, 63) notes, that "the results of sin intentionally committed (such as Hell and the like) are not got rid of."

This suggests that penances have only a social, and not a spiritual, reference inasmuch as they do not "remove sins" but merely reverse excommunications resulting from sinful contaminations. This is seemingly implied in Yājñavalkya's statement (3.220) that a sinner should perform penances "for his own purification here and in the next world," for the sake of his own composure and for social relations with his own people. Kane (History of the Dharmaśāstra [1973], Vol. IV, 65) moreover takes this statement as definitive of the function of penances according to the smṛtis, namely as means of purification for the sake of relieving troubled consciences and enabling readmission to social communion. For:

---

[a]"Akāmataḥ kṛtaṃ pāpaṃ vedābhyāsena śudhyati; kāmatastu kṛtaṃ mohāt prāyaścittaiḥ pṛthagvidhaiḥ" (Manu 11.46, The Dharmaśāstra, Vol. II [1909], 198).

> The potentialities and consequences of sins are twofold, viz. those leading to Hell and the others preventing intercourse with members of the society to which the sinner belongs. Therefore, even though a *prāyaścitta* may not be efficacious to prevent the first-mentioned consequence (viz. falling into Hell), there is nothing improper in *prāyaścitta* being effective in removing the obstacle to association with other people.

Yet immediately following Kane admits that this is only the case for sins which cause "loss of caste," whereas penances do remove sins which do not cause "loss of caste." In this case his argument regarding the limited efficacy of penances for intentional sin appears to break down entirely. For the efficacy of any penance is governed not by the intentionality or accidence of a misdeed, but by the gravity of the deed it is intended to remedy. Taking Āpastamba's guidance (1.9.24.24-5) as a starting point, it appears that there are grave sins such as slaying a guru, a parent, a Vedic teacher, and so on, which are unexpiable by any special penance. Expiation must take the form of a "lifelong" penance understood as penance of such severity that it causes the sinner's death. The belief that a grave sin can be removed by the sinner's voluntary or punitive death provides a rational basis for a range of specific "death-penances" authorized in smṛtis and accepted by commentators and "by most medieval writers." "Penance-unto-death" is prescribed by Manu (11.73, 90-91, 99-100, 103-104), Yājñavalkya (3.247-248, 253 and 257), Gautama (22.2-3; 23.1, 8-11), and Āpastamba (1.9.24.25 and 1.10.28.18). Hence where Manu (in 11.89) states that for slaying a brāhmin no penance is acceptable, this only means that no "special" or "occasional" penance--but only a life-consuming one--will suffice. Hence while admittedly many penitential regulations and their interpretations have a seeming contradictoriness which occupied the commentators in ingenious explanations and special pleadings in support of the ancient smṛti writers and their rulings on which acts are sins and which penances are efficacious for removing sins, those regulations imply the relative efficacies of penances as self-administered punishments for all kinds of sins. The apparant confusions and contradictions, accordingly, are resolved when, for want of contrary evidence, it is recognized that the smṛti-writers and commentators perceived the composite nature of acts and determined that penances would be considered efficacious for treating moral and spiritual elements and penalties the criminal elements of acts. This resolution of the problem of contradictory statements would be consistent with the extensive śāstrika discussions of the penitential and the penal modes of treating transgressional acts and the role of the king in buttressing by sanctions the penitential system, as well as with their understanding of the expiational character of civil penalties when these are conscientiously administered, and their penitential character whenever the execution of them is willingly accepted and submitted to by an offender. One further resolution of the apparent contradiction is the privilege which brāhmins are allowed to exercise of submitting to capital penances in lieu of the prescribed capital punishments executed by the king's officers.

While sufficient examples in the literature of these interrelations imply an early recognition of the equivalence-relation of penances and penalties, it is hardly possible, for want of certain historical evidence, to ascertain the extent to which substitutions from penalties to penances were actively allowed. The problem is that, while some textual statements imply a general recognition of such equivalences, their literary contexts appear to qualify the extent of such equivalence. The texts only indicate that certain acts, whether they happen to be sinful, immoral, or criminal in nature, require voluntary submission to penances. But this is in order that the penitent may avoid the future karmic consequences of his offence, and that he may realise certain positive benefits of penances, quite above and beyond any rehabilitative and other benefits which may arise from his subjection to judicial punishments. In this case, penances would be supplementary to and not substitutional for penalties. The only clear instance of penitential substitution is the rule that corporal punishments may not be inflicted on brāhmins who choose the prescribed penances which have been approved for their crimes.

If, on the other hand, it is recognized that penances and penalties treated different intrinsic dimensions of any unlawful act, then questions concerning the historic relations of the two systems of retribution need only be considered in the light of the spirit and not of the letter of the śāstras. The scholarly arguments of whether or not traditional Indian law arose as one or other system or as a dual system, might be brought to rest. In Hindu Law and Custom [1928], 263, Julius Jolly rejected Burnell's contention (Sāmaveda, xivff.) of the primacy of an ecclesiastical retributive system which supplied the matrix of a later, secular system. Jolly supported the contentions of Weber, Barth, and Konow, that the two systems arose contemporaneously and developed independently prior to their unification into a dual system. The forcefulness of Jolly's argument is a probable over-reaction to Burnell's hypothesis that two originally independent systems became, in course of time, integrated into a dual system. For, the "thorough parallelism" which Jolly found (p.269) between the two systems, may merely be apparent if one ignores or overlooks the textually more supportable probability of definitional diversification and compilative organization in the smṛti manuals and digests evidenced by the *vyavahāra* and the *prāyaścitta* chapters of the major lawbooks. In any case, the manifestly mixed character of the regulations and sanctions in the manuals is more readily explicable as reflecting a synthetic view of law rather than a historical development, and a complexity of administrative organization rather than of a singular civil system. The precedence of the ecclesiastical administration over the secular one would not be the same as its historical primacy. The parity and interfunctionality of the two systems best explains the apparent confusion of principles and prescriptions in the smṛtis as supported by the following considerations:

a. The spiritual sanctity of the lawcourts and their processes. [Not only were the judges learned brahmins, but the law which they interpreted was perceived to have divine authority and to embrace spiritual sanctions. Thus: "headlong in utter darkness shall the sinful man tumble into hell, who, being interrogated in a judicial enquiry answers one question falsely."[16]]

b. The interfunctionality of spiritual and civil penalties on account of being tied to regulations which carry simultaneously both secular and religious dimensions.

c. The manifest parity of penances to penalties in treating transgressions, there being no mitigation of severity in penances in comparison with penalties.[17] [The religious penance for adultery, for example, stated in Gautama-dharmasūtra (23.14ff.) and the Mahābhārata (12.165.64ff.) carries similar physical pains as the civil penalty enunciated by Manu (8. 371ff.) for this crime.]

d. The spiritual merits of submitting to penalties are the same as those from penances. Both punishments "purify sinful men" (Manu 8.318).[18]

e. Penitential prescriptions carry the force of law and accordingly are supported by royal sanctions.[19] [Yājñavalkya is of the opinion that penances of any kind are properly allowable only for unintentional or accidental transgressions, criminal acts being those which are intentionally committed and are expiable only through civil penalties. But penances are prescribed for intentional faults (e.g. Manu 11. 46),especially when the offender expresses willingness to make amends. In such cases, the prescribed penance is double the severity of one ordained for an accidental fault.[20] The king provides the supportive role, however, to both agencies of the law, the civil and the ecclesiastical, while instrumenting directly the punishment of capital crimes and of mortal sins which cannot be corporally punished by religious officers.]

In the matter of the integrality of the two administrations, Julius Jolly (Hindu Law and Custom, [1928], 265ff.) contributes the following observations:

i) "the conceptions of *dolus* (evil design) and *culpa* (crime) are as much in evidence in the religious law as in the secular law."

ii) Joint participation in a crime "is judged likewise from the same point of view both in the religious law and in the secular law."

iii) "The repetition of a crime is taken into consideration both in [civil] punishments and in penances."[21]

iv) "In this thorough parallelism of the two systems it is quite natural that they should have very many particular sins and crimes in common with one another . . . ."

v) "There being no fine line of demarcation between penances and punishments both may be applied indiscriminately."

It is, however, doubtful, that penances and punishments were applied indiscriminately in the light of the clear and specific directives on their utilization in the smṛtis. On the whole, it can be said, that while the nature and the respective roles of civil and religious tribunals were never apparently confused in smṛti regulations, it is historically probable that, in the course of the definitional clarification of the respective functions and relations of the distinctive religious, civil, legal, and social institutions, their integrality emerged as a comprehensive traditional Indian system of government. However, on the specific matter of the interrelation of penances with punishments, the final word may fairly be allowed to the Indian jurists themselves such as Nārāyaṇa's comment on Manu 8.336 that "although pecuniary punishment [i.e. fines] are weightier than such gifts [i.e. penances in the form of a gifting of cows to brāhmins], yet punishment and penance have been laid down as alternative methods of correction of a criminal [emphasis added]. If it is further said that substitutes are substitutes only and not the real things, then the answer is that (if that view was right) then prescription of the gift of cows would not have been laid down."[22]

Yet, arguments have been raised against the justicial commensurality of the two systems. Robert Lingat (J. D. N. Derrett, trans., The Classical Law of India, [1973], 64) argued that the penitential system "is imperfect and incomplete" since the quality of "chastisement" [i.e. retribution] is only secondary to it,"its real object being to cleanse the sinner of his guilt." But, in this statement, Lingat appears to be confusing a utilitarian purpose in penances from their essential character as "chastisements". Since, in the treatment of guilt by penitential means, the element of chastisement would be expectedly most weak when appertaining to minor faults, one should not be surprised to find forms of penances which meet Lingat's criticism that they "often attenuate or even reduce to vanishing point whatever penal content they may have." Lingat's point is not carried by G. Bühler's reference (SBE II; 82 n.8) to Haradatta's comment on the *kṛcchra* penances referred to in Āpastamba-dharmasūtra 1.9.25.8, that the applicability of this one penance to "all kinds of sins" is that "the penances must be heavy for great crimes and lighter for smaller faults," this adjustment being made by prescribing the number of days or months or a full year in which one or another *kṛcchra* penance [such as the twelve-day *prājāpatya-kṛcchra* penance in Āpast.Dhs.1.9.27.7, after Manu 11.212 and Yājñ.Dhs.3.320] must be performed.

The traditional penitential system could be said to be ethically unsound inasmuch as its voluntary aspect is diminished even to vanishing-point when brāhmins are compelled by the threat of penalties for noncompliance, to apply the penitential prescriptions of an ecclesiastical court. But it is unclear whether noncompliance with the directives of an ecclesiastical court is a criminal act properly subjectable to civil penalties. There is a strong, if not stronger compulsion for the careful performance of penances in the form of the hellish and other after-death consequences of omissions. Clearly, the ethical distinction lies somewhere in the moral necessity over against the civic necessity of the correction of misdeeds.

Lingat also thinks that the penitential system is ethically deficient insofar as it is not purely expiatory but is also deterrent; yet, even as a deterrent, a monetary penance secures no compensation to the injured parties inasmuch as the monetary element is donated to brāhmins. Here too, the question of ethicality is a complex one. For while penitential amercements occur as donations to worthy brāhmins, it appears that some penances specifically include compensations to injured parties "in order to escape vengeance." These are additional to *prāyaścittārtham*, levies "to expiate one's sin" (Baudh.Dhs.1.10.19.1, and Āpast.Dhs. 1.9.24.1).[23] But here one may argue that even compensational or restitutional levies comprise a form of retribution whenever their amount and other criteria relating to damages to the victim of a crime, are calculated and considered in the affirmation of the principle of justice. The basic ethical distinction between a penance and a penalty, however, lies in the voluntary character of the former in recognition of the principle of justice and the compulsive character of the latter as an assertion and asseveration of the authority of the law upon unwilling acknowledgers of it. Yet the assertion of the law against its violators, is not the primary duty of the king, but rather to protect the commonwealth of the society and the wellbeing of its members. On the basis of Manu 8.1, Medhātithi, perceived the king's duty to include not only keeping his subjects out of the conditions under which they might bring penalties as well as natural evils upon themselves, but also from acts which might bring them torments in hell in the hereafter. This comprehensive duty, moreover, was emphasized by the śāstrikas in the form of the retributions in this world and in the hereafter which the king would bring upon himself and his household if he was negligent. For his own good, accordingly, the king had a kind of vested interest in serving both systems of social control even as the officers of both courts were expected to look to him for support in the fulfilment of their public duties. In other words, the king's responsibilities as defined in the manuals on *rājanīti* admitted no options beyond his commitment to upholding the decisions of ecclesiastical courts as well as of the civil courts in order that their officers could act with confidence as well as authority. As the Āpastamba-dharmasūtra (2.5.10.12-16) reads:

> The spiritual guide shall order those who (while) participating according to sacred law (in the rites of their caste) have gone astray through weakness of their senses, to perform penances proportionate to (the greatness of) their sins, according to the precepts (of the Smrti). If (such persons) transgress their (*Ācārya's*) order, he shall take them before the king. The king shall (send them) to his domestic priest, who should be learned in the law and the science of governing. He shall order (them to perform the proper penances if they are Brāhmanas). He shall reduce them (to reason) by forcible means, excepting corporal punishment and servitude.

Āpastamba's directive would be mistakenly interpreted as a subjection of the king's office to the ecclesiastical authority when considered outside of its textual contexts.[24] Moreover, however minimal the voluntary participation of the penitent in his own punishment, the directive reflects concern for an exact and impartial administration of justice.[25] This being so, then any justicial "discrepancies" which Lingat (The Classical Law of India, [1973], 56) can be said to have noticed in the matter of penances are fairly correctable by their interpretation as variational specificalities intended to meet extenuating conditions bearing upon the guilt of punishable acts.

Inasmuch as the penitential system is described in relation to degrees of guilt in offences, it cannot be argued justifiably that penances afforded to brāhmins a softer or less stringent or justicially less exact mode of expiation. The suggestion of penances as a softer alternative to penal retributions is removed by the numerous examples of "equivalences" identified between penances and penalties. The justicial equality becomes evident, for example, when one compares the penitential section of Āpastamba's dharmasūtra (1.9.25) with the criminal section (1.10.26). In the former section, the penance prescribed for a brāhmin who consorts adulterously with his guru's wife, is that he shall "cut off his organ together with the testicles, taken them in his joined hands and walk towards the south without stopping, until he falls down dead."[26] In the latter section, the penalty prescribed is that a "young man" adulterously behaving in this manner shall be punished in the manner that "his organs shall be cut off together with the testicles." This verbal similarity between the penitential and the penal prescriptions is complemented by a provision in the criminal section of the dharmasūtra that, should the young man "agree to undergo the (prescribed) penance," then the king shall hand him over to his lawful guardian.

In the light of such identities, it cannot be said that there is a mitigation of severity of punishments in the penitential system in contrast to the secular one even though the resort to penances is proffered as a more desirable optional alternative to judicial penalization. The reason for this, however, lies in certain important extrinsic factors in penances which are not fully present in judicial punishments. A particular merit of the penitential treatment of wrongdoing is that it removes the spiritual and moral taints of the sin and permits restoration to social communion unlike penalties which only vindicate the law and uphold the social order which is in the king's guardianship. Hence, when comparing penances and penalties, it would be a mistake to assume that penances are always the lighter punishments, although this appears to be the case if one compares the penance prescribed for the slaying of a brāhmin with the penalty for this crime in Manu 8.380f., because there are lighter and heavier penances even as there are lighter and heavier penalties which are governed by the mitigative factors of extenuating conditions of a wrongful act which the commentators (Medhātithi, Govinda, Kullūka, Nārāyaṇa, and others) pointed out in reference to this prescription of Manu as grounds for ascertaining the different degrees of guilt and severities of punishment for the deliberate or the accidental slaying of righteous or of reprobate brāhmins.[27]

Nevertheless, since transgressions of any kind, done

knowingly and deliberately, or relunctantly under forceful compulsion, or through ignorance, error, or accident, all violate the Dharma and therefore incur guilt, they are all in principle, punishable inasmuch as punishment alone can negate, neutralize, or remove the guilt, which itself is qualified according to the understanding that wilful transgressions carry a greater weight of guilt than accidental ones, and accordingly are fully compensated only by relatively heavier penances or penalties. The broad range of lighter and heavier penances illustrate this understanding, and the *kṛcchra* penance pronounced for brāhmins who wrongly prescribe punishments, and the penances for accidental consumption of forbidden foods, are cases in point.[28] The principle is recognized even by the penitential provisions made by Manu (11.47) for example, for acts "committed in a former life" or "by fate." Since in each case, the penances prescribed are retributive of the guilt incurred, they are in effect, purifications, and they do their job, as it were, no more efficiently than their commensurality with the kind and circumstances of the acts which they are designed to expiate.

The factor which determines that the penances are not magical purifications but are intended as punishments is their painfulness, which accordingly will be light if the guilt is light through the selective adjustment of penances befitting the crimes. The thirty-day lunar (*cāndrāyaṇa*) penance described in Manu 11.217-220 is evidently painful, and so are the penitential purgations of boiled *kuśa* grass, bovine excrements, etc. mentioned in Manu 11.213 which could not have been self-administered without a strong sense of guilt and a concern for purification in the mind of the penitent.

It is probable that the forms of these penances were intended to serve other useful functions such as deterrence or the discouraging of future repetitions of acts requiring such expiations, and restoration to community life and the rights and privileges of caste reinstatement as described by Manu 11.197. Indeed, the conditions of formal readmission to a community explained by Manu, appear to have imposed such a necessity upon the submission to penances, that their implicit voluntary nature may be doubted. Inasmuch as they were ordained by ecclesiastical courts and carried the force of law buttressed by sanctions and compelled under the threat of publicly shameful judicial penalties and the present inconvenience and spiritual dangers of social or communal exclusion, few brāhmins could have felt that penances were merely convenient available options in meeting the requirements of the punishment of crimes. The compulsory element of involuntariness can be seen, for example, in the Manusmṛti (11.209ff.) where penances are prescribed for threatening, striking, wounding, and shedding the blood of a brāhmin, and a provision is made that "for the expiation of offences for which no atonement [penance] has been prescribed, let him [i.e. the ecclesiastic] fix a penance after considering (the offender's) strength and the (nature of the) offence."[a] Yet the moral distinction between the penances and the penalties lies in the recognition by the penitent of the principle and the processes of justice by which he becomes a willing participant in his expiational retribution in contrast to the vindication of the authority of the law by the king's officers with, or without the acknowledgement of that authority and the order it serves, by the offender.

It is not always the case, on the other hand, that penances were perceived as 'alternatives' for penalties, since sometimes they are ordained as expiations for acts whose punishment is not within the law. For, after comparing the smṛtis, certain jurists concluded that whenever an act causes hurt or harms to persons, but under excuseable circumstances such as self-defence, police-duties, and suchlike which exclude him from judicial punishment, the doer is not to construe that his "immunity from punishment" is the same as "absence of sin". He is bound to submit himself to penitential expiations not only to remove the moral and spiritual taints of his act, but also to prevent any revenges which might be taken by his victim in a future life.[29] For the most part, however, penances are prescribed alongside of, or in addition to penalties, with the development of a complete

---

[a] "Anuktaniṣkṛtīnām tu pāpināmapanuttaye; śaktiñcāvekṣya pāpaṃ ca prāyaścittaṃ prakalpayet" (Manu 11.209; Chowkhamba, 226; 645).

penitential "penology" in tandem with the judicial penology or even integral with it at a very early period of Indian history. The integrality of the two penologies is clearly apparent not only in such general statements as are found in the smṛtis, for example in Manu 11.209ff., but in the specificalities of the relationship such as Paiṭhīnasi's regulation in Bhattacharya's translation of the Daṇḍaviveka that, for a felony such as murder:

> . . . the actual murderer, the adviser (i.e. the instigator), the supporter (*sampratipādakaḥ*), the encourager, the assistant, the adviser of methods (of committing the offence), the winker, though capable (of stopping the commission of the offence), the falsely deposing (witness) and the approver -- all these persons should be compelled to perform penances and should be punished appropriately and in conformity with their (physical and financial) capacity [emphasis added].[30]

By way of contrast, the propriety of penances rather than of penalties in certain cases, comes into focus in the question of Manu (8.336 and 9.249) of whether corporal and pecuniary punishments (such as fines, confiscation of property, and banishment) might be more or less appropriate than penances for restoring dutifulness in wayward and lawbreaking rulers. Nārāyaṇa is of the opinion that most kings "desist from the commission of crimes . . . from the fear of hell (after death), from (visualizing) the rigours of the performance of penances or from the fear of censure (in this life) and of infamy (after death)." But when kings become immune to such constraints, they are to be subjected to pecuniary penances in the form of "gifted articles or animals" made over to "Brāhmaṇas and other worthy recipients." Such penances, however, are to be undergone only when the king "is not physically fit to undergo (corporal) penances."

Both Nārāyaṇa and Halāyudha agree in their interpretation of Manu's regulations on the punishment of kings, namely that "when a king goes on committing crimes, forgetting the fear of hell, owing to the intensity of his addiction (to material pleasures) which action on his part amounts to an aversion to punishment [correction] owing to the absence of anyone protesting against it," then "the remedy left for the king's actions" is the punishment of the king, and this "should be administered by the courtiers."[31]

Here too, submission to penances is not a convenient or

purely voluntary option but is instead in the nature of a dutiful atonement for a real crime or offence such as theft (Manu 11.162-166) committed either knowingly or unknowingly. For this reason the crime of *prāyaścitta-vyatikrama*, that is, non-performance of the penitential rites, itself became a subject of penal legislation. The Daṇḍaviveka, following Kātyāyana and "an anonymous Smṛti text on the above offence," says that "(the king) should devise appropriate corporal and pecuniary punishments for those members of the four *varnas*, who do not undergo expiatory rites (for their lapses)."[32] Hence the question of whether or not such forceful impositions should properly be called penances is not answerable in reference to the will of the authorities who instrument the sanctions, but by reference to the voluntary will of the recipient in subjecting himself to them in expiation of his guilt and in recognition of the justice of his punishment. The impositions accordingly, are most fully penitential when an offender does not wait to be convicted of guilt, but freely confesses his guilt prior to any process of judicial enquiry. Such a person may even be less guilty, as Nārada explains, being "he who, having committed a reprehensible crime, confesses his guilt, i.e. himself speaks out before an assembly" such a one "is to be awarded half the prescribed punishment." Halāyudha interprets Nārada's statement to mean that "he who undergoes *pratyāsatti* which means *prāyaścitta* or himself reports to the assembly by saying, 'I am the author of such and such crime. Please inflict the (proper) punishment upon me' gets half of the prescribed punishment."[33] In such instances it clearly follows that either confession of guilt OR self-submission to penance have the effect of mitigating by half the social dimension of the guilt of the felony. This is because a penance is understood as a means of purification of guilt. For, the Daṇḍaviveka concludes as "being the settled conclusion of the several digests by means of reconciliation of the texts of Bṛhaspati, Yama, Śaṅkha, Vasiṣṭha and other sages" that a woman mistakenly or forcibly led into adultery is purified by her subsequent menstrual discharge; but should she become pregnant then only by the "*Caṇḍāla* penance." Expiations serve in other cases where wives of brāhmins, kṣatriyas, and vaiśyas are guilty of felonious sexual connections provided such acts have not been accompanied by physical violence.[34] The applicability of penances to other crimes which are not considered totally expiable by juridical penalties is recognized as serving the purpose of effecting purification--by means of painful self-inflicted punishments--from all remaining stains of guilt. The effectiveness of any penance, however, depends upon the voluntary submission of the penitent "by confession, repentance, austerity, and reciting the Veda" (Manu 11.228). So where the will is weak one may have to compel him to undergo penance by causing him to imagine terrifying judicial consequences (11.232). As Manu (11.228-231) says:

> In proportion as a man who has done wrong himself confesses it, even so far he is freed from guilt . . . . In proportion as his heart loathes his evil deed, even so far is his body freed from that guilt. He who has committed a sin and has repented, is freed from that sin; but he is purified only by (the resolution) of ceasing (to sin and thinking) I will do so no more.[a]

If however, a firm purpose for self-amendment is not present, then the penance has no power of inducing a purified conscience. In this regard, Manu (11.234) decrees that, "if his mind be uneasy with respect to any act, let him repeat his austerities (prescribed as a penance) for it until they fully satisfy (his conscience)."[b] On the other hand, where there is conscientious performance (Manu 11.240 and 242):

---

[a] "Yathā yathā naro 'dharmaṃ svayaṃ kṛtvānubhaṣate; tathā tathā tvacevāhistenādharmeṇa mucyate. Yathā yathā manastatya duṣkṛtaṃ karma garhati; tathā tathā śarīraṃ tattenādharmeṇa mucyate. Kṛtvā pāpaṃ hi santapya tasmātpāpātpramucyate; naivaṃ kuryyāṃ punariti nivṛttyā pūyate tu saḥ. Evaṃ saṃcintya manasā pretya karmaphalodayam; manovāṅmūrtibhirnityaṃ śubhaṃ karma samācaret" (Manu 11.228-231; Chowkhamba 226; 650-651).

[b] "Yasminkarmaṇyasya kṛte manasaḥ syādalāghavam; tasmiṃ-stāvattapaḥ kuryyādyāvattuṣṭikaraṃ bhavet" (Manu 11.233; Chowkhamba 226; 651).

> . . . those who have committed mortal sin(*mahāpātaka*) and all other offenders are severally freed from their guilt by means of well-performed austerities . . . . Whatever sin men commit by thoughts, words, or deeds, that they speedily burn away by penance, if they keep penances as their only riches.[a]

However, were one to admit to a limited extent the substitutional equivalence of penalties and penances, this would not displace the prior reference of penalties to crimes and penances to sins. Accordingly, the śāstrikas cannot be said to have confused penal and penitential expiations when granting the king authority to enforce implementations of penances and thereby to uphold the authority of the penitential court or *pariṣad*. If they considered that all crimes are also sins, they were not of the opinion that all sins are crimes. They did, however, recognize the complementarity of penances and penalties as treatments of offences which are both sins and crimes. They acknowledged the expiational capability of penalties for removing spiritual/moral guilt and they interpreted penitentially those penalties for crimes which the offender accepted voluntarily. Manu (8.314-316) framed this acknowledgement in the rule that a thief should present himself early to the king, and confessing his guilt, say, "I have done this, punish me," knowing that whether or not the king punishes him, he nevertheless is purified. The principle is (Manu 8.318; Vasiṣṭha Dharmasūtra 19.45, and the Nārada Smṛti) that men voluntarily submitting to the king's punishment "are purified and go to heaven like those who have performed good deeds."

The transmutation of the penalty into a penance through the voluntary submission of the offender introduces an expiational capability for annihilating karmas which produces beneficial effects for the recipient beyond the

---

[a]"Mahāpātakinaścaiva śeṣāścakāryyakāriṇaḥ; tapasaiva sutaptena mucyante kilbiṣāttataḥ . . . . Yatkiṃcidenaḥ kurvanti manovāṅmurtibhirjanāḥ; tatsarvaṃ nirdahantyaśu tapasaiva tapodhanāḥ" (Manu 11.239 and 241; Chowkhamba 226; 652-653).

judicial ends related to the public interest, although a specific qualification follows from Vijñāneśvara's Mitākṣarā on Yājñavalkya 3.359, and Medhātithi's comment on Manu 8.318 that this expiational power is only effective in corporal punishments, since when a fine is prescribed, then also a penance must be performed. Why is this so? Robert Lingat (as translated by J. D. M. Derrett in The Classical Law of India [1973], 235) cites Medhātithi on Manu 8.316 on "the invisible effect produced in the person of the convict by the application of punishment" analagous to the effect (*karma*) of an act of *dharma*. The dutiful enactment of a chastisement in conformity to the precepts of *smṛti* by one who personifies *dharma* effects a removal of sins. Even the physical gesture of touching the criminal in an act of pardon purifies the offender of his sin, since the king's touch transfers to himself the criminal's guilt. In this case, it is the power implied in the king's office which removes sin, not the penitential act of the sinner. But Lingat (page 236) may be over-straining his argument that this explanation, and not the principle that a penalty is equivalent to a penance, is the true interpretation. A corporal punishment whether of a penal or a penitential kind is a direct act upon the body of a producer of negative karmas, while a fine is not. The inadequacy of fines for effecting a moral recompense could sufficiently explain the absence of references to fines for expunging guilt.

On the whole, however, the evidence surrounding the formulation of a penitential system in the smṛti literature is conclusively on the side of the argument that the penitential system is not a secondary, but an essential part of the body of teaching on law, morality, and custom. This is perceptible in strongly worded endorsements of the system by the smṛti writers, and in the sanctions enunciated for infractions of penitential regulations. Both Manu (12.54ff.) and Yājñavalkya (3.206ff.), for example, set the expediency of penance against the terrors of unexpiated sins. Grave sinners, after passing many years in hells, are reborn in this world for the remainder or "the remnant" of their evil actions as lower animals, or as trees or shrubs. Manu

(11.53) asserts that unexpiated sins cause a sinner to be reborn with "disgraceful marks" such as bodily deformities, ugly birthmarks, or repellent features which are indicative of the former sins. The Viṣṇudharmasūtra (44.1-10) contains the same doctrine with the refinement that the consequences of unexpiated sins are in the order first of hellish torments, next of rebirths in "despised wombs," and then rebirth as disformed human beings marked by signs of former sins. The Manusmṛti's conclusion (11.54) of its listing of sanctions is that penances have to be performed for the sake of purification because, those persons whose sins remain unexpiated during the present life are certainly reborn with "disgraceful marks."

C. Expiational Suicide

The prestige surrounding ascetical suicide among Hindus, Jains, and Buddhists is amply testified in their literatures. The ascetical intensification of the expiational process toward the final culminative act of self-destruction found recognition as a permissible expedient for dedicated ascetics who become discouraged by frequent lapses in mental concentration and moral purity and the prospect of many life-times of faltering penitential programmes. The attraction of expiational suicide as the final emancipative penance may account for its regulation in Jain texts[35] such as the permission being granted to an ascetic only after he has pursued ascetic disciplines for at least twelve years.

Even if the Buddha discouraged religious suicide as much as he is said to have discouraged all extremism, its popularity was nevertheless strong enough for its acceptance to emerge among the Buddha's followers.[36] Yet, although the ethics of religious suicide came to occupy the interest of Buddhist scholars, textual discussions suggest that it was largely an academic problem revolving around the idea of rebirth (*saṃsāra*) rather than a pastoral problem relating to the spiritual life of a monk. For, if it is assumed that suicide is sinful and causes a degraded rebirth, then what happens in the case of a person who, at the precise moment of winning perfect sainthood (*arhatship*) commits suicide? Since by having reached the goal of *nirvāṇa* he had already transcended the round of rebirth, how then by acting in this way can he be thought to have perpetuated it!

The brāhmaṇic perception of the retributive character of expiational suicide is clearly apparent in smṛti references to certain grave sins which are thought to be inexpiable in this life.[37] Murder of a brāhmin, adultery with the wife of one's guru, gold theft, and liquor drinking, for example, are beyond the reach of available means of expiating guilt. The agent of them, according to one sense of Āpastamba's statement (1.9.24.24ff.), "cannot be purified in this life; but his sin is removed (after death)."[38] But Āpastamba's regulations are not uniform nor unambiguous. The statement could merely mean, as Haradatta explains, that the offender could not be restored to the full dignity and privileges of his caste in his present lifetime. However, the prescriptions for treating grave sins are not apparently standardized and uniform. Sometimes, lifelong penances or three-year penances or violent self-destruction are enjoined.[39] While Haradatta suggests that the different regulations of Āpastamba are due to different sources from which he culled his information—the lighter penalties being culled from a *purāṇa*—it is more likely that Āpastamba, like Manu, distinguished varying degrees of guilt even for brāhmin-murder, and prescribed different severities of treatment for them.[40] Nevertheless, whenever a crime warranted the prescription of capital punishment, a brāhmin, at least, had the option of imposing the death sentence upon himself in the form of an expiational penance, and as a sacrificial act having such additional benefits as the expunging of all guilts, restoration to caste dignity, and the securing of that dignity for a future life, as Haradatta explicitly recognized.[41] Āpastamba (1.9.25.12) likens an act of expiational suicide to "a burnt-offering" which atones for all sins. "Such a sinner," writes Āpastamba (SBE.II), "may tear from his body and make the priest offer as a burnt-offering his hair, skin, flesh, and the rest, and then throw himself into the fire."[42] Such a sacrifice is different from the regular burnt-offerings in atonement for sins which Āpastamba prescribes but which do not entail the forfeiture of human life. Concerning the latter kind, Vasiṣṭha (Vas.Dhs.20.26) is more detailed. He decrees that the slayer is to kindle the sacrificial fire himself, and is to make eight oblations of portions of his body, saying with each portion respectively, "I feed Death with my hair, I offer my skin to Death . . . my blood . . . my flesh . . . my sinews . . . my fat . . . my bones . . . my marrow to Death." Vasiṣṭha also prescribed alternative forms of capital penance for murder (20.27ff.) and other grave sins (20.13ff.) explaining that thereby the sinner "becomes pure after death." In some cases of capital punishment, on the other hand, the sacrificer is the king and the criminal is the sacrificial victim. A. B. Keith (The Religion and Philosophy of the Veda and Upanishads, Cambridge, Mass.: Harvard University Press [1925], 31) is of the opinion that the punishment of a crime sometimes took the form of a human sacrifice, though this practice was isolated and rare.

In this connection also may be noted Āpastamba's (1.9.25.4) prescription for gold-theft which is a capital crime carrying the death sentence. The thief should go to the king, carrying a club on his shoulder, pronouncing as he runs the nature of his criminal deed. The king is then required to give him a blow with the club, from which, "if the thief dies, his sin is expiated." Should he survive, then factors must be present either mitigating the gravity of his crime and requiring him to submit to other expiations or even a lifelong penance.[43] Vasiṣṭha (Vas.Dhs.20.41-42) may have consciously modified the directive so as to make the king the official witness of the thief's penitential self-destruction. For the thief is enjoined to announce his own guilt [as Āpastamba prescribed], then receive from the king an instrument or club with which he is to administer upon himself a deadly blow which will instantly expiate his sin.

Manu's directives (6.23-32) on expiatory suicide show that he permitted suicide by anyone who, on account of physical or moral inability to persist in his austerities, sought leave to foreshorten the "ascetical stage" of his life-vocation. The preliminary austerities here enjoined for the procuring of this fatality are manifestly those which are liable to reduce his physical stature and stamina to such an extreme condition as to bring on naturally but prematurely his physical death without any resort to a violent act against his own body. Should an ascetic feel that the time is ripe for him to terminate his life by a final penance, then "in summer let him expose himself to the heat of five fires, during the rainy season live under the open sky, and in winter be dressed in wet clothes, (thus) gradually increasing (the rigour of) his austerities."[a] Or else:

> Let him receive alms (barely sufficient) to support life . . . . Or let him walk, fully determined, and going straight on, in a north-easterly direction, subsisting on water and air, until his body sinks to rest . . . .[b] A Brāhman, having got rid of his body by one of these modes practised by the great sages, is exalted in the world of Brahman, free from sorrow and fear.[44,c]

Medhātithi explains the phrase *tyaktvānyatamayā* (one of these modes) as meaning drowning of oneself in a river, casting oneself over a precipice, self-immolation, or fasting unto death.[45] According to Govinda and Kullūka, the "great departure" (*mahāprasthāna*) could properly be undertaken by one who is incurably diseased or meets with great misfortune, because it is taught in the śāstras. On the other hand, there is damnable suicide which both Manu (5.89ff.) and Āpastamba (1.10.28.17) condemn by coupling

---

[a]"Grīṣme pañcatapāstu syādvarṣāsvabhrābakāśikaḥ; ārdravāsāstu hemante kramaśo varaddhayaṃstapaḥ" (Manu 6.23, Chowkhamba 226; 297).

[b]"Aparājitāṃbāsthaya vrajeddiśamajihmagaḥ; ānipātāccharīrasya yukto vāryyanilāśanaḥ" (Manu 6.31; Chowkhamba 226; 297).

[c]"Āsāṃ mahirṣacaryāṇaṃ tyaktvānyatamayā tanuṃ; vītaśokabhayo vipro Brahmaloke mahīyate" (Manu 6.32; Chowkhamba 226; 299).

compulsive suicidals with grave sinners, shamefully-born persons, heretics, lustful and alcoholic or murderous women, and outcasts. As Āpastamba asserts: "he who takes his own or another's life becomes an *abhiśasta* (cursed, outcast)." In contrast, expiational suicide is a courageous virtue to which Manu (6.76-78) calls the most determined spiritual warrior.

> Let him quit this dwelling, composed of the five elements, where the bones are the beams, which is held together by tendons, where the flesh and blood are the mortar, which is thatched with the skin, which is foul-smelling, filled with urine and ordure, infested by old age and sorrow, the seat of disease, harassed by pain, gloomy with passion, and perishable. He who leaves this body, (be it by necessity) as a tree (which is torn from) the riverbank, or (freely) like a bird (that) quits a tree, is freed from the misery (of this world, dreadful like) a shark.

D. Sacrificial and Devotional Expiation

If expiational suicide is the grand finale of the spiritual way in the dharmasmṛtis, it could be seen as being transcended by the way of devotion in theological literature. The surrender of one's self and of one's life to God is a spiritual self-sacrifice which expiates all sins. This idea of self-offering to God which the Śrīvaiṣṇavas eventually formalized in the concept of *prapatti*, at least from the eleventh century A.D. onwards, is apparently only a spiritualized formulation of sacrificial ideas and practices formulated in early Indian texts.

The harmonization of retributional ideas and sacrificial ideas is apparent in explicitly expiational sacrifices. The senses, however, in which certain Vedic sacrifices can be said to have been retributional and not substitutional evasions of punishments, are not explicit in the Vedic texts themselves. Yet such connotations as are discernible in the texts add facets to the conception of Punishment reflected in early Indian literature. Inexplicit punitive elements are discernible, for example, in the many *śrāddha*-rituals treated in early liturgical texts. Superficially regarded, the rituals appear to be merely devices for procuring from the male ancestors (*pitṛs*) and their ruling deities--the Vāsus, the Rudras, and the

Ādityas--such material benefits as long life, male progeny, good health, successful enterprises, and other blessings. But indications that the rituals are contrivances for neutralizing or transmuting into favourable conditions, circumstances which have arisen through the fruitions of inherited karmas, certainly brings those rituals within the perspective of the Indian conception of Punishment. For insofar as the rituals perform a substitutional function, as an alternative to penances, for example, there is at least some degree of awareness of moral operations related to the justicial concerns of the divine guardians of Order, or taking effect through the principle of Karma. Since the most central aim of the rituals is to "render satisfaction" to the superintendent deities, among whom the Ādityas, as chiefly represented by Varuṇa, are prominent, they are not far removed from the Ṛgvedic penitential hymns to Varuṇa intended for the removal of his chastisements of sinners. This means, of course, that the Ṛgveda as a whole, supplies a wider literary context in which punitive elements of the śrāddha-rituals become discernible.

An unobvious yet material sense in which *śrāddha*-rituals can be considered to be retributional relates to the pecuniary costs of the purificatory and other preparations, including the hiring of officients, supplying of provisions and accommodations, payments of special fees, gifts, giving of honoraria, as well as specific charges connected with the ceremonies themselves. The cost could easily have been sufficiently great for one to feel that he was "paying the price" for his sins, that they were a kind of "fine" which was a necessary part of the expiation for those misdeeds whose karmic fruitions were being painfully experienced. Such a "cost aspect" is easily overlooked in determining the punitive factors in such rituals, although formal payments or "fines" as the costs of the correction of civil wrongs is recognized. By connecting civil 'fines' and sacrificial 'costs', costly sacrifices can be seen as a similar but religious kind of substitutionary payment with the remedial prescription pronounced and the satisfaction rendered, not in a civil court but in the place of sacrifice. And if one adds to the rituals themselves any preliminary rituals related to purification, then one has an equivalent act of confessing of sins, acknowledgement of guilt, and acceptance of the approved remedies with the pains and personal sacrifices which are required to be made.

As a religious method for dealing with sin, ancient sacrifices (*yajn̂ā*) are still practiced in India. During the sacrifice mantras are read which emphasize the moral as well as the spiritual conditions required for the proper performance of an effective sacrifice. Before making oblations to a sacred fire, the worshipper must purify himself, every part of his mind and soul and body, and at every step of his purificatory process must repeat to himself *jyotir aham virajā vipāpma bhuyāsam svāhā*, that is, "Let me be pure light, free from all defilement and sin." When making the offerings to the sacrificial fire, he is required to recite the following text (*mantra*): "Let fire lead me to the place where the knower of Brahman (*brahmavido*) goes with his devotion (*dikṣā*) and penance (*tapasā*)." All this suggests an integration of sacrifice, austerity and penance, on account of which one cannot say that sacrifice might have been resorted to as a convenient escape from the just retribution of sinful actions. More explicitly, the word *tapas* with its close etymological connections with *tejas* (heat) unites sacrifice and expiation in the same paradigm of fire. Just as fire transmutes a gross mass into its "essential substance" of light and heat, so also sacrifice and penance burn up the dross of sin and ignorance, and transmute the soul's condition into its pristine translucent purity. Just as in Indian punitive asceticism the self-sacrifice is a willed enactment for expunging guilt which anticipates, intensifies, and accelerates a purgative process, so also ritual sacrifice anticipates and accelerates an expungement which could be expected otherwise to determine transmigrations through many centuries of retributive life-conditions. In this case, penance and sacrifice stand as complementary modes of dealing with sin. Penance deals with the subjective conditions of sin, and sacrifice deals with its objective conditions. Penance treats the inward state of a guilty conscience, and sacrifice affirms the transcendental Law or Order of which God is the guardian. Each in its distinctive way acknowledges the principle of just punishment.

The connection between Sacrifice and Punishment may not be merely metaphorical in sacerdotal statements of the dharmasmṛtis in reference to civil penalties and to the role of the king as the guardian of the social order.[46] The metaphor of sacrifice as a figure for punishment would be the converse of punishment as a dimension of expiatory sacrifices. However, explicit analogies appear in the smṛtis between the sacramental "courts" in which the expiational sacrifices are performed and the civil courts through which penalties are administered, and between penalties and expiational rituals. Recognition of the sacrificial character of civil punishments is evident in Manu's statement (8.302-311) on the king's necessary social role:

> Let the king exert himself to the utmost to punish thieves; for, if he punishes thieves, his fame grows and his kingdom prospers. That king indeed is ever worthy of honour who ensures the safety (of his subjects); for the sacrificial session (which he, as it were, performs thereby) ever grows in length, the safety (of his subjects representing) the sacrificial fee.[a] . . . A king who protects the created beings in accordance with the sacred law and smites those worthy of corporal punishment, daily offers (as it were) sacrifices at which hundreds of thousands (are given as) fees . . .;[b] by punishing the wicked and by favouring the virtuous, kings are constantly sanctified, just as are twice-born men by sacrifices.[c]

---

[a] "Paramaṃ yatnamātiṣṭhetstenānāṃ nigrahe nṛpaḥ; stenānāṃ nigrahādasya yaśorāṣṭraṃ ca vardhate. Abhayasya hi yo dātā sampūjyaḥ satataṃ nṛpaḥ; satraṃ hi varddhate tasya sadaivābhayadakṣiṇam" (Manu 8.302-303; Chowkhamba 226; 450-451).

[b] "Rakṣandharmeṇa bhūtāni rājā badhyāṃśca ghātayan; yajate 'haraharyajñaiḥ sahasraśatadakṣiṇaiḥ" (Manu 8.306; Chowkhamba 226; 451).

[c] "Nigraheṇa hi pāpānāṃ sādhūnāṃ saṃgraheṇa ca; dvijātaya ivejyābhiḥ pūyante satataṃ nṛpāḥ" (Manu 8.311; Chowkhamba 226; 452).

The connection between expiational sacrifice and civil punishment is evident in the sacrificial rites which formally precede "trials by ordeal," which invoke the attendance at court of the guardian deities of justice, deities who are believed to make the ritual effective not only to prove an accused's guilt or innocence but also to effect a just retribution of his guilt. Even the ordeal itself is a ritual which effectually carries, or transforms itself into an instrument of retribution, particularly when it causes the death of a guilty person, either directly as the outcome of the ordeal by fire or the ordeal by poison, or through subsequent processes since in the latter case, once the signs of guilt become evident, an antidote is administered and capital punishment is judically administered at a later time, after inquiries into the degree of guilt, the number of persons involved with the accused, and other factors bearing upon the degree of culpability.

In several textual contexts, the receiver of a capital punishment is represented as an atonement offering to the retributing deities, his "penal immolation" itself being perceived as an intensive expiation of his sin, and its execution a great sacrifice. Awareness of this sacrificial character of capital punishment in early texts has already been indicated, as in Āpastamba's statement (1.9.24.24) followed also by Vasiṣṭha (20.13ff. and 27ff.) that a sinner whose sin is too grave to be completely expiable in this life, manages it through the 'rite' of capital punishment. But the sacrificial expiation appears even more explicit in acts of penitential self-destruction. Both the king who strikes the penitent a deadly blow with a sacrificial axe, and the penitent who immolates himself in a sacred fire, perform ritual acts of punishment. But whereas in such "cosmic" sacrifices as the great royal Aśvamedha Sacrifice it is the divine creation of the universal order which is dramatically re-enacted and upheld for the sake of all beings, in the retributional sacrifices it is the justicial dimension of that order which is affirmed and vindicated for the sake of all heavenly beings as well as for the sake of mankind. It is in this latter respect that capital punishment in particular, following Haradatta's comment on

Āpastamba 1.9.25.12 (SBE Vol. II), is perceived as the great "burnt offering" (*tapas*) which atones for all sins.

The relation of sacrifice and asceticism which has been indicated reaches its finest expression in the supreme sacrifice in which the officient and the offering are the same person. This is realized through the "spiritual sacrifice" in which a devotee presents himself as a holy offering to God. Insofar as such a self-offering could be motivated by the desire to escape the judgemental wrath of God, it could be perceived as an evasion of just punishment. Moreover, the teaching that God even removes the sins of His devotees, and treats them as if they had never sinned at all, implies that He also waives the instruments of His justice and even the principle of Karma itself, of which He is sometimes said to be the governor, supervisor, or controller. But while it has been shown that Hindu theologians recognized conditions under which God does not waive Karma but transforms it into an instrument of redemptive grace in and for His devotees, it is also apparent that the life of devotion itself embraced by the word *bhakti* and the word *prapatti* with the sense of unconditional wholehearted self-surrender to God, which Rāmānuja in the eleventh century developed on the basis of devotional concepts and beliefs in early and contemporaneous literary sources, demands physical and mental self-disciplines which set it plainly within that ascetical tradition in which the notion of Karmic expiation is central. This acknowledgement of the principle of Karma even in devotional asceticism rules out the probability that in devotion to God, a circumvention of the principle of justice is intended. True *bhakti* is a devotional austerity which affirms the justice as well as the goodness of God in the spirit of the inspired lines of the Bhagavadgītā:

> "Yatkaroṣi yadaśnāsi yajjuhoṣi dadāsi yat;
> Yattapasyasi kaunteya tatkuruṣva madarpaṇam."
>
> ("Whatever you do, whatever you eat, whatever you offer in sacrifice, whatever you gift away, whatever your austere practice, O Kaunteya, do it as an offering to Me") (Bhagavadgītā 9.27; Sri Ramakrishna Tapovanam [1974], 514-515).

CONCLUSION: THE STRUCTURE OF PUNISHMENT

The search for the conception which early Indian writers had in mind when they wrote descriptively and prescriptively on punishment has entailed a thematic compilation of the manifold retributional data under metaphysical, ethical, judicial, and experiential headings, and an elucidation of the different theories of law, morality, and retribution, in which the conception was expressed by vedic, upanishadic, and smṛti writers.

The assumption that those writers had in mind a general conception of punishment as a metaphysical reality, a cosmic law, an ethical principle, and a divine activity, is warranted by the unifying sense that such a complex conception gives to the myriad diversity of otherwise seemingly contradictory and dischoate retributional sentences. It may be assumed that many, if not all, of the statements carried conceptual allusions familiar to or understood by the readers as well as the authors, and that statements about punishment implied understanding of what punishment is both as an instrument of social control, and/or as a divine operation, and even as a principle of life outworking itself in human experience. In this case, they would have received even judicial statements or penal prescriptions as modes or forms of expression of the higher principle of retribution. Only when the conception was forgotten would there have remained for the reader a discrete manifold of retributional statements manifesting contradictions of meaning which could not be logically reconciled.

The complexity of the conception, however, would hardly allow its comprehensive definition in a simple statement. Instead, one would look for a schema of statements which would embrace its substantial and contextual facets and would bring out by implication at least, if not explicitly, the subtlety of manifold detail which belongs to the essential meaning of punishment as they understood it when drawing their regulative principles and directives from it. In the light of the reconstructed theories and forms of the conception drawn in preceding pages, their definitional statements would reasonably be expected to include the following:

1. Punishment is a manifestation of, or an affirmation of, a transcendent Order referred to as Rta and perceived to be a reality supported, protected, and served by a host of guardian deities whose principals are referred to as "charioteers" or "guardians of Rta." [These guardians establish the transcendent Order through lesser orders in the world of finite moral beings, particularly those of Dharma, Karma, and the social order. Their guardianship is expressed by their actions against violations of these orders, which are perceived, not only as manifestations of the transcendent Order, but also as either autonomous dynamic principles, as personalized divinities, as instruments of the divine Will, and as embodiments of justice in rulers and judges when these are dedicated to the principles of law and justice for the suppression of crimes, the restraint of criminals, the promotion of morality, and the material benefit and good order of their societies.]

2. Punishment is a negative manifestation of the transcendent Order in Nature and in human societies. [Both the beneficial and the adverse phenomena of Nature, the political and economic fortunes of societies, and the experiences of human individuals, are realizations of the outworkings of the transcendent Order through the principles of Dharma and Karma, just as the actions of kings and judges when protecting the social order, manifest that Order or Rta, and its Dharma, in the society. Inasmuch as they serve the order of mankind, they embody within themselves and their offices the principles of Dharma and Danda, of Law and Punishment, under the auspices of the guardian deities of Rta.]

3. Punishments are retributions of acts (rather than of persons). Punishments are negative acts, processes, or instruments which 'negate' wrongful acts. [All acts are 'moral' acts inasmuch as the doers of them are answerable for them from the lowest to the highest degrees of responsibility ascertainable by examination. All acts are, accordingly, retributable between the lightest to the heaviest retributions with respect to rewards for meritorious deeds and punishments for demeritorious acts.]

4. Punishments are treatments of guilt. Since there are no 'non-responsible' acts, there are no acts which are devoid of moral deserts. There are only degrees of responsibility or answerability governed by a variety of mitigative circumstances or qualifying conditions of responsibility. [The mitigative conditions arise from infancy, juvenility, mental infirmity, pecuniary necessity, and so forth. These govern the degree of responsibility for an act, not the fact of it, and the severity of deserved punishment. Guilt however, is a qualitative factor which is also transferable between persons happening to fall within a specified range of personal

relations such as occur between a king and his subjects, a parent and his children, husbands and their spouses, teachers and their disciples, judges and the criminals whom they punish, and others. Guilt-transference may occur accidentally between a thief and the owner of his stolen possessions; or it may be formally transferred as by a deathbed ritual in which a father transmits his merits and demerits to his sons, or a dying ascetic transmits the remainder of his demerits to his enemies. In each instance of such transference, the recipient is believed to experience the retributive outworkings of his acquired demerit, as if they had been entirely his own.

Punishments are justicially equated with guilt. The mechanisms of Karma effect the equation automatically or under the control of a supervisory deity. The justiciary deities effect the equation when they punish wrongdoers. Judges instrument the equation when they calculate degrees of guilt and apportion commensurate severities of penalty. The punishments and penalties accordingly realize the justicial equation between retribution and retributability.

As instrumentations of justice, punishments are essentially retributive. (Retribution is only another word for punishment where the just treatment of wrongful acts is concerned. It is not a 'form of punishment' distinguishable from 'other forms' of punishment, such as restraint, deterrence, and reformation, which are really useful things which punishments can do. Imprisonment is not a 'form of punishment' governed by a system of prison-terms or jail-sentences on par with the lists and tables of fines and corporal punishments given in the law-chapters of the dharmasmṛtis.)]

5. Punishments are equivalentially interrelated. Corporal punishments, fines, and penances are ethically distinguishable in terms of the kinds of transgressions which they correct, corporal punishments being explicitly directed to the correction of injuries to persons, fines to property damages, and penances to moral and spiritual transgressions not in the category of crimes, and to moral and spiritual dimensions of crimes already subject to penalties. [Ascetical practices, and certain sacrificial rites, are inexplicitly retributional inasmuch or insofar as their performance causes expiational purificatory pains or pecuniary costs similar to fines inasmuch as they are demanded as a necessary condition of making amends for wrongdoing.]

The conception of punishment represented in the data is an ideic complex whose constituents have integral ramifications of metaphysical, religious, and ethical connotations which inform the total meaning of any retributional statement. A statement that judges ought to punish wrongdoers is not simply a statement about law but also a statement about the nature and the importance of justice and of civil order and of dutifulness in judges as divine concerns related to Order as an ultimate value. Sentential correlations between Dharma-, Karma-, and Yama-statements also reflect their mutual, yet qualifying, retributional correlations. Sentential correlations, likewise, between penal, pecuniary, and penitential statements, indicate their ideic correlation within a general conception of punishment. The resultant manifold of ideic, sentential, and contextual interrelations, both explicit and implicit, prevents an overly simple representation of that conception of punishment which the theorists on law and conduct in ancient India expressed in their writings. Even a verbal account would have to be extremely lengthy to provide more than a skeletal definition of the complex conception. A visual summarization can be useful, however, in providing a general indication of the interrelations of the different ideic facets of the conception which have been amplified through the explanations and descriptions of the earlier pages of this work. The following "open-grid" configuration (which represents the interconnections and interchangeabilities of the elements of the conception) is only a tentative summarization through a visual representation of the integral totality of principles, powers, agents, processes, and operations, perceived to negate, correct, compensate, counteract, and neutralize, such acts of self-willed beings as are adversative toward that universal Order upon which the world and the wellbeing of all finite creatures is believed primarily and ultimately to depend.

THE TRADITIONAL INDIAN CONCEPTION OF PUNISHMENT

	ṚTA (UNIVERSAL ORDER)				
Spheres/Orders Of Ṛta	THE SUPERNATURAL SPHERE/ORDER	THE RITUAL SPHERE/ORDER	THE MORAL-SOCIAL ORDER	THE JUDICIAL ORDER	THE PSYCHOPHYSICAL SPHERE
Supervisory Deities Of Ṛta	VARUṆA BRAHMĀ	AGNI MITRA SŪRYA	DHARMA INDRA	DAṆḌA VYAVAHĀRA	YAMA (Lord Of Conscience)
Non-Capital Retributions	DIVINE AFFLICTIONS (Tapiṣṭhena)	PENAL-CURSES	KARMAS, SOCIAL EVILS	PENALTIES	DISEASES AND DEFORMITIES
Capital Retributions	ETERNAL DAMNATION (Madhva) REPEATED DEATH	CAPITAL PENANCES	DESTRUCTIVE EPIDEMICS	CAPITAL PUNISHMENTS	FATALITIES
Equivalential And Voluntary Retributions	FATES, ECONOMIC MISFORTUNES	MONETARY-ATONEMENTS (Gifts To Brāhmins)	PENANCES	FINES, COMPENSATIONS	AUSTERITIES, YOGA, DEVOTIONAL SELF-SURRENDER (Prapatti)

NOTES

[Numbers in parentheses indicate page references]

Introduction: The Indian Conception of Punishment

1 [17] John Kleinig's critique of J. Rawls' criteria of punishment as being inapplicable to self-inflicted, divine, and parental punishments appears in John Kleinig, Punishment and Desert (The Hague: M. Nijhoff [1973], 18-20).

2 [17] Antony Flew, "The Justification of Punishment," in 29 Philosophy 291 [1954].

3 [17] G. W. F. Hegel, The Philosophy of Right, tr. T. M. Knox (London: Oxford University Press [1942], note to paragraph 99).

4 [17] Kleinig would have the "forms" of punishment labelled as "penalties" as being "the form which punishment takes" (Punishment and Desert [1973], 28-31).

5 [18] This utilitarian sense of "the justification of punishment" as an instrument of social control is explored from a wide variety of philosophical, religious, and social perspectives in Rudolph J. Gerber and Patrick D. McAnany (eds.), Contemporary Punishment: Views, Explanations and Justifications (Notre Dame, Indiana: University of Notre Dame Press [1972]). The arrangement of the essays suggests that the writers perceived punishment as an unnecessary evil, which in the public interest, could better be replaced by rehabilitative and prophylactic "treatments."

6 [18] This aspect of the problem of punishment is treated in detail in John Kleinig's brilliant essay, Punishment and Desert [1973], specifically with respect to the moral justification of punishment. But even here the distinction is made between "just" and "unjust" punishment, where "just punishment" is perceived as punishment of an offender for an offence, and is not in excess of what is commensurate with the offence, where "offence" and "offender" are to be interpreted in the morally relevant senses of those expressions, and where "unjust punishment" is either in excess of or less than what is commensurate with the offence, but is morally justified by "the good it achieves," which however "must be so great that it outweighs the evil of the injustice involved." H. J. McCloskey, "Utilitarian and Retributive Punishment," Journal of Philosophy, Vol. LXIV [1967], pp. 91, 92 and discussed at length in John Kleinig (Punishment and Desert [1973], 82-87).

7 [18] K. G. Armstrong appears to hold this view in "The Retributivist Hits Back," Mind, Vol. LXX [1961], p. 476,

which may be contrasted with Sir Walter Moberley's argument in The Ethics of Punishment (London: Faber and Faber [1968]) for judicial punishment as a means of expiation.

8 [*18*] Hegel's Philosophy of Right, para. 99 may be compared with his description of punishment as "an injury of an injury," para. 101, p. 72.

9 [*18*] Many writers, contrary to the views of retributionists, have characterized punishment as a necessary evil. Many definitions include the infliction of pain as a necessary element of punishment as if supporting J. M. Smith's argument that "if an act which we took to be an act of punishment could be shown to be not painful or coercive, we would or at least should, withdraw the name 'punishment'" (J. M. Smith, "Punishment: A Conceptual Map and a Normative Claim," Ethics, Vol. LXXV [1964-1965], p. 285). But as Kleinig points out, a fine may not be painful yet both by act and intention it would still be a punishment. A hardy schoolboy caned by the headmaster would hardly contend that he had not been punished "because the caning did not hurt!"

10 [*18*] In this case the notion of "unjust punishment" entertained by H. J. McCloskey ("Utilitarian and Retributive Punishment," Journal of Philosophy, Vol. LXIV [1967], 91, 92) is not an ethical conception, since even its motivation is not with reference to a wrong done but to an end "so great that it outweighs the evil of the injustice involved." The question of whether there can be "undeserved punishment" is fully discussed by John Kleinig in Punishment and Desert [1973].

11 [*19*] While it is probable that most of the major literary sources of the Indian conception of Punishment might have been composed prior to the fourth century B.C. in classical or "Pāṇinian" Sanskrit, most of the early minor sūtras and smṛtis which only survived as portions of later writings prior to their modern restoration through synoptic analysis probably existed only in vernacular languages. The Epics had certainly been current in Prākrit for some centuries prior to their rendition into Sanskrit "perhaps shortly after the Christian era" (A. Berriedale Keith, Classical Sanskrit Literature, New Delhi: Y.M.C.A. Publishing House [1966], 1) even as the earliest Jain and Buddhist texts also appeared firstly in Prākrit vernaculars. Keith's references include Indian Antiquities xxiii.52; JRAS [1914], 102ff. and JRAS [1915], 382ff. and 799ff.

12 [*22*] The 1909 edition of the Manusmṛti by the Elysium Press of Calcutta for the Society for the Resuscitation of Indian Literature provides an example of this early title of the work as the Manusaṃhitā consistent with the repetition of this title at the close of each section (*adhyāya*). The compilative character of this dharmaśāstra is consistent with other titles such as Viṣṇusaṃhitā and Parāśarasaṃhitā in this two-volume collection of dharmaśāstra works.

13 [*23*] The source of Müller's thesis and Bühler's defence is in Bühler's Introduction to the SBE, Vol. XXV.

Arguments against the thesis appears in P. V. Kane's History of the Dharmaśāstra [1968], Vol. I, Pt. I, 143-149; Jayasval, Manu and Yājñavalkya [1930], 21; S. Y. Banerjee, Dharmasūtras [1962], 39-44, and D. F. Mulla, Principles of Hindu Law [1960], 20.

14 [25]J. D. M. Derrett has described the functions of the commentator in settling the order of texts, explaining the succession of topics, and distinguishing injunctions from declamations (*arthavāda*), the force of the injunctions, and particularly their applicability to court cases, in Essays in Classical and Modern Hindu Law [1976], Vol. I, 143-149.

15 [25]In a highly readable account of Medhātithi's use of Bhāruci's Manu-śāstra-vivaraṇa, Derrett (Essays in Classical and Modern Hindu Law [1976], 151) shows that the "south Indian, Mālayāli-speaking" Bhāruci (c. A.D. 750) was already a widely reputed authority by the time that Medhātithi (c. A.D. 850), a north-Indian, wrote. This illustrates the roles of the commentators as disseminators of authoritative texts and promoters of their authority. On the date of Bhāruci, Kane's discussion in History of the Dharmaśāstra should be compared with Derrett's discussion in Essays in Classical and Modern Hindu Law [1976], Vol. I, 125ff.

16 [25]Kane (History of the Dharmaśāstra [1975], Vol. I, Pt. II; [1975], Vol. III; [1962], Vol. V, Pt. II, gives the following dates for the leading commentators: Medhātithi (A.D. 900), Govindarāja (A.D. 1080-1140), Kullūka (A.D. 1150-1300), Nārāyaṇa (A.D. 1100-1300) (Kane, History of the Dharmaśāstra [1968], Vol. VII, Pt. I, 348), Vijñāneśvara (A.D. 1070-1100), Viśvarūpa (A.D. 800-850), and Aparārka (A.D. 1125). For the authors of the widely-known digests (*nibandhas*) Kane gives broad dates as: Caṇḍeśvara (A.D. 1290-1370), Ballāla Sen (A.D. 1161), Lakṣmīdhara (A.D. 1100-1150), Gopāla (Kāmadhenu, Kane, Vol. I, Pt. II [1968], 616-622) (A.D. 1000-1100), Halāyudha (A.D. 950), Hemādri (A.D. 1260-1270), and Nīlakaṇṭha (A.D. 1615-1645).

17 [26]J. D. M. Derrett (Essays in Classical and Modern Hindu Law [1976], 142) explains that certain eighth- or ninth-century jurists declared that specific practices amounting to thirty or so in number and authorized by the dharmaśāstra were deemed obsolete or void in the present degenerate age. Derrett says: "This was accepted by jurists all over India with some alacrity" on the principle that "any rule which met the determined opposition of any section of the public, was to be ignored and was not to be enforced."

PART I, Chapter 1. The Concept of Rightness.

1 [27]M. Bloomfield, The Religion of the Veda [1908], p. 12.

2 [28]Śat.2.3.4.4-5; 2.3.1.5; 4.3.1.9-10; 4.3.2.5; and 1.6.3.8. J. C. Tavadia explained the conception of ṛta as "Order" in his essay "The Meaning of ṛta" in ABORI 35; 27-34. G. P. Conger has related the cosmic and the social orders in an interesting essay for UNESCO in "Ṛta: Cosmic Structure and Social Order" in "Human Relations and International Obligations" (Report of UNESCO--Indian Philosophical Congress Symposium, Ceylon [1954]), Bangalore, [1956].

3 [28]As in RV 5.63.7; 1.161.9 and other Ṛgvedic hymns.

4 [28]RV 4.23.8-10.

5 [29]As in RV 10.87.11. H. D. Velankar however has presented a somewhat de-ethicalized connotation of *satya* (truth) in relation to Ṛta in "Ṛta and Satya in Ṛgveda" in the Summary of Papers of the 20th AIOC in Bhubaneshwar [1959], p. 11.

6 [29]Modern studies of the major vedic deities, particularly in their ethical roles as agents of Varuṇa and as instruments of Ṛta, are noticeably few in R. N. Dandekar's Vedic Bibliography [1956-1973]. Though apparently in three volumes, each volume of the bibliography in effect revises and updates the previous volume. Useful sources of reference and critical discussion in Dandekar's list are: Y. R. Vipradas, "Agni in the Ṛgveda" (in the summary of Papers of the 18th AIOC, Annamālanagar [1955]; 19-20); H. Heras, "The Personality of Yama in the Ṛgveda" (in the Jandunath Sarkar Commemorative Volume II [1958]; 191-197); H. Lüders, Varuṇa: Varuṇa und das Ṛta (Göttingen: Vandenhoeck and Ruprecht [1959]; XXIII and 339-765); J. J. Meyer, "Varuṇa" (in WZKM 46; 138ff.); P. Thieme, "Mitra and Aryaman" (in Transactions of the Connecticut Academy of Arts and Sciences, Vol. 41, New Haven [1957], 96); M. D. Balasubrahmanyam, "Ethics of the Ādityas in the Ṛgveda" (in the Summary of Papers of the 19th AIOC, Delhi [1957], 5-6); T. V. Kapali Sastry, "Godhead and the gods in the Rigveda" (in the Sri Aurobindo Mandir Annual, Jayanti No. 6 [1947], 82-108); and A. N. Pande, "Role of the Vedic gods in the Gṛhya-Sūtras" in JGJRI 16 (1-2); 91-133. According to P. Thieme, "Varuṇa in the Mahabharata," SP, 26, ICO [1964], 252, the fundamental conception of Varuṇa is an ethical one, not that of a nature deity, since his primary role is the guardianship of truth expressed by speech, and all other traits are connected with, and follow from, this basic character. Dr. C. Kunhan Raja's substantial and richly supported reconstruction of the mythology of Yama in

Poet-Philosophers of the Ṛgveda, Madras [1963], unfortunately lacks sufficient treatment of Yama's ethical attributes and role.

7 [29] As in RV 1.1.8; 2.29.1; 5.63.1; 7.66.12; and 9.73.8.

8 [30] RV 2.27.8; 5.68.4; and 10.85.1.

9 [30] S. Bhattacharji's study of the etymology and religious history of Varuṇa in *The Indian Theogony* [1970], 23ff. proved most useful here.

10 [30] Śat.5.3.3.9; also MS 2.6.6; TS 1.2.11; and JB 3.11.4.2.

11 [30] As in RV 1.24.9 and 4.24.8.9, also TS 1.5.11.

12 [31] E.g. in Śat.2.5.2.20.

13 [31] RV 1.122.9; 2.28.5-8.

14 [33] RV 8.35.13; also MS 3.9.1.

15 [33] TB 1.2.5.5; JB 2.230.

16 [34] TS 4.4.8.3; also 2.1.9.3.

17 [34] So S. Bhattacharji, *The Indian Theogony* [1970], 223.

18 [37] Mait.Br.4.2(SBE XV); Vas.Dhs.18.18-19; Manu 7.7.

19 [37] RV 10.11-12, cf. BhP.6.1ff. and Mbh.3.200.49.

20 [37] Vas.Dhs.20.3; Nār.Dhs., appendix 50 in SBE XXXIII.

21 [37] Manu 12.17 and 22; Mbh.3.237.11.

22 [37] AV 4.6.110.2 and 5.8.8.11; RV 1.38.5 and 10.165.4.

23 [37] AV 2.7.53.1 cf. RV 10.154.4-5; 10.123.6.

24 [38] Mbh.3.11.66 cited E. W. Hopkins, *The Religions of India* [1895]; 380.

25 [38] Mbh.1.9.11ff. (where "king Dharma" is mentioned in place of Lord Yama); cp. also Mbh.1.108.8ff.

26 [38] Manu 8.173; 9.303 and 307; Nār.Dhs.18.26 and 30.

27 [38] Manu 8.92; Nār.Dhs., Quotations from Nār.Dhs.5.9, in SBE XXXIII, p. 247.

28 [38] Nār.Dhs. Quotations from Nār.Dhs.5.4, in SBE XXXIII, p. 245.

29 [38] From the Daṇḍaviveka, Bhattacharya's trans., p. 9.

Chapter 2. The Concept of Obligation

1 [42] G. H. Mees (Dharma and Society, London: Luzak [1935]; 8-9) listed eleven connotations of the word *dharma*: an aspect of Ṛta, ethical duty, virtue or propriety, good works, religious obligation, the ideal, truth, universal law or principle, divine justice, "a compromise between the ideal and actual conditions," convention or code of customs and traditions, common law, "international" or "intertribal" law. Varma remarks (Studies in Hindu Political Thought [1974], 113 n.1) that "these several and diverse meanings do not signify any lack of the logical faculty of discrimination but indicate the dominance of a principle or primeval norm," that is, "the underlying law or principle." Balbir Singh Gauchhwal, "The Metaphysical Foundations of Hindu Ethics and Religion" in PEW 16 (3-4) [1966], 143-159, states that Dharma in its metaphysical aspect is a specific mode of Ṛta, which latter in turn is the determinate mode of the indeterminate reality of Brahman. John M. Koller in PEW 22 (2), April 72, 131-144 also states that "Dharma: [is] an expression of universal order." Clearly, a short essay in the context of Punishment could not do justice to the concept in its manifold contexts, nor even attempt to meet the problems to be faced in treating the historical development of this fundamental presupposition of Indian philosophy. These problems were cogently felt by Sternbach (Bibliography on Dharma and Artha in Ancient and Medieval India, Wiesbaden: Otto Harrassowitz [1973]) in attempting to compile a bibliography which would take into consideration the historical continuity of the conception of Dharma without the guidance of clear historical demarcations. Such difficulties would justify the restriction of this discussion of the concept of Dharma to the dimensions of religion, law, regulation, and custom in general and with particular reference to its penal and penitential bearings. For this reason, however, valuable historical studies of Dharma have been hardly more than consulted for relevant information. They include G. Mees, Dharma and Society (Le Haye [1935] and London [1946]), Julius Jolly, Hindu Law and Custom (Calcutta [1928]), V. P. Varma, Studies in Hindu Political Thought and its Metaphysical Foundations (Delhi [1954]; 3rd revised edn. [1974]), and P. V. Kane's History of the Dharmaśāstra (Poona [1930-1968]).

Sternbach's bibliography, though not a complete reference-source, has an extensive list of works relating to the history of Dharma, of which the following appear to be particularly noteworthy: B. Bhattacharya, "Hindu Conception of dharma in the fourteenth century" (in Indian Culture, 6.1.67-70); A. L. Basham, Studies in Ancient Indian History and Culture (Calcutta [1964]), chaps. 6 and 9; and Aspects of Ancient Indian Culture (Bombay [1966]), chap. 2; T. Chakravarti, "Dharma in the Mahabharata" (in RMIC 4.11); R. K. Chowdhury, "Conception of Law in Ancient India" (in JBRS 33; 183-192); "Theory of Punishment in

Ancient India" (in Proceedings of the 10th Session of the IHC, Bombay [1947]); "Indian Crime, Punishment and Justice through the Ages" (in OT 1 (2), 153-160); R. N. Coomeraswamy, Spiritual Authority and Temporal Power: the Indian Theory of Government (New Haven [1942]); J. N. C. Ganguly, "Philosophy of dharma (law)" in IHQ 2; 575-586; 809-825; B. G. Gokhale, Indian Thought through the Ages: a Study of some dominant Concepts (Bombay [1961]); N. N. Ghose, "Law and Morals" (in CR 30.3; 283-293); U. N. Ghoshal, "The Relation of the dharma Concept to the Social and Political Order in Brahmanical Thought" (in BORS 38.190-202); R. C. Harza, "Dharma--Its Significance and Scope" (in OH 7.1; 15-36 and 8.1; 7-34; and in JRAS [1962]); D. H. H. Ingalls, "Authority and Law in Ancient India" in "Authority and Law in the Ancient Orient" JAOS 17 [1954], 34-45; C. Kulkarni, "Hindu Dharma" (in Bhāratīya Vidyā Bhavan, Bombay); V. A. Ramaswami Śāstri, "Dharma--its Definition and Authority" (in JGJRI 7.29-42); L. Renou, "La Société et le droit dans l'Inde ancienne; le dharma" (in Sanskrit et Culture, Paris [1950], ch. X, 126-136).

2 [44]J. D. M. Derrett's rich knowledge of the concept of Dharma appears in such works as Hindu Law Past and Present [1957] and The Classical Law of India [1973], and in the journal articles which are compiled in Essays in Classical and Modern Hindu Law ([1973]; I.80-85).

3 [44]Also as a personification of Punishment (*Daṇḍa*).

4 [45]RV 8.89.4.

5 [45]The problems arising from depending exclusively on etymological analyses and philological comparisons of words while ignoring their ideic, sentential and contextual correlations are illustrated by Kane's extensive controversy with the Sanskritist, Vaman Shivram Apte, former Professor of Sanskrit at Ferguson College, Poona, over the meaning of the word *vrata*.

Kane (History of the Dharmaśāstra [1958], Vol. V, Pt. I, 1-32) acknowledges the authority of "the great Petersburg Dictionary" where the meaning of *vrata* is derived from the root *vṛ*, and at least eight specialized and general senses are given including: "(1) will, command, law, prescribed order; (2) subservience, obedience, service; (3) domain; (4) order, regulated succession, realm; (5) calling, office, customary activity, carry on, custom; (6) religious duty, worship, obligation; (7) any undertaking, religious or ascetic performance or observance, vow, sacred work; (8) vow in general, fixed purpose; (9) other specialized senses."

Max Müller appears to have accepted the root *vṛ* as the proper source of the meaning of *vrata* with the general sense of "to protect" first in its ordinary meaning of "to enclose in a safe place, to pen, to set apart" and then in the sense of "what is settled or determined," that is, "decided upon," hence "law or ordinance," and finally "sway or power."

Professor Apte followed Professor Whitney in deriving the word from the root *vṛt* in the sense of "to turn around, move on," "to revolve" or "to roll onward," in specific reference to "the heavenly routes, the divine rounds, the periodical movements round the sky" which are performed by the planetary deities, and not in the sense of any "holy laws" thought to have been "laid down" by particular deities.

Apte also discredited the notion of *vratas* as "ordinances" which the deities institute for worshipping beings to follow. Of particular interest in Kane's repudiation of Apte's thesis is his repeated reference to ideic and sentential contexts of the word *vrata* as disproofs of Apte's arguments. In the light of these, Kane insists that the sense of "command" or "law" is quite appropriate in more than half of the Ṛgvedic passages in which the word *vrata* occurs without prefixes. Furthermore, in numerous places where *vrata* is found with prefixes (*upasargas*) such as *abhi*, *ā*, *ni*, *pari*, *pra*, or *vi*, the meaning is changed so completely that any inferences drawn solely from the supposed root-meaning are totally useless (Vol. V, Pt. I, 2), while in several places in the Ṛgveda, *avrata*, *apavrata*, and *anyavrata* occur in the sense of "the mode of worship, or ethical or religious practices of the Vedic worshippers."

The question of whether the gods are the law-makers and all other beings are required to be law-abiders appears irrefutably answered by the Ṛgvedic references which Kane presents to demonstrate that deities are both creators and subjects of *vratas* in the sense of Ṛgveda 3.7.7; "the gods observe the *vratas* of gods."[a] As Kane (History, Vol. V, Pt. I, 9) comments: "The passages clearly show that the Vedic sages believed that not only did the several gods observe or carry out the immutably fixed ordinances laid down by themselves or by any one of them but that even wily demons had to observe them and the waters or rivers flow as ordained by gods."

Coupled with this belief in the obligatoriness for deities of *vratas* is the belief that human beings who violate or transgress "the *vratas* of the gods" are liable to be punished, which constrains them to offer penitential intercessions for release from punishments, as in the well-known Ṛgvedic prayer (1.25.1-2): "Whatever ordinances of thine, O Varuṇa, we may break day to day, give us not as prey to death, to be destroyed by thee in wrath, to thy fierce anger when displeased."

Hence both in the Ṛgveda and the other Saṃhitās, and in the Brāhmaṇas, *vrata* generally means "divine ordinances" or "ethical precepts" or "patterns of conduct." Moreover, the word implies ritualistic duties or obligations in ritualistic formularies as in the Atharvaveda (e.g. 6.64.2 in the sense of "religious observance" and in 4.15.13; 19.59.2; and 20.109.3 where the words *vrata*, *vatrāni*, and *vratānyasya* occur with the sense of "religious vow,") and the Śrauta- and Gṛhyasūtras.

---

[a]"deva devānāmanu hi vrata guḥ . . .".

The sense of ritualistic obligation is carried over into the Brāhmaṇas of which the statement of the Taittirīya Āraṇyaka (1.26.6) quoted by Kane [1974] (Vol. V, Pt. I, p. 24) is typical "This is the *vrata* for him"--i.e. one who has performed *Aruṇaketukacayana*, a dawn-ritual--"viz. he should not run while it is raining, should not urinate or void ordure in water, should not spit, should not bathe naked, should not step over lotus leaves or gold, should not eat (the flesh) of a tortoise."

Upanishadic uses of the word not only repeat the earlier senses but also supplement these by significations which reflect the philosophical and meditational features of this literature. The statement of the Bṛhadāraṇyaka Upaniṣad (1.5.21-23) that "one should perform only one *vrata*," namely, one should only breathe in and emit breath "for fear that Death may seize him"[a] reflects a yogic specificality in the usage of the word *vrata*. But since in the Taittirīya Upaniṣad (3.7-10) several *vratas* are mentioned--namely, one should not speak ill of food; one should not shun food; one should not refuse accommodation to a needy stranger, etc., it appears that *vrata* applies not only to strictly religious or liturgical procedures, observances, and obligations, but to propriety itself in the sense of the conduct proper to each situation which arises. There are *vratas* for kings which appear in the Aitareya Brāhmaṇa (8.28) to be strategic in character such as never resting before an enemy settles to rest, never sleeping before an enemy sleeps, etc. if the king wishes to overcome his enemy.

But it is not surprising if proprieties and rules which are separately treated as *vratas* appear together in the dharmaśāstra literature with meanings approximating to those of *dharma* in the same literature, though with specific reference to dharmas, duties, obligations, or commitments which are religious or ritualistic in nature, especially those which, according to Śabara (on the Jaiminīya Brāhmaṇa 6.2) and the Mitākṣarā on Yājñavalkyasmṛti 1.129, and other references cited by Kane (History of the Dharmaśāstra [1958], Vol. V, Pt. I, 28-29), imply negative self-determinations in the mode of *niyama* or self-restraint. In this category penances (*prāyaścittas*) are also referred to as *vratas*--since they are formalized procedures of self-imposed restraints--in the Manusmṛti (11.117, 170, 176, and 181), in the Yājñavalkyasmṛti (as in 3.251, 252, 254, and 258), and in Saṅkhalikhita [17.6, 22, 42, 61, 62). Vows or formal resolutions to observe certain customs or restrictions about diet, personal hygiene, or general conduct are also called *vratas*, as, for example, in the Mahābhārata 2.58.16; 3.296.3; and 12.35.39. Again, the ritualistic

---

[a] "Tasmādekameva vratam caretprāṇyāccaivāpānyācca nenmā pāpmā mṛtyurāpnuvaditi . . ." (Bṛhad.1.5.23, Daśopanishads, Vol. II [1936], 217).

character of these is evident in their observance on certain lunar days--*tithis*--or at other auspicious times, for the procurement of material objectives especially when accompanied by worship of a deity.

A further qualification, suggested by a footnote in Kane ([1974], Vol. V, Pt. I, 29 note 57) is that *vratas* are not "paramount duties" and in this respect are like the ten "restraints" (*niyamas*) and unlike the ten *yamas* mentioned in Manu (4.204) and Yājñavalkyasmṛti (3.312-314) on chastity, nonviolence, self-restraint, compassion, and others whose negligence could cause a brāhmin's excommunication. On the other hand, *vratas* appear to refer to more than merely formal performances of a restraintive or of a cultic kind, since they appear to be articulated resolutions to perform such duties as are enjoined. In this case, *saṃkalpa* or "firm mental resolve" is the hallmark of a *vrata*, and which resolve need not be present in the formal obligations comprised in the *varṇāśramadharma*. Kane cites some verses of the Agnipurāṇa (175.10-11), which are in the Bhaviṣyapurāṇa and are quoted in the Kṛtyakalpataru, in support of this view. Hence *vratas* apparently comprise a distinctive type of *dharma* despite a range of content which is so vast, even in the citations from the dharmaśāstra literature alone, that Kane [1974], Vol. V, Pt. I, 60, admits that the tabulation of all the sources of *vrata* would entail a "large team of workers" engaging in "a huge amount of labour" which would be "spread over many years," but which when completed would comprise "a monumental one (work) on the social anthropology of India."

6 [45] Kane (History of the Dharmaśāstra [1974], Vol. V, Pt. I, 20) insists that "in the Ṛgveda the word is *dharman* and not *dharma*, and that *dharman* is sometimes used as a masculine noun or an adjective with the sense of "upholder and sustainer" (as in RV 1.187.1; 10.92.2). At least sixty times (Kane, History of the Dharmaśāstra [1968], Vol. I, Pt. I, 1) it is found in the neuter form without prefixes, about eighteen times with the prefixed particle *vi*, and fifty-six times in combination with *sva* and/or *satya* in connection with religious rites or sacrifices "thus approaching *vrata* in one of its senses." In a few sentential contexts (eg. RV 4.53.3 and 5.63.7) it has the sense of "fixed principles or rules of conduct," and in some places its use is explicitly the same as *vrata*. For example RV 7.89.5, "When we destroy (or violate) your *dharmans* through heedlessness (or infatuation), do not harm us, O God, on account of that sin."[a] This may be compared with RV 1.25.1-2, "Whatever ordinance (*vrata*) of thine, O God Varuṇa, we may break day to day . . . give us

[a] "acittī yattava *dharmā* yuyopima mā nastasmādenaso deva rirīṣaḥ" (RV 7.89.5 in Kane, History of the Dharmaśāstra [1974], Vol. V, Pt. I, 30, note 31).

not as a prey to death, to be destroyed by thee . . . ."[a] Moreover, not only are there passages of the Ṛgveda "in which the senses of *vrata* and *dharman* have coalesced," but also statements where "all the three words--*Ṛta*, *vrata*, and *dharman*--or two of the three occur together" such as RV 5.63.7, "O wise Mitra and Varuṇa! according to your fixed rule of conduct (*dharman*) you guard your ordinances (*vrata*) with the wonderful power of an *asura*; you rule over the whole world according to the principle of cosmic order (*Ṛta*); you establish in the heaven the Sun that is a brilliant chariot."[b] In RV 5.72.2 and 6.70.3 *vrata* and *dharman* occur together, while in RV 1.65.2; 2.27.8; 3.4.7; and 10.65.8, *Ṛta* and *vrata* occur together in a manner which suggests that they carry equal force with *vrata*, meaning divine laws or ordinances, and with *dharman*, meaning religious rites and sacrifices. In later texts however *dharman* appears as the all-encompassing conception, with *vrata*, according to Kane, "restricted to sacred vows and rules of conduct to be observed by a person as a member of a community or as an individual."

7 [*49*] Varuṇa alone is styled *dhṛtavrata* in RV 1.25.8-10; 1.44.14; 1.141.9; 2.1.4; 8.27.3; and 10.66.5. He shares the title with Mitra as *dhṛtavrata* in RV 1.15.6; 8.25.2 and 8; and with Indra in 6.68.10. Indra alone is so styled in 6.19.5 and 8.97.11. Viśvedevāḥ has the title in 10.66.8, Agni in 8.44.25, Savitṛ in 4.53.4, and the Ādityas as a group (who include Varuṇa and Mitra) in 2.29.1. The inclusion of the title *kṣatriya* (ruler) along with *dhṛtavrata* in some passages such as 8.25.8 and 10.66.8 suggests dual functions both of divine rulership and divine guardianship of ordinances and commands against transgressions by self-willed creatures. On this matter, Kane (History of the Dharmaśastra [1958], Vol. V, Pt. I, 16-19) strongly contended against those interpretations of Professor Apte which reduced *dhṛtavrata* and *vrata* to merely constellational connotations.

8 [*52*] Robert Lingat, Les Sources du Droit dans le Système Traditionnel de L'Inde (La Haye: Mouton [1967], 166) notes that the Nītisāra of Kāmandaki is generally dated in the 8th century of our era. Kane however (History of the Dharmaśāstra [1973], Vol. III, xvii) dated it between A.D. 400 and 600.

---

[a] "yacciddhi te viśo yathā pra deva Varuna *vratam* minīmasi dyavidyavi, mā no vadhāya hatnave jihīḻānasya rīradhaḥ" (RV 1.25.1-2, Kane, History of the Dharmaśāstra [1974], Vol. V. Pt. I, 9, note 12).

[b] "dharmanā Mitrāvaruṇā vipaścitā vratā rakṣethe asurasya māyayā Ṛtena viśvaṃ bhuvanaṃ vi rājathaḥ sūryamā dhattho divi citryaṃ ratham" (RV 5.63.7, Kane, History of the Dharmaśāstra [1958], Vol. V, Pt. I, 20, note 33).

9 [52]The exact meaning of the science of *Ānvīkṣikī* appears to be in doubt since Kane (History of the Dharmaśāstra [1973], Vol. III, 46-47) devotes an extensive discussion to it, and accepts the meaning indicated by the Kauṭilīya Arthaśāstra as being the Sāṅkhya-Yoga philosophy plus "Lokāyata" in the sense of "logic based on premises derived from ordinary (*loka*) experience."

10 [55]Lingat (Les Sources du Droit dans le Système Traditionnel de L'Inde [1967], 166, note 1) places the date of the Śukranītisāra some time prior to or close to the sixth- or eighth-century date of the Nītisāra of Kāmandaki, apparently in contradiction of an essay on the date of the Śukranīti by Lallanji Gopal in "The Śukranīti, a nineteenth century text."

11 [62]Mbh.12.59.74.

12 [63]As in Mbh.12.69; Nār.Dhs. Intro. 1.34 in SBE XXXIII, p. 14; and Matsya-purāṇa 226 (Allahabad [1916]).

13 [63]Manu 7.3-7.

14 [63]Manu 7.8.

15 [63]Manu 7.11.

16 [63]Manu 7.2.

17 [63]Manu 7.3.

18 [63]Manu 7.10.

19 [64]A. L. Goodhart, English Law and the Moral Law (London: Stevens and Sons [1953], Preface p. ix).

Chapter 3. The Concept of Retribution

1 [71] Kane criticizes Deussen's presentation of the Karma theory at some length.

2 [72] The sacrificial or ritualistic origins of the theory of Karma are assumed by many scholars on the basis of the Śatapatha Brāhmaṇa text, as in J. M. McKenzie, Hindu Ethics (London, N.Y.: Oxford Univ. Press [1922], 15) and E. J. Thomas, The History of Buddhist Thought (London: Kegan Paul, Trench and Trubner [1933], 108ff.).

3 [73] A phrase by which S. Radhakrishnan translates the theory of Karma.

4 [76] Manu gives the names of twenty-one hells in 4.88-90.

5 [83] Pillai Lokācharya in M. Yamunacharya, Ramanuja's Teachings in His Own Words [1963], 105.

6 [83] M. Yamunacharya, Ramanuja's Teachings in His Own Words [1963], 106.

7 [84] The Vaiṣṇavite and Śaivite conceptions of divine Grace are fully discussed by S. N. Dasgupta (A History of Indian Philosophy, Vol. II, 922-955, Vol. III, 452ff., and Vol. IV, 410ff.), upon which I have drawn substantially for the discussion of this topic.

8 [84] This is based on the Śiva Jñāna Siddhiyar 1.37 in J. A. Nallasvamypillai's translation cited by S. Kulandran, Grace in Hinduism and Christianity (London: Lutterworth Press [1964], 203ff.).

9 [86] Max Warren, Interpreting the Cross [1960], chapter 2.

10 [88] Manu 7.27-28. Such relationships and their bearings upon punishment are discussed in greater detail on pages 106-112.

PART II. Ethical Dimensions of Punishment

1 [93] In the Daṇḍaviveka the etymology of the word *enas* is explained as being a vedic word meaning both "sin" or "vice" according to the context (Bhattacharya's trans. p. 5).

2 [97] Mbh.2.209, 29-32 in E. W. Hopkins, The Religions of India [1895], 381.

3 [97] Sir Patrick Devlin attempted to distinguish crime from sin in The Enforcement of Morals (London: Oxford University Press [1965]).

4 [98] Yājñ.Dhs.2.231, Daṇḍaviveka, GOS, LII [1931]; 75 and Bhattacharya's trans., p. 65.

5 [98] Daṇḍaviveka, Bhattacharya's trans., p. 15.

6 [99] Priya Nath Sen, Hindu Jurisprudence, Lecture XII, pp. 335ff.

7 [99] Sir Henry Maine (1858-1958). His Ancient Law [1861] chap. X, 307. This text was to become "a set-book for law-students in India" despite its many errors and lacunae. An insightful critique of Maine's contribution to jurisprudence in India as a Professor of Civil Law then as Vice-Chancellor of Calcutta University, and finally as Corpus Professor of Jurisprudence at Oxford, is found in J. Duncan M. Derrett, Essays in Classical and Modern Hindu Law ([1977]; II.260-275), originally published in the Juridical Review, April 1959; 40-55.

8 [100] Eg. Medhātithi's Manu-bhāṣya on Manu 2.28.

9 [100] Eg. Manu 5.110 and Medhātithi's comment on this.

10 [100] Manu 2.12, also followed by Yājñ.Dhs.1.7.

11 [102] The play of these factors in mitigating the gravity of an offence and its punishment is indicated by Manu (9.230), Yājñavalkya (2.298-299), Bṛhaspati (19.27-28), Kullūka on Manu 9.271-278, Kauṭilya (Arthaśāstra 4.13), in the Matsya-purāṇa (227.165-177), in the Agni-purāṇa (162), and in other texts.

12 [103] In the Kātyāyanasmṛti, as cited in the Daṇḍaviveka, and Paiṭhīnasi, are distinguished several kinds of aider and abettor of criminal or punishable acts such as the commencer, the assistant, the adviser, the protector (who offers asylum), the supplier of weapons, food, and material support of any kind, the planner or mastermind, the winker (*upekṣākarī* = the bystander who "turns a blind eye"), and others. Vyāsa in particular distinguished between assistants (*sa-sahāya*)--persons very intimate with

the culprit--and friends (*sa-bandhava*), the former being active partners effecting a joint criminal enterprise, and the latter comprising those who "though knowing (full well) the perpetrator of the crime as such, do not avoid his company" (Daṇḍaviveka on the basis of the Ratnākara, p. 377) and who therefore pay lip-service or provide surreptitious support for a crime. Thus any aider or abettor or friend of a murderer becomes in effect a partner in his crime and thereby a kind of murderer though not in the same degree. For although a murder may be one of five kinds--(a) by direct action, (b) by offering advice, (c) by showing favour, (d) by according permission, and (e) by acting accidentally or unknowingly becoming an occasion or cause of a murder--the gravity is self-evidently not the same in each case. The range of prescribed penalties take note of this graduation, and include consideration of the degree of guilt of each participant in order to apply with due moderation the following formula:

(a) the murderer: "death by various tormenting methods;"
(b) the adviser: three-fourths of the above;
(c) the favourer: one-half of the "first" or highest measure;
(d) the permitter: one-quarter of the "supreme" measure;
(e) the accidental occasioner: one-half of one-quarter of the first measure; (so Daṇḍaviveka, Bhattacharya's trans. 62-63).

13 [*103*] The Daṇḍaviveka cites Kullūka and other authoritative commentators as translating *mohāt* as "perverse knowledge," and the Ratnākara as giving its meaning as "wrong knowledge," *ajñānāt* as being either "temporary loss of understanding" (according to Kalpataru) or "non-maturity of understanding" (according to the author of the Mitākṣarā which is a commentary on Dharmaśāstra); and *bāliśyāt* as "infatuation due to youth" (citing Caṇḍeśvara's Ratnākara), or "non-generation of knowledge" (according to the Mitākṣarā as explained in the Daṇḍaviveka [Bhattachārya's trans. pp. 288-289].

14 [*103*] In fact, the prescribed penalty for a criminal act is the maximum penalty to be imposed when the act is wilfully entertained and carried out. For this reason the Hindu jurisprudents follow the Manusmṛti in distinguishing different penalties for intentional and unintentional acts. The Kātyāyanasmṛti (cited on page 66 of the Sanskrit edition of the Daṇḍaviveka), prescribes solitary confinement and "similar other penalties" for intentional commission of grave sins. Whereas Manu (9.238-239) exempted brāhmins from this penalty, ex-communication from caste rights and privileges, family ostracism, and even branding with hot-irons are substituted for intentionally indulged grave commissions (*mahāpātaka*) which he specifies as being (9.235-6) brāhmin-murder, drunken disorderliness, theft of gold, and sexual violation of a guru's wife.

Unintentional acts on the other hand appear to be treated as sins, although both intentional and unintentional acts by brāhmins are expiable by penances according to the Manusmṛti (9.90). Unintentional acts by "untouchables" which cause hurts to superior caste persons are only expiable through fines (Manu 5.73-74) whereas intentional acts of this kind must be punished by public flogging or capital punishment.

15 [*104*] Manu 8.293-294. The guilt of accidental transgressions appears to have been recognized in the early Vedic period according to references such as RV 1.185.8 and 5.85.7-8. Manu, however, summarized the expiations requisite both for deliberate and for unintentional or accidental transgressions, while enjoining manifestly lighter penalties or penances for unintentional defaulting in social obligations and breaches of etiquette.

16 [*107*] Manu 8.12 and 137; Viṣ.Dhs.3.28; Yājñ.Dhs.1.337 [teacher and disciple].

17 [*107*] Āpast.Dhs.2.6.14.15-18; 2.11.29.3; Kāty.Dhs. 488-489 [husband and wife].

18 [*107*] Manu 3.100 and 195; Āpast.Dhs.2.36.19-20 [a brāhmin guest and his host].

19 [*107*] Yājñ.Dhs.2.75 cf. Manu 8.96; Viṣ.Dhs.8.26 [a perjuror and the party injured by him].

20 [*107*] Manu 9.137-138; Āpast.Dhs.2.9.24.1-11 [father and eldest son].

21 [*107*] Bṛhas.Dhs.16.9. A striking instance of the justicial implications of a criminal master-servant relationship appears in the Daṇḍaviveka in reference to masters who engage their servants in committing, or who order their servants to commit, criminal acts. The rule appears on pages 63-64 of Bhattacharya's translation and is to the effect that any person in a fiduciary relationship acting on evil orders "incurs the <u>sin</u> of transgression of legal injunction but invites no punishment on himself" [emphasis added]. But just as fathers are liable to face punishment for the delinquencies of their sons, "so here also on equitable principle, the offerer of the evil advice and not the person acting under that advice, is to be punished."

22 [*107*] See Ait.1.1ff. and Āpast.Dhs.2.9.24.1-11.

23 [*108*] That is, the father must leave home, turn his back on his sons, and never see them again during the remainder of his life.

24 [*108*] On the matter of parental responsibility for the actions of their children, see also, Baudh.Dhs.2.1.2.18-20 and Bühler's footnote (SBE II) to Āpast.Dhs.1.10.29.9-10.

25 [*108*] Āpast.Dhs.2.9.24.1-10; compare Nār.Dhs.16.32 which says that "a father is not liable to be punished for an offence committed by his sons unless he should have set them to do it" (SBE, Vol. XXXIII).

26 [*110*] Āpast.Dhs.4.201-202 which should be compared with Yājñ.Dhs.1.159-160, Baudh.Dhs.2.5.6.29, and Viṣ.Dhs.64.1.

27 [112] Compare H. D. Lewis, Morals and Revelation (London: Allen & Unwin [1951], pp. 113ff.) with H. D. Lewis, Morals and the New Theology (London: Gollanz [1947], 80ff.), and N. H. G. Robinson, Faith and Duty (London: Gollanz [1950], 135ff.).

28 [112] Viṣ.Dhs.5.73-74, 195; Gaut.Dhs.3.19; and Yājñ.Dhs.2.221.

29 [112] An informative discussion of the British law pertaining to "conspiracies" as joint criminal enterprises is found in D. W. Elliott and J. C. Wood, A Casebook of Criminal Law (London: Sweet & Maxwell [1968]) and also in an article by D. W. Elliott in the Listener (London: British Broadcasting Corporation, January 6 [1966]) with the title "The Criminal Company."

30 [113] As in Yājñ.Dhs.2 and other references cited in the Sanskrit edition of the Daṇḍaviveka (Bhattacharya's trans. pp. 216 and 217).

31 [113] The rulings of different authorities on these are concisely summarized in the Daṇḍaviveka (Bhattacharya's trans. p. 61).

32 [113] Bhattacharya (Daṇḍaviveka, p. 61).

33 [114] The Ratnākara ([1931]; 374, note 2) explains this instigation as being "by verbal suggestion" or by persuasion according to the model: "I would pay you . . . (followed by a stipulated amount) . . . for committing this offence." In such a case, the penalty is four times the prescribed punishment which is to be interpreted by reference to the prescriptions for the different castes of the participants.

34 [114] In a lengthy note on the criminal bearings of these words, the explanation is provided in the Daṇḍaviveka (Bhattacharya's trans. pp. 62-63) that *sahāya* means a person who is closely associated with the offender as an accomplice. It is distinct from *bandhava* which means a friend who associates with a publicly known offender instead of avoiding his company. The penalties for criminal associations are in relation to the degrees of involvement, admission or non-admission of such involvement, and the gravity of the involvement itself, i.e. whether the crime was particularly grave or not, since association with a murderer by maintaining him in hiding is understandably graver than socializing with a petty thief.

35 [115] According to interpretations in the Ratnākara, the Kalpataru and the digest of Halāyudha referred to in the Daṇḍaviveka, pp. 61ff.

36 [115] Daṇḍaviveka (Bhattacharya's trans. pp. 61ff).

37 [116] E.g., RV 5.2.7 and 7.86.5.

38 [117] E.g., RV 6.51.7 and 10.15.6.

39 [117] As in RV 10.14.6-8.

40 [117] As in RV 7.58.5.

41 [118] So the Nārada Smṛti states following Manu. If, however, an injured party forgives the offenders, that is meritorious (so the Daṇḍaviveka [Bhattacharya's trans. p. 25] interprets on the authority of the Ratnākara).

42 [118] D. W. Elliott, "The Criminal Company" in the Listener (London: British Broadcasting Company, January 6 [1966]).

43 [119] A judge might be led by compassion, to reduce the prescribed penalty, fearing that if the discouraged criminal were to be driven through despair, rage, or desperation to commit suicide, this would cause the judge to commit a crime by inciting or causing a homicide. The Daṇḍaviveka quotes Bhavadeva Bhaṭṭa as treating this matter:

When a culprit, having been penalized with admonition, fine or any form of corporal punishment, appropriately applied to him for his specific offence, commits suicide . . . (the king or the judge) thereby incurs no fault whatsoever, as even though punishments enrage criminals, there is no valid reason for withholding them . . . owing to the Shastric injunction viz. 'One should not kill anybody' (since) the agency of directly bringing about the death of a person is only prohibited.

The Daṇḍaviveka continues:

There is also no authority (of the judge) to administer on the accidental perpetrator of a crime a heavier punishment than admonition. Similarly, why should there be any prohibition (imposed on the judge) to inflict punishment on a convict, even though such punishment may arouse anger in him and indirectly result in his death (by committing suicide)?

44 [119] See, for example, Manu 12.62.

45 [120] Majjhima-nikāya 1.389; 3.202ff. which should be compared with Manu 12.62.

46 [120] The Bible, Deuteronomy 19:21, which may be compared with Leviticus 24, and Viṣ.Dhs.5.19.

47 [121] E.g., Āpast.Dhs.1.9.24.24-25.

48 [122] Kāty.Dhs.956 based on Manu 9.275.

49 [123] Manu 9.224. But Yājñ.Dhs.2.304 sets a fine of 800 copper *paṇas* for this. Bhattacharya (in the Daṇḍaviveka) explains *vipratvena* as meaning "the sacred thread and other insignia of a Brāhmaṇa." He cites the Mitākṣarā as prescribing or interpreting the lesser penalty of 800 *paṇas* as applicable to a Śūdra who uses the insignia to steal an entrance into a feast which is intended solely for brāhmins.

But should he use them to gain admittance to a memorial (*śrāddha*) ceremony, the penalty must be branding with a hot iron. Should he use it to procure gainful employment reserved solely for brāhmins, a death penalty must be imposed.

50 [*123*]As in Yājñ.Dhs.1.368; Manu 8.126 and 9.262.

51 [*123*]An informative historical study, by a political scientist in the University of Florida, of legislation against "cruel and unusual punishment" arising in 1689 with the English Bill of Rights followed by its introduction into the American Bill of Rights in 1777 is found in Larry Charles Berkson, The Concept of Cruel and Unusual Punishment (Lexington, Mass.: D. C. Heath [1975]).

52 [*125*]Manu 7.27; Yājñ.Dhs.1.357 and 359.

53 [*125*]Ramprasad Das Gupta, Crime and Punishment in Ancient India (Varanasi: Bharatiya Publishing House [1973], 13) is of the opinion that "the Hindu theory of Punishment is mainly deterrent."

54 [*125*]According to the Daṇḍaviveka (Bhattacharya's trans. p. 42).

PART III, Chapter 1. Retribution in Human Experience

1 [130]E.g., RV 7.104.3, 7, 11; 2.29.6; 9.73.8; 4.5.5. See also W. N. Brown, "The Ṛgvedic Equivalent for Hell" in JAOS, Vol. 61 [1941], pp. 76-80.

2 [131]See W. Kern, Manual of Indian Buddhism (Strassburg [1896]) and S. Bhattacharji, The Indian Theogony (London: Cambridge University Press [1970]), 68-69.

3 [131]S. Bhattacharji, The Indian Theogony, 105; also B. C. Law, Heaven and Hell in Buddhist Perspective (Calcutta: Thacker and Spink [1935]).

4 [131]Śat.2.1.9.3 and 11.2.7.33.

5 [132]Śat.2.3.3.8; cp. Bṛhad.1.2.6 and 1.5.2.

6 [133]E. W. Hopkins (The Religions of India [1895], 252) suggests that this text is pre-Buddhistic.

7 [133]Gaut.Dhs.21.20; Manu 11.207; Yājñ.Dhs.3.293. Haradatta interprets "loss of heaven" (*asvargyam*) as meaning a period in Hell (SBE II, p. 283 footnote).

8 [134]This is in contrast to Mbh.1.90.6ff; cp. Manu 4.166-168 and Manu 11.207-208 (where hell is equated with rebirth) and Manu 4 and 11, where they appear as alternative retributions for injuring a brāhmin.

9 [134]As in Mbh.3.127-128; 3.209.29-32; 8.69.53; and 12.298.7.

10 [135]As in Manu 12.54.

11 [135]E. W. Hopkins, The Religions of India [1895]; 261. For an example of the parallel presentation which Hopkins has described compare Vas.Dhs.11.34 with Manu 5.35 and 38.

12 [136]Śrīmad Bhāgavatam 6.1ff. Prabhavananda's trans. p. 85.

13 [136]E.g., RV 10.14.10-12; AV 17.11.13. A detailed discussion of the significance of the canine imagery in ancient literature is found in S. Bhattacharji's book, The Indian Theogony, pp. 70ff.

14 [136]Sūtrakṛtāṅga 1.5.1.19; 1.5.1.26 to end; Uttarādhyayaṇa 19.69ff.

15 [137]Sūtrakṛtāṅga 1.5.1.1, 12, 19, and 26.

16 [137]Madhvāchārya, Tattva-saṁkhyāna, cited by S. Dasgupta, A History of Indian Philosophy, Vol. IV, 57ff. A

discussion of *bhavya* and *adbhavya* by P. S. Jaini (Berkeley: University of California) could be a challenge to this assertion.

17 [*138*]According to J. N. Farquhar, Outline of the Religious Literature of India (London: Oxford University Press [1921], 239, note 6).

18 [*139*]The reference is Śat.1.5.3.14.

19 [*140*]Vāsubandhu (4th c. A.D.) in Vijñaptimātrata-viṃśatikā IV, cited by S. Dasgupta (A History of Indian Philosophy, Cambridge: The University Press), Vol. IV.

20 [*140*]H. Zimmer, Philosophies of India (London: Routledge and Kegan Paul, 579).

21 [*141*]Patañjali, Yoga-sūtras 3.51, Vyāsa's comment, Harvard Oriental Series, Vol. XVII, 286.

22 [*142*]See Max Weber, JRAS, Vol. I [1865], p. 306ff.

23 [*145*]Śaṅkara's *bhāṣya* on the Vedānta-sūtras 3.1.4-8.

24 [*147*]Banishment is decreed specifically for brāhmins in Kāty.Dhs.967-968 and also in 823-824. The textual basis for this sanction could be a regulation in the Bṛhaspati Dharmasūtra 9.25-26.

25 [*148*]Daṇḍaviveka (Bhattacharya's trans. p. 16).

26 [*148*]Bṛhas.Dhs.27.4-12 and Ratnākara p. 629 (Bibliotheca Indica).

27 [*150*]Daṇḍaviveka (Bhattacharya's trans. pp. 55-56) on the ground of Āpast.Dhs.2.10.27.18-20.

28 [*150*]Āpast.Dhs.2.10.27.18-19 substitutes banishment if moral correction or reform is not effected by a period of imprisonment.

29 [*150*]Kāty.Dhs.670 according to the Daṇḍaviveka (Bhattacharya's trans. p. 228).

30 [*152*]The dilemma of an ambiguous role for prisons and imprisonment in modern societies is illustrated by an interview with Jacques Leyre, the noted French psychiatrist and criminologist and one-time Chairman of the French Ministry of Justice Committee on Violence, published in "L'Express" of Paris, and excerpted in Atlas World Press Review, March [1979], Vol. 26/No. 3. The question is whether or not, or in what respects, prisons are or ought to be places of "quarantine" where the "antisocial individual" is "isolated like a virus" for five or twenty years, or is a place of rehabilitation, or whether "society hasn't the courage to tell the convict that prison is a punishment, that it is a sanction," that is, a "retributive sanction."

Chapter 2. Penal Instruments of Retribution

1 [156] Manu 8.82 contrast also 8.106 and 9.308.

2 [157] E. W. Hopkins, "Modifications of the Karma Doctrine" in JRAS [1906], 581-593 and 665-672.

3 [157] Following Mbh.12.153.56.

4 [157] So E. W. Hopkins, The Religions of India [1895], 369, 417, and 41.

5 [158] Dhātṛ is mentioned in RV 10.18.5 and 10.190.3, and is an epithet for Brahmā or for Viṣṇu in some texts.

6 [160] From E. W. Hopkins (The Religions of India [1895], 385ff.).

7 [160] This faith, flowering into the religion of *bhakti*, found a beautiful expression in Tulsidas' Rāmāyaṇa (as in Growse's tr., Vol. I, 19 and 27), in the idea that all principalities and powers are subject to Rāma's commands.

8 [161] A concise account of the leading exponents of medical science is found in S. N. Dasgupta, A History of Indian Philosophy, Vol. II, 318-339.

9 [162] These, with salvation (*mokṣa*) included, comprise the four "aims of life" (*puruṣārthas*) in Indian ethics.

10 [162] These are *vāyu*, *pitta*, and *kapha* which are bodily secretions having noxious influences if deficient or excessive.

11 [162] This compares with the Sāṃkhya-Nyāya theory of diseases as presented in S. N. Dasgupta (A History of Indian Philosophy, Vol. II, 325ff.).

12 [162] Caraka-saṃhitā 6.1.3 and Cakrāpani's commentary on this in the Āyurveda-dipikā.

13 [164] Manu 11.54, footnote to Manu 11.47 in SBE XXV; also Vas.Dhs.1.18; 20.6; 21.43-44; Viṣ.Dhs.45.2-33; Yājñ.Dhs. 3.207-215; and Manu 11.49-53.

14 [164] Manu 11.49-52 cf. Viṣ.Dhs.45.2-31.

15 [164] As in Manu 8.22 and 11.49.

16 [164] As in Manu 9.262-263.

17 [165] Manu 8.22; cf. Manu 9.247.

18 [165] Manu 11.53.

19 [165] Bhāgavata Purāṇa, "The Tale of King Parakshit and the Bull" in Prabhavānanda, Śrīmad Bhāgavatam, Book II, chap. 3, 11.

20 [168] J. D. M. Derrett, Essays in Ancient and Modern Hindu Law, Vol. I, 27ff.

21 [170] Manu 8.124 followed by Bṛhas.Dhs.9.12-13 and 29.2. The Daṇḍaviveka cites Bṛhaspati, Nārāyaṇa, and other authorities (Bhattachārya's trans. p. 16) for the form of an "admonition" (*vāg-daṇḍa*) being rebuking and warning a person with such words as "You have acted improperly etc." and the form of a "reproof" (*dhik-daṇḍa*) as being framed in such words as "shame upon you, you perpetrator of evil deeds."

Fines (*dhana-daṇḍa*) are explained as being of two kinds: "fixed" and "fluctuating." The fixed kind correspond with the three degrees of amercement related to the intensification of guilt arising from the frequency of the offence. The different kinds and degrees of fines approved by different Hindu jurisprudents, however, are not identical. The prescriptions of these major authorities are indicated in summary form in a table at the end of this section, on pages 273-4.

According to Manu 8.125 there are ten kinds of corporal punishment (*vadha-daṇḍa*) embracing tortures and mutilations of limbs and organs as well as death-sentences. Torture is of four kinds, namely, beating or whipping, restraint by imprisonment, putting in fetters, and harassment or public disgracing. Mutilation of limbs or organs is of fourteen kinds related respectively to the fourteen different parts and organs of the body--hand, leg, eye, ear, tongue, thumb, finger, etc. The death-sentence is of two kinds--"pure" and "mixed"--that is, of itself or in conjunction with torture, mutilation or other punitive acts. The "pure" variety is "simple" or "complicated"--that is immediate, as, for example, with a single stroke of sword, or prolonged, as in a lengthy agonizing capital punishment.

22 [170] This is discussed at some length in pages 180ff.

23 [171] Manu 8.321-332; 9.293; Yājñ.Dhs.2.275; Kāty. Dhs.5.793; Nār.Dhs.(sāhasa)14.21, and the commentaries of Kullūka, Halāyudha, Vācaspati Miśra, and explanations in the Ratnākara, and the Saṅkhalikhita.

24 [171] Manu 9.293 and the Daṇḍaviveka on Manu (Bhattacharya's trans. p. 123).

25 [171] Kāty.Dhs.950-958.

26 [171] Manu 8.339-341; 11.16; Gaut.Dhs.2.3.25; Kāty.Dhs.959.

27 [171] Kāty.Dhs.960.

28 [171] Yājñ.Dhs.1.368; Manu 8.126, which is different from the capacity of an offender to undergo punishment

"physically (for undergoing the rigours of punishment) or financially (for paying the fines imposed)" (Manu 9.262, in Bhattacharya's translation of the Daṇḍaviveka, p. 67).

29 [171] Bhattacharya (Daṇḍaviveka, p. 40) explains that the word *paryāpta* in this statement is an adjective derived from the verbal-noun *paryāpti* which means "the operation of all the criminal actions, necessary for the successful commission of the intended crime." The *paryāpta* (?) in this case is the criminal "who has perpetrated all the component actions."

30 [172] Daṇḍaviveka (Bhattacharya's trans. p. 42).

31 [175] Manu 8; Viṣ.Dhs.5.8.7; and the Ratnākara.

32 [176] Yājñ.Dhs.2.216 which may be compared with Bṛhas.Dhs.21.8 and which states that a fine of the first amercement should be imposed on one who attempts an assault with stones, slabs of stone, and/or wood. The Viṣṇu Dharmasūtra 5.60-62 and 64 prescribes the fines as ten and twenty *kārṣāpaṇas* with the lesser and greater amercements according to the weapons taken in hand for the unsuccessful attempts cited by Yājñavalkya. The latter's prescription, however, contrasts with his ordering of dismemberment of the hand for a non-brāhmin who inflicts injury on a brāhmin, but fines of one and one-half times the first amercement where weapons are seized and/or brandished threateningly (Yājñ.Dhs.2.215). Both the Daṇḍaviveka (Bhattacharya's trans. p. 209), the Mitākṣarā, and Saṅkhalikhita, amplify Yājñavalkya's statement. The jurisprudents frequently prescribed specific penalties for accomplished assaults depending on the objects or instruments used, such as "ashes and other objectionable things (*amedhya*)" (Bṛhas.Dhs.21.6-7); "ashes, mud and dust" and saliva (Yājñ.Dhs.2.213-4); "vomitings etc." (Kāty.Dhs.784), insolent urinating, defecating, or breaking wind (Manu 8.282; Nār.Dhs.5.27); assaulting with bricks and stones etc. (Bṛhas.Dhs.21.10) or by touching with hands or legs (Yājñ.Dhs.2.217; Manu 8.279-283; Nār.Dhs.5.28; Viṣ.Dhs.5.66); shouting abusing, insulting (Yājñ.Dhs.2.232); causing breaking of the flesh or bones, causing agony and/or bloodshed (Manu 8.284; Bṛhas.Dhs.21.11-12; Yājñ.Dhs.2.219-220; Viṣ.Dhs.5.68-72) or any dismemberment (Kāty.Dhs.781) according to the degree of pain intentionally caused (Manu 8.286) and other considerations allowed by law.

33 [180] Each of these categories of relationship and the penalties prescribed are amplified by the commentators including Karpardin on the directives of Āpastamba on this case, the Kalpataru, the Kāmadhenu, the digest of Halāyudha, and the Ratnākara.

34 [182] See for example, Manu 8.337-339 and Gaut.Dhs. 12.13-16.

35 [183] Manu 11.127-131; Āpast.Dhs.1.9.24.1-4; and Yājñ.Dhs.3.266.

36 [183]E.g., Viṣ.Dhs.5.1-3; but cp. Manu 8.124; 9.239 and Kāty.Dhs.483 and 806.

37 [183]E.g., Kāty.Dhs.806.

38 [183]Manu 9.238ff.; 11.181-188.

39 [183]Manu 11.183-186.

40 [185]This is supported by Bühler's note on Vas.Dhs.21.1-5 in SBE XIV.

41 [186]M. Bloomfield in SBE XLII translates this differently.

42 [187]In the Judaic religious tradition the retributive functions of curses are plainly stated in the extensive curse-passage of the Book of Deuteronomy, chapters 27 to 30. The distinctive retributive features of the curses include the curser as being God himself whose curses are set over against the blessings of God: the curses are penal sentences pronouncing the evils of natural calamity, foreign invasion and oppression, physical diseases, epidemics, mental and social confusions, which must befall the evildoer, much as Manu, Caraka, and others also interpreted these as penal consequences of sin, but which the Jewish Testament consistently interprets as punishments for disobeying the law of God. In Chapter 27 of the Book of Deuteronomy where a ritual-cursing ceremony is prescribed, it is ordered to be recited by the priests and affirmed by the people. The priests are to cry, "Cursed be the man who makes a graven or a molten image . . . . Cursed be he who dishonours his father and his mother . . ." To each of the curses "all the people shall say 'Amen, Let it be so.'" This ceremony is clearly an invocation to the Lord of Justice who is expected to act on the curses in the face of all violations of His ordinances.

The tone of the curse-ritual suggests that it is intended to deter God's people from sinning through visions of the terrible calamities and miseries which would befall those who err from God's way. Yet their deterrent mode is not their only or even their primary function, since there are explicit warnings of real consequences from the violation of God's commandments.

In the only case of a "trial by ordeal" in the Jewish Testament (Numbers Chapter 5) a curse and an oath are linked together by the words, "If you have gone astray though you are under your husband's authority then . . . the Lord make you an execration and an oath among your people, when the Lord makes your thigh fall away and your body swell; may this water that brings the curse pass into your bowels and make your body swell and your thigh fall away. And the woman shall say 'Amen, Amen.'" (Numbers 5:20-22, R.S.V.).

43 [188]According to Max Weber, <u>The Religion of India</u> (Illinois: The Free Press [1958], 60) which may be compared with the Bible, Deuteronomy 27:11-26. According to the Śat.1.4.3.11-22, the priest formally pronounces the

retributions in the form of reversing the curses upon those who curse him.

44 [188] Bühler's comment on Manu 9.290 in SBE in the light of the commentaries of Kullūka and Medhātithi.

45 [190] Rāmāyaṇa, Chapter II, Rajagopalachari's trans. p. 21.

46 [190] A. E. Crawley notes (ERE, Vol. IV, Art. "Cursing and Blessing," part 6) that "in the Old Testament the undeserved curse has no effect, or may be turned by God into a blessing." Curses therefore are understood to be effective only as instruments of divine judgement and justice.

47 [190] In the English language, the words "curse" and "oath" are commonly confused. The general Hebrew word for "oath" is *ālāh* or *shebūāh*. The New Testament Greek word for "oath" is *horkos*, and for "oath-taking" is *horkomosia*. The Hebrew word for "curse" in the sense of divine judgement or punishment is *ārar*. This must be distinguished from other words which mean to devote, abuse, execrate, damn, vilify, etc. which are also found in the Biblical text. The word *ārar* is found, for example, in Genesis 3, 4, 9, 27, and 49; in Numbers 24:9; in the great "curse" passage of Deuteronomy 27-30; in Jeremiah chapters 11, 17, 20 and 48, and elsewhere. Its equivalents in New Testament Greek are *katarāomai* which means to wish a curse to fall on someone, *epikataros* meaning "one who is cursed," and *katāra* meaning "a curse" (2 Peter 2:14). An interesting illustration of the retributive function of oaths can be found in I Kings 8:31ff. as a means by which God is provoked into exposing and then punishing a guilty person by bringing his conduct upon his own head.

48 [191] Oaths are ordered to be used only to decide doubts in minor criminal cases. Doubts in cases of grave criminality are to be settled through "trial by ordeal" according to Nār.Dhs.1.249ff.

49 [195] J. Morgenstern, "Trial by ordeal among the Semites and in Ancient Israel," Hebrew Union College Jubilee Volume, Cincinnati [1925]; 113-143.

50 [195] J. Duncan M. Derrett, "Ancient Indian Nonsense Vindicated" in JAOS 98.1 [1978], 100.

51 [196] Faith in the power of rituals to influence court proceedings and events is still evident, even with or without knowledge of the theoretical background of its judicial bearings, as R. S. Khare shows ("Lawyer's Law in India," Comparative Studies in Society and History, Vol. 14, Cambridge: The University Press [1972], 76, notes 3 and 4):

Priests (*purohits*), temples, scriptures, sacrifices, and spiritual *gurus* 'help' in influencing the court proceedings and events. In this sense, legal action resembles an unpredictable crisis like sickness, where again all these techniques are resorted to for obtaining health . . . . The ritual techniques may be supposed to function for, as well as against, the litigation victory, depending on the interest of the party. A defeated party may invoke supernatural power to see that the opponent is defeated in cases with a third party.

52 [197] Saṅkhalikhita Dhs. quoted in Devaṇṇa Bhaṭṭa's Smṛticandrikā (trans. by J. R. Gharpure, Vol. ii, p. 96, Bombay, [1954]).

53 [197] As in Manu 8.109-116; Āpast.Dhs.2.11.29.6; Viṣ.Dhs.9-14; and Nār.Dhs.1.239-348.

54 [197] Derrett in "Ancient Indian Nonsense Vindicated" (JAOS 98.1 [1978]) discusses the conflicting interpretations of ordeals.

55 [199] Bṛhas.Dhs.10.16-17 should be compared with Nār.Dhs.1.316.

56 [199] Nār.Dhs.1.257. The reference to punishment here means that the plaintiff is not "ready to take the punishment on himself in case of defeat" (footnote to Nār.Dhs.1.257 in SBE).

57 [200] Nār.Dhs.1.313ff. contrasts with Viṣ.Dhs.9.2.18 and 21-22 where the "trial by ordeal" does not appear to allow this element of personal choice.

58 [200] This interesting argument appears to remove from law-officers responsibility for seeking indisputable proof of a person's guilt. But it is counter-balanced by the general regulations already provided concerning scrupulous concern for justice. The appeal to supernatural mechanisms for explaining the imperfections of normal court proceedings may not be as archaic as one would suppose judging by the following statement of Pope Pius XII to the Catholic Jurists of Italy:

> One should not forget that no human sentence finally and definitively settles the fate of a man, but only the judgement of God, both for single acts and for those of a lifetime. Consequently, in every case where human judges have erred, the Supreme Judge will re-establish equilibrium first of all immediately after death with the definitive judgement . . . and then later and more fully in the final and universal judgement . . . . This is not to be understood as though it dispenses a judge from conscientious and exact efforts in ascertaining the facts. Still, there is something magnificent in the realization that there will be a final equation of guilt and punishment which will be absolutely perfect. (Pope Pius XII, "The Function of Punishment" in Dublin Review, No. 471, Section II [1956], 70ff.)

59 [200] This contrasts with Julian Morgenstern's statement on "trial by ordeal" among the Semites. "In fact in no sense is the entire procedure of the ordeal religious in character. In no case is any particular deity invoked by name, or called upon to decide the guilt or innocence of

the persons, accused or suspected." Morgenstern concludes from "a minute analysis of every detailed description of the administration of the ordeal" that "the entire procedure is not only not religious, having no connection whatsoever with either deity or sanctuary, but is wholly and entirely magical." (Julian Morgenstern, "Trial by Ordeal among the Semites," in Hebrew Union College Jubilee Volume (1875-1925), [1925], New York: KTAV Publishing House [1968], 125-126.) But so many explicitly religious connotations can be found in his own essay, such as note 21 on page 127, that it is difficult to accept his argument for the non-religious character of "non-Israelite" Semite "trials by ordeal."

60 [201] A pre-Independence, partly nationalistic, and partly moral-social voice and public lobby for the survival and restoration of the traditional Indian legal system based on dharmaśāstra in order to overcome the demoralizing "maze of artifice and fraud" arising from "the whole elaborate machinery of English Law" in British India, is the subject of a substantial and richly documented historical essay by Marc Galanter of the University of Chicago, titled: "The Aborted Restoration of 'Indigenous Law' in India" in Comparative Studies in Society and History, Vol. 14, Cambridge: The University Press [1972], 53-70. The survival of the tradition of the ancient juridical schools is reflected in Khare's brief account of a retired judge, aged seventy-two, who in 1962, regularly met with former colleagues--priests and lawyers--to discuss their (day's) "experiences with court law," and who drew on readings of "the Mahābhārata and several Purāṇas," "as an exercise in delineation of how good and bad are to be separated through their contexts" (R. S. Khare, "Lawyer's Law in India", op. cit., Vol. 14 [1972], 82 note 17).

TABLE A. AMERCEMENTS OF FINES

Amercements	first amercement	= *prathama-sāhasa*
	middle amercement	= *madhyama-sāhasa*
	highest amercement	= *parama-sāhasa*
1. Saṇkha-likhita:		
	first amercement	between 24-91 *paṇas*
	middle amercement	between 200-500 *paṇas*
	highest amercement	between 600-1000 *paṇas*
2. Nārada:	first amercement	between 40-96 *paṇas*
	middle amercement	between 200-500 *paṇas*
	highest amercement	between 500-1000 *paṇas*
3. Manu (8.120-138) and Viṣṇu:		
	first amercement	250 *paṇas*
	middle amercement	500 *paṇas*
	highest amercement	1000 *paṇas*
4. Yājñavalkya (1.366):		
	first amercement	252 *paṇas*
	middle amercement	504 *paṇas*
	highest amercement	1008 *paṇas*

5. Bṛhaspati (7.11):
highest amercement 1000 *kārṣāpaṇas*

(The Daṇḍaviveka explains that a *kārṣāpaṇa* is nothing but a *paṇa*).

Coins (*paṇas*, *māṣās*, etc.) (Manu 8.131-137; Vis.Dhs. 4.1-14; Yājñavalkya 1.361-365; and Nārada 55-60 in the Nepalese ms.)

1. Copper Coins	1 *kārṣa* = 1 *kārṣāpaṇa* = 16 *māṣas*
	4 *kārṣas* = 1 *dhānīkā*
	12 *dhānīkas* = 1 gold-*dīnāra*
	16 *māṣas* = 80 *kṛṣṇalas*
	1 *kṛṣṇala* = 1.875 grains
2. Silver Coins	2 *kṛṣṇalas* = 1 *māṣa* (ka)
	16 *māṣakas* = 1 *dharaṇa* (dharaṇaka or purāṇa)
	10 *dharaṇas* = 1 *śatamāna*
	1/4 *māṣa* (silver or gold) = 1 *kākinī*
3. Gold Coins	5 *kṛṣṇalas* = 1 *māṣa*
	16 *māṣā* = 1 *suvarṇa*
	4 *suvarṇa* = 1 *niṣka*

Note: There are gold and silver *māṣas* and *kṛṣṇalas*. But all these categories are distinguished as coin or currency weights from the smallest (a white or light-brown mustard seed of which 8 comprise a *taṇḍula* or *godhūma*) up to the higher multiples of *guñjās*, *māṣas*, *akṣas*, *palas*, *tulās* and *bhāras*). (Daṇḍaviveka [Bhattacharya trans.], p. 18).

TABLE B. GRAIN MEASURES

In the largely rural societies of ancient and medieval India, controlling the widespread problem of grain-theft required a detailed range of penal amercements. The grain-measures used in the texts however are sufficiently complicated for a table of measures for reference, and illustrations of some penalties for different degrees and circumstances of grain-theft, will be found useful. Since grain was an ancient form of currency, the connection of grain-measures with coin-measures in Table A is not surprising.

1. An anonymous text (cited in the Daṇḍaviveka [Bhattacharya's trans.], pp. 112ff).

5 *kṛṣṇala* = 1 *māṣaka*
64 *māṣaka* = 1 *pala*
32 *pala* = 1 *prastha*
4 *prastha* = 1 *āḍhaka*
4 *āḍhaka* = 1 *droṇa*

2. Skandapurāṇa

2 *pala* = 1 *kuḍava*	
4 *kuḍava* = 1 *prastha*	
4 *prastha* = 1 *āḍhaka*	
4 *āḍhaka* = 1 *droṇa* (*sūrya*, *sūrpa*)	
2 *droṇa* = 1 *kumbha*	
16 *droṇa* = 1 *khārin*	

3. The Varāhapurāṇa

1 *pala* = 1 *muṣṭi*	
2 *pala* = 1 *prasṛti*	
8 *muṣṭi* = 1 *kuñci*	
8 *kuñci* = 1 *puṣkala*	
4 *puṣkala* = 1 *āḍhaka*	
4 *āḍhaka* = 1 *droṇa*	

4. The Ratnākara and the Mītākṣarā

20 *prastha* = 1 *kumbha* (Rat.)	
20 *droṇa* = 1 *kumbha* (Mīt. & Kullūka Bhaṭṭa)	
1 *droṇa* = 200 *pāṇas* (palas?)	

5. Ćandesvara in the Bālabhuṣaṇa gives *kuḍava*, *prastha*, *āḍha* (*āḍhaka*), *droṇa*, and *khārin* successively four times the one immediately following, and makes a *kumbha* worth twenty *khārins*. Hemādri in the Caturvarga-cintāmani, and the Kalpataru, identify the *kuḍava* with a *serikā* and say the latter is comprised of twelve *prasṛti*. They are supported by such commentaries as the Samaya-prakāṣa, the Ratnākara, and the Smṛtisāgara, which add that four *serikā* make a *prastha*. The variations in weight values however is dependent upon regions (such as the standard measures of Magadhā and Mithilā according to the Gopatha-Brāhmaṇa and the Daṇḍaviveka) and also by the particular grains (rice, paddy, *dhānya* etc.) referred to, since the Viṣṇu-dharmasūtra states that 16 *droṇa* make a *khārin* and 20 *droṇa* make a *kumbha* except in the case of paddy (*dhānya*) for which a *khārin* comprises only 10 *kumbha*.

Bṛhaspati, Manu and other authorities prescribe penalties for grain-theft. Bṛhaspati 22.24 states that theft of paddy (i.e., rice in the straw or in the husk) is fined ten times the value of the stolen item as compensation for its owner and twice this amount (being 2 x 10 = 20 times) as a fine to the king. Manu 8.320 declares that thefts valued at more than ten *kumbha* are to carry a death-sentence. Thefts of less than ten *kumbha* are to be fined eleven times the value of the stolen paddy (*dhānya*) and the paddy restored to its owners. The Ratnākara of Caṇḍeśvara (1931 Sanskrit edition, pp. 320-321) reconciles the statements by explaining Bṛhaspati's prescription as referring to repeated commissions of the offence. It is followed also by the Kalpataru, Nārāyaṇa, Kullūka, and others in including the condition of the paddy and the place from which it was stolen as circumstantial considerations in the awarding of higher or lower fines ranging from as high as fifty or a hundred *paṇas* and as low as five silver or gold *kṛṣṇala*.

Part III. Chapter 3. Modes of Self-Retribution

1 [*202*] Tom Hadden, "The Other Side of Penal Reform," in New Society Journal, no. 453, 3 June 1971, 952ff.

2 [*202*] Tom Hadden, op. cit., 954.

3 [*204*] In this connection C. S. Lewis' striking critique of "The Humanitarian Theory of Punishment" published in an Australian journal in 1956, in an Anglican Journal, The Churchman, in 1959, and later in God in the Dock (Eerdmans), is still pertinent for the contention that those who would "treat" crime as a sickness and would "cure" criminals compulsorily with a deliberate avoidance of reference to just deserts, manage, despite their avowed or assumed humanitarianism, to act "as cruelly and unjustly as the greatest tyrants" and "they might in some respects act even worse." Lewis argues that "to be 'cured' against one's will . . . of states which we may not regard as disease is to be put on a level with those who have not reached the age of reason or those who never will; to be classed with infants, imbeciles, and domestic animals." On the other hand, "to be punished, however severely, because we have deserved it, because we 'ought to have known better,' is to be treated like a human person made in God's image." Lewis may have read Aquinas' argument that punishment is for the reformation of the criminal, but in order to be effective, it must be accepted by the offender as truly deserved (Charles Burns, Dublin Review [Special issue on Punishment] No. 471 [Summer 1956], 95).

But one might go further than Lewis in contending that the imposition of a punishment denies one's *humanitas* by classing him with domesticated animals and children. The truly adult way of punishment is where he makes voluntary restitution and effects by his own hand his atonement with the society, reconciliation with the members he has injured, and a settling of his own conscience. A penal system for such adults would provide for the freely willed and voluntary imposition of judicially-approved and even judicially-prescribed punishments in the spirit of a self-imposed penance. (Lewis' statement in full is found in Rudolf J. Gerber and Patrick D. McAnany [eds.], Contemporary Punishment: Views, Explanations and Justifications, Notre Dame; University of Notre Dame Press [1972], 194-199).

4 [*205*] Srīmad Bhāgavatam, Book VI, Chapter I, Introduction to the story of Ajāmila, Prabhavananda's trans., p. 83.

5 [*205*] See S. B. Dasgupta, Aspects of Indian Religious Thought (Calcutta: Mukherjee [1951], 3) who developed this connection.

6 [*205*] RV 10.16.4 (= heat) and 10.83.3 (= fervour or zeal).

7 [205] RV 10.109.4 (= austerities).

8 [206] RV 7.59.8.

9 [206] Chānd.3.16.3 and Mahānār(āyana) Up.8.

10 [208] The context suggests that here the word *tapas* applies to the four stations-in-life: studentship, householder, etc.

11 [210] Tattvathādhigama-sūtra (post-3rd cent. A.D.), in Radhakrishnan & Moore, A Sourcebook in Indian Philosophy (Princeton: Princeton University Press [1957], 256).

12 [210] Uttarādhyayana Sūtra 2.21.42ff.

13 [213] An important study of the concept is W. Gampert, Die Sühnezeremonien in der altindischen Rechsliteratur (Oriental Inst. [Monografie Archivu Orientalniho 6], Prague, [1939]), in which *prāyaścitta* has been critically, systematically, and historically studied in relation to the Indian conceptions of crime, sin, atonement, expiation, etc. Kane (History of the Dharmaśāstra [1953], Vol. IV), in the section on *Prāyaścitta* does not cite it, but Dandekar (Vedic Bibliography, Second Volume [1961], 477) mentions a review of this work of X + 279 pages by Luigi Heilmann in BIIEME (sic, should be BIISMEO?) 8.61-62, and by Sten Konow in AO 19.100.

14 [214] In Bühler's footnote to Vas.Dhs.6.22 (SBE XIV) *vrata* is stated to mean penances. Dandekar (Vedic Bibliography [1961], 572) cites H. Lüders' etymological essay on this word in Philologica Indica, p. 765. In opposition to the interpretation of *vrata* as vow or holy ordinance, Dandekar mentions V. M. Apte's essays: "The *vi-vrata*, *śuci-vrata*, and other *vrata* passages in the Ṛgveda favouring the derivation of the word *vrata* from the root *vṛt*" in QJMS 47(1), 38-46; and "*Vrata* in the Ṛgveda" in QJMS 49(3), 176-182. There Apte argues that *vrata* means some kind of "physical activity," "practice," path, route, or "track." Accordingly, penance is a form of *vrata* since it is a kind of physical activity, as Kane shows (History of the Dharmaśāstra [1958], Vol. V, Pt. I, 27).

15 [214] E.g. Vas.Dhs.6.22-25; and *vrata* in Apte's Sanskrit-English Dictionary [1975].

16 [218] Manu 8.94.

17 [219] Manu 9.240; Baudh.Dhs.1.19.4; and Nār.Dhs.12.77.

18 [219] Manu 8.318; also Vas.Dhs.19.45; and Nāradīya appendix, 48 in SBE Vol. XXXIII.

19 [219] E.g., Āpast.Dhs.2.10.24; Manu 9.236; Viṣ.Dhs. 5.3-7 etc.; see also Julius Jolly, Hindu Law and Custom [1928], pp. 293-296).

20 [219] According to the Mitākṣarā on Yājñ.Dhs.3.226.

21 [219] Cp. Yājñ.Dhs.3.294 and 1.367.

22 [220] Nārāyaṇa's comment on Manu 8.336 with reference to the punishments which are applicable to kings, discussed by Bhattacharya in Daṇḍaviveka, p. 45.

23 [221] But see Bühler's note (SBE II) on Baudh.Dhs. 1.10.19.1 and Derrett's observation in Lingat (The Classical Law of India [1973], 65, n.51) that the exactions go to the king's treasury, not to the injured party. Each is therefore, a penalty and not a compensation.

24 [222] Āpastamba's statement is followed also by Nārada (Nār.Dhs.18.3), Bṛhaspati (Bṛhas.Dhs.29.3), and the Kātyāyana-smṛti (in P. V. Kane's edn. and trans. [1933], 949).

25 [222] Āpast.Dhs.1.29.1 and 7; Vas.Dhs.3.15.

26 [223] Āpast.Dhs.1.9.25.1; also Gaut.Dhs.23.10 and Vas.Dhs.20.13.

27 [223] Following Bühler's footnotes to Manu 11.73-78 in SBE XXV, pp. 444-445.

28 [224] Vasiṣṭha Dharmasūtra 20 according to the Daṇḍaviveka [Bhaṭṭācharya trans. p. 6]; and Manu 11.147 & 153.

29 [225] The matter of "crimes" (such as homicide) for which the doer is excused punishment (as when committed in self-defence) received specific attention from Baudhāyana, whose regulations on the matter (extensively quoted in the Rājadharmakāṇḍa of the (Kṛtya-) Kalpataru) were supported by texts of the major authorities, namely, Bṛhaspati, Nārada, and Kātyāyana (as noted in the Daṇḍaviveka pp. 202-233, and given in translation in Bhaṭṭācharya's text of the Daṇḍaviveka, pp. 206-209). It is in the statement of the (Kṛtya-) Kalpataru (p. 132) in Bhattacharya's trans. of the Daṇḍaviveka (p. 206), that the phrase occurs: "Absence of sin cannot be presumed from immunity from punishment, as in spite of such immunity . . . penances have been prescribed."

30 [226] Daṇḍaviveka (Bhattacharya's trans., p. 62). Paiṭhīnasi's statement may be based on a statement of the Manusmṛti.

31 [226] A lengthy discussion of the subjection of kings to law appears in the Daṇḍaviveka (Bhattacharya trans., pp. 43-45).

32 [227] Daṇḍaviveka (Bhattacharya trans., p. 226).

33 [227] These quotations of Nārada and Halāyudha are taken from Bhattacharya's translation of the Daṇḍaviveka, pp. 64-65.

34 [228] Daṇḍaviveka (Bhattacharya trans, pp. 196-197).

35 [231] Three Jain canonical works regulate expiational or ascetical suicide: the _Chausarna_, the _Aurapacchakkhana_, and the _Battaparinna_.

36 [231] In praise of ascetical suicide see _The Questions of King Milinda_ (SBE XXXV) 4.4.13 where expiational suicide is contrasted with impulsive suicide which is a criminal act such that "whosoever does so shall be dealt with according to the law."

37 [232] See for example, Manu 11.89-90; 11.104 and 146; cf. with Yājñ.Dhs.3.269 and Āpast.Dhs.1.9.25.1-12. Note also _The Questions of King Milinda_, 4.3.37 in which capital punishment is said to be _self-caused_ (SBE XXXV, p. 257).

38 [232] Compare Āpast.Dhs.1.9.24.24ff. with 1.9.25.1-7 and 1.10.28.18, and with Vas.Dhs.20.41ff.

39 [232] E.g., Āpast.Dhs.1.9.27.6-8, and 11ff.

40 [232] See, e.g., Āpast.Dhs.1.10.29.6-8 and compare this with the footnote in SBE to Āpast.Dhs.1.9.25.9 and with Baudh.Dhs.2.1.1.6ff.

41 [232] The footnote to Āpast.Dhs.1.9.24.25 in SBE Vol. II indicates this.

42 [232] Bühler remarks (SBE II; 83) that "the Mantras given in the commentary, and a parallel passage of Vasiṣṭha XX.25-26, show that this terrible penance is not altogether a mere theory of Āpastamba."

43 [232] But compare this with Vas.Dhs.20.28, which states that a murderer who survives _three_ penalties "becomes pure."

44 [234] Manu 6.27 and 6.31ff.; compare this with Āpast.Dhs.2.9.23.2.

45 [234] So Bühler, SBE XXV, 204, note 32.

46 [238] E.g., Manu 11.246; cp. with 8.302ff., 306, 311 and Vas.Dhs.19.1ff.; Viṣ.Dhs.5.196 and Yājñ.Dhs.1.335ff. and 358.

* * * * * * * * * *

SELECTED REFERENCES

Indian Texts: Sanskrit editions, translations, commentaries, and compilations.

Aitareya Brāhmaṇa, R. Anantakrisṇa Sastri and P. K. Narayana Pillai, eds., Aitareya Brāhmaṇa. University of Trivandrum Sanskrit Series no. 149 and 167, Trivandrum, India: [1942] and [1952].

Aitareya Brāhmaṇa, Arthur Berriedale Keith, trans., HOS, Vol. XXV, Cambridge, Mass.: Harvard University Press [1920].

Aitareya Brāhmaṇa, Martin Haug, ed., The Aitareya Brahmanam of the Rigveda. SBH, extra volume 4. Allahabad: The Panini Office [1922]; NY: First AMS ed., [1974].

Aitareya Upaniṣad, C. Kunhan Raja, supervisor of trans., Daśopanishads. Adyar, India: The Theosophical Society [1935] and [1936].

Aṅguttara Nikāya, H. C. Warren, trans., Buddhism in Translations. HOS, Vol. III. Cambridge, Mass.: Harvard University Press [1915].

Āpastamba Dharmasūtra, G. Bühler, trans., The Sacred Laws of the Aryas. SBE, Vol. II, Oxford: The Clarendon Press [1886].

Arthaśāstra, R. P. Kangle, ed., trans., The Kauṭilīya Arthaśāstra. Parts I & II, second ed. Bombay: University of Bombay Press [1972].

Atharvaveda, Pt. Shrirāma Sharma Ācārya (sampādaka), Atharva-Veda. Bareilly, India: Saṃskṛti Saṃsthana [1962].

Atharvaveda, R. T. H. Griffith, trans., The Hymns of the Atharvaveda. SBE, Vol. XLII, Oxford: The Clarendon Press [1886].

Baudhāyana Dharmasūtra, Karmakāṇḍa section No. 11, Kashi Sanskrit Series No. 104, Varaṇasi: Chowkhamba Sanskrit Series Office [1934].

Baudhāyana Dharmasūtra, G. Bühler, trans., The Sacred Laws of the Aryas. SBE, Vol. XIV, Oxford: The Clarendon Press, revised ed. [1953].

Bhagavadgītā, Sri Swami Sivananda, ed., trans., comm., Srimad Bhagavad Gita. Durban: Divine Life Society of South Africa [1962].

Bhagavadgītā, Swami Chidbhavananda, ed., trans., Srimadbhagavadgītā/The Bhagavad Gita. Tamil Nadu: Sri Ramakrishna Tapovanam [1974].

Bhagavadgītā, W. D. P. Hill, trans., The Bhagavadgītā. Oxford: The Clarendon Press, revised ed. [1953].

Bhāgavata Purāṇa, Swami Prabhavananda, abbrev. trans. Mylapore, Madras: Sri Ramakrishna Math [1944].

Bṛhadāraṇyaka Upaniṣad, C. Kunhan Raja, supervisor of trans., Daśopanishads. Adyar, India: The Theosophical Society [1935] and [1936].

Bṛhaspati Dharmasūtra, Julius Jolly, trans., The Minor Law-Books. SBE, Vol. XXXIII, Oxford: The Clarendon Press [1886].

Carakasaṃhitā, T. K. Yādavasharma, ed., Carakasaṃhitā. Bombay: Nirnaya Sagar Press [1933].

Carakasaṃhitā, The Caraka Saṃhitā. Jamnagar, India: Shree Gulabkunverba Ayurvedic Society [1949].

Chāndogya Upaniṣad, C. Kunhan Raja, supervisor of trans., Daśopanishads. Adyar, India: The Theosophical Society [1935] and [1936].

Citralakṣaṇa, B. N. Goswamy and A. L. Dahmen-Dallapiccola, trans., An Early Document of Indian Art, The 'Citralakṣaṇa' of Nagnajit. New Delhi: Manohar Book Service [1976].

Daṇḍaviveka, B. Bhattacharya, trans., The Daṇḍaviveka of Vardhamāna Upādhyāya. Calcutta: The Asiatic Society [1973].

Dhammapada, F. Max Müller, trans., The Dhammapada. SBE, Vol. X, Oxford: The Clarendon Press [1886].

Dharmaśāstra, Manmatha Nath Dutt, trans., The Dharmaśāstra. Calcutta: Elysium Press [1909].

Gautama Dharmasūtra, Gautamapraṇītadharmasūtrāṇi. Poona: Ānandāśrama [1959].

Gautama Dharmasūtra, G. Bühler, trans., The Sacred Laws of the Aryas. SBE, Vol. II. Oxford: The Clarendon Press [1886].

Kaṭha Upaniṣad, C. Kunhan Raja, supervisor, trans., Daśopanishads. Adyar: The Theosophical Society [1935] and [1936].

Kātyāyanasmṛti, P. V. Kane, trans. Bombay: Hindu Law Quarterly [1933].

Kauṣītaki Brāhmaṇa, Arthur Berriedale Keith, trans., HOS, Vol. XXV. Cambridge, Mass.: Harvard University Press [1920].

Kauṭilīya Arthaśāstra, R. Shamaśāstry, trans. Mysore: Wesleyan Mission Press, 2nd edn. [1923].

Kauṭilīya Arthaśāstra, R. P. Kangle, ed. and trans., The Kauṭilīya Arthaśāstra. Second ed. Bombay: University of Bombay Press [1969] and [1972].

Mahābhārata, Rāmanārāyaṇadatta Pāndeya, ed., trans. Gorakhpur: Gita Press [1911-1964].

Mahābhārata, Pratap Chandra Roy, trans., The Mahabharata of Krishna-Dwaipayana Vyasa. Calcutta: Bharata Press [1899] and Oriental Publishing Co., nd.

Mahābhārata, The Mahabharata of Krishna Dwaipayana Vyasa. New Delhi: Munshiram Manoharlal Publishers Prt. Ltd., 3rd improved edn. [1972-1975].

Majjhima-Nikāya, Lord Chalmers, trans., *Further Dialogues of the Buddha, II*. SBOB, Vol. VI, London: Oxford University Press [1927].

Māṇḍūkya Upaniṣad, C. Kunhan Raja, supervisor of trans., *Daśopanishads*. Adyar: The Theosophical Society [1935] and [1936].

Manusmṛti, Sri Haragovinda Shastri, *Manusmṛti*. Chowkhamba Sanskrit Series, Vol. 226, Varanasi: Chowkhamba Sanskrit Office [1952].

Manusmṛti, G. Bühler, trans., *The Laws of Manu*. SBE, Vol. XXV, Oxford: The Clarendon Press [1886].

Matsya-Purāṇa, A. Talaqdar of Oudh, trans., Allahabad [1916].

Milindapañhā, W. Rhys Davids, trans., *The Questions of King Milinda*. SBE, XXXV and XXXVI, Oxford: The Clarendon Press [1886].

Mitākṣarā, Śriśa Chandra Vasu, trans., *Yājñavalkya's smriti with the commentary of Vijñāneśvara called The Mitākṣarā*. Part I, Bahadurganj, India: The Panini Office [1909].

Muṇḍaka Upaniṣad, C. Kunhan Raja, supervisor of trans., *Daśopanishads*. Adyar: The Theosophical Society [1935] and [1936].

Nārada Smṛti, Julius Jolly, trans., *The Minor Law-Books*. SBE, Vol. XXXIII, Oxford: The Clarendon Press [1886].

Rāmāyaṇa, R. T. H. Griffith, *The Ramayana of Valmiki*. London: Trubner; Banaras: E. J. Lazarus [1868].

Rāmāyaṇa, C. Rajagopalacharya, abbrev. trans., Bombay: Bharatiya Vidya Bhavan, 3rd edn. [1958].

Ṛgveda, F. Max Müller, ed., *Rig-Veda-Saṃhitā*. 4 vols., Varanasi: Chowkhamba Sanskrit Series No. 99, 1st Indian Edition [1966].

Ṛgveda, R. T. H. Griffith, trans., *The Hymns of the Ṛgveda*. Chowkhamba Sanskrit Studies, Vol. XXXV, Benares: E. J. Lazarus, 3rd edn. [1920-1926] and Varanasi: Chowkhamba Sanskrit Series Office [1963].

Sāmaveda, Śrirāma Śarma Ācārya, ed., Bareilly: Saṃskṛti Sansthāna [1962].

Sāmaveda, Theodore Benfey, ed., *Die Hymnen des Sāma-Veda*. Darmstadt: Wissenschaftlich Buchgesellschaft [1968].

Sāmaveda, R. T. H. Griffith, trans., *The Hymns of the Sāmaveda*. Benares: E. J. Lazarus [1907].

Saṃyutta-Nikāya, H. C. Warren, trans., *Buddhism in Translations*. HOS, Vol. III, Cambridge, Mass.: Harvard University Press [1915].

Śaṅkara Bhāṣya, G. Thibaut, trans., *The Vedānta-Sūtras with the Commentary by Śaṅkarācārya*. SBE, Vols. XXXIV and XXXVIII, Oxford: The Clarendon Press [1886].

Śatapatha Brāhmaṇa, Albrecht Weber, ed., *The Śatapatha Brāhmaṇa*. Varanasi: Chowkhamba Sanskrit Series Office [1964].

Śatapatha Brāhmaṇa, J. Eggeling, trans., The Śatapatha-Brāhmaṇa according to the Text of the Mādhyandina School. SBE, Vols. XII, XIV, XXVI, XLI, and XLIII, Oxford: The Clarendon Press [1886].

Śrī Bhāṣya, G. Thibaut, trans., The Vedānta-Sūtras with the Commentary of Rāmānuja. SBE, Vol. XLVIII, Oxford: The Clarendon Press [1886].

Sūtrakṛtāṅga, Hermann Jacobi, trans., Gaina Sutras, Part II, The Sūtrakritāṅga Sūtra. SBE, Vol. XLV, Oxford: The Clarendon Press [1886].

Śvetāśvatara Upaniṣad, Swami Tyāgīśānanda, trans., Śvetāśvataropaniṣad. Mylapore, Madras: Sri Ramakrishna Math [1957].

Taittirīya Upaniṣad, C. Kunhan Raja, supervisor of trans., Daśopanishads. Adyar: The Theosophical Society [1935] and [1936].

Upanishads, C. Kunhan Raja, supervisor of trans., Daśopanishads. Adyar: The Theosophical Society [1935] and [1936].

Upanishads, F. Max Müller, trans., The Upanishads. SBE, Vols. I and XV, Oxford: The Clarendon Press [1886].

Upanishads, R. E. Hume, trans., The Thirteen Principal Upanishads. London: Oxford University Press, 2nd edn. [1931].

Uttarādhyayana, Hermann Jacobi, trans., Gaina Sutras, Part II, The Uttarādhyayana Sūtra. SBE, Vol. XLV, Oxford: The Clarendon Press [1886].

Vasiṣṭha Dharmasūtra, G. Bühler, trans., The Sacred Laws of the Aryas. SBE, Vol. XIV, Oxford: The Clarendon Press [1886].

Viṣṇu Dharmasūtra, Manmatha Nath Dutta, The Dharmaśāstra. Calcutta: Elysium Press [1909].

Viṣṇu Dharmasūtra, Julius Jolly, trans., The Institutes of Vishnu. SBE, Vol. VII, Oxford: The Clarendon Press [1886].

Viṣṇusmṛti, Julius Jolly ed., Viṣṇusmṛti. Chowkhamba Sanskrit Series, No. 95, Varanasi: Chowkhamba Sanskrit Series Office [1962].

Yājñavalkyasmṛti, Narayan Ram Acharya, ed., Yājñavalkyasmṛti. Bombay: Nirnaya Sagar Press [1949].

Yājñavalkyasmṛti, Śriśa Chandra Vasu, trans., Yājñavalkya smṛti with the commentary of Vijñāneśvara. Allahabad: The Panini Office [1908] and [1918].

Yoga Sūtras, James Haughton Woods, trans., The Yoga-System of Patanjali. HOS, Vol. XVII, Cambridge, Mass.: Harvard University Press [1914].

Indic Studies

Apte, V. S. The Practical Sanskrit-English Dictionary. Revised edn., Delhi: Motilal Banarsidass [1975].

Banerjee, S. G. Dharmasūtras: A Study in their Origins and Development. Calcutta: Punthi Pustak [1962].

Basham, A. L. The Wonder that was India. 3rd revised edn., N.Y.: Taplinger [1968].

Bhattacharji, Sukumari. The Indian Theogony. London: Cambridge University Press [1970].

Bloomfield, Maurice. A Vedic Concordance. HOS, Vol. 10, N.Y.: Harvard University Press, [1906] and Delhi, India: Motilal Banarsidass [1964].

Bloomfield, Maurice. The Religion of the Veda, The Ancient Religion of India (from Rigveda to Upanishads). New York, London: G. P. Putnam's Sons [1908].

Bobilli, The Maharajah of. "There is No Modification of the Karma Doctrine," in JRAS, London: [1907].

Brown, D. Mackenzie. The White Umbrella: Indian Political Thought from Manu to Gandhi. Berkeley, California: University Press [1953].

Brown, W. N. "The Ṛgvedic Equivalent for Hell," in JOAS Vol. 61 [1941].

Cambridge History of India. London: Cambridge University Press [1921]; First Indian Reprint, S. Chand, Delhi [1955].

Chakravarti, A. The Religion of Ahimsa. Delhi: Ratanchand Hirachand [1957].

Chatterjee, S. C. The Fundamentals of Hinduism. Calcutta: Dasgupta [1950].

Crawley, A. E. "Cursing and Blessing," in The Encyclopaedia of Religion and Ethics, 3rd impression [1955], Vol. II.

Dandekar, R. N. Vedic Bibliography, Poona: University of Poona, and Bhandarkar Oriental Research Institute, Second Volume [1961]; Third Volume [1973].

Daniélou, Alain, Hindu Polytheism. London: Routledge & Kegan Paul [1964].

Dasgupta, Ramprasad. Crime and Punishment in Ancient India. Varanasi: Bharatiya Publishing House [1973].

Dasgupta, Shashi Bhusan. Aspects of Indian Religious Thought. Calcutta: Mukerjee [1957].

Dasgupta, Surendra Nath. A History of Indian Philosophy. Cambridge: The University Press [1922-1955].

____________________. Yoga Philosophy in Relation to Other Systems of Thought. Calcutta: The University Press [1930].

Dass, Sukla. Crime and Punishment in Ancient India (c. A.D. 300 to A.D. 1100). New Delhi: Abhinav Publications [1977].

Derrett, J. Duncan M. Essays in Classical and Modern Hindu Law. Leiden: Brill [1976].

____________________. Religion, Law and the State. NY: The Free Press [1968].

Deussen, Paul. The Philosophy of the Upanishads. The Religion and Philosophy Series. Edinburgh, New York: T. & T. Clark [1906] and [1908].

Eliot, Sir Charles Norton Edgecumbe. Hinduism and Buddhism: A Historical Sketch. London: E. Arnold [1921].

Farquhar, John Nicol. An Outline of the Religious Literature of India. The Religious Quest of India Series. London: Oxford University Press [1921].

Galantar, Marc. "The Aborted Restoration of 'Indigenous' Law in India," in Comparative Studies in Society and History, Vol. 14, Cambridge: The University Press [1972].

Geden, A. A. "Asceticism (Hindu)," in The Encyclopaedia of Religion and Ethics, 3rd impression [1955], Vol. II.

Griswold, H. D. "The God Varuna in the Rig-veda," in Bulletin No. 1 of The Society of Comparative Theology and Philosophy. Cornell University Press [1910].

____________. The Religion of the Rigveda. London: Oxford University Press [1923].

Gupta, R. K. "Hindu Vratas (Fasts) (II)," in Indian Cultures Quarterly. Jabalpur, India: Leonard College Press [1964].

Hardman, Oscar. The Ideals of Asceticism. London: S.P.C.K. [1924].

Hiriyanna, M. Popular Essays in Indian Philosophy. Mysore: Kavyalaya [1952].

Hopkins, Edward Washburn. The Religions of India. New York: Ginn & Co. [1895].

____________. "Modifications of the Karma Doctrine," in JRAS [1906] and [1907].

Jacob, G. A. A Concordance to the Principal Upaniṣads and Bhagavadgītā. Delhi: Motilal Banarsidass [1891].

Jacobi, Hermann. "Death," in Encyclopaedia of Religion and Ethics, 3rd impression [1955], Vol. IV.

____________. "Jainism," in Encyclopaedia of Religion and Ethics, Vol. VII.

Jayaswal, K. P., Manu and Yājñavalkya. Calcutta: Butterworth [1930].

Jolly, Julius (trans.). Ghosh, Batakrishna. Hindu Law and Custom. Calcutta: Greater India Society [1928]; and Delhi: Bharatiya Publishing House [1975].

Kane, Pandurang Vaman. History of the Dharmaśāstra. Bombay: Bhandarkar Oriental Research Institute [1930-1962], Vols. I-V; revised, enlarged, and second editions [1968-1974]: Vol. I Part I [1968], Part II [1975]; Vol. II, Second edn. Parts I & II [1974]; Vol. III, second edn. [1973]; Vol. IV, second edn. [1973]; Vol. V, Part I, second edn. [1974].

Khare, R. S. "Indigenous Culture and Lawyer's Law in India," in Comparative Studies in Society and History, Vol. 14, Cambridge: The University Press [1972].

Keith, Arthur Berriedale. "Suicide (Hindu)," in Encyclopaedia of Religion and Ethics, Vol. XII.

________________. The Religion and Philosophy of the Veda and Upanishads. HOS, Vols. XXXI & XXXII. Cambridge, Mass.: Harvard University Press [1925].

________________. Classical Sanskrit Literature. The Heritage of India Series, New Delhi, 6th edn. [1966].

Kern, W. Manual of Indian Buddhism. Strasbourg [1896].

Kulandran, Sabapathy. Grace in Christianity and Hinduism. London: Lutterworth Press [1964].

Kunhan Raja, C. Poet-Philosophers of the Ṛgveda, Vedic and Pre-Vedic. Madras: Ganesh [1963].

Law, B. C. Heaven and Hell in Buddhist Perspective. Calcutta: Thacker and Spink [1935].

Lefever, Henry. The Vedic Idea of Sin. Travancore, India: London Mission Press [1935].

Lingat, Robert, Les Sources du Droit dans le Systѐme Traditionnel de l'Inde. Paris: Mouton [1967].

________________ (trans.), Derrett, J. Duncan M. The Classical Law of India. Berkeley: University of California Press [1973].

Macnicol, Nicol. Indian Theism. London: Oxford University Press [1915].

McKenzie, John M. Hindu Ethics: A Historical and Critical Essay. The Religious Quest of India Series. London, New York: Oxford University Press [1922].

Mees, G. H. Dharma and Society. London: Luzac [1935].

Mudaliyar, Ṣ. Sabāratna. Essentials of Hinduism in the Light of Śaiva Siddhānta. Madras: Meykandan Press [1913].

Mulla, D. F., Principles of Hindu Law. Bombay: N. M. Tripathi Prt. Ltd. [1960].

Müller, F. Max. The Six Systems of Indian Philosophy. London, New York: Longmans, Green [1928] ed.

Murti, T. R. V. The Central Philosophy of Buddhism. London: Allen & Unwin [1955].

Parrinder, E. G. Upanishads, Gita and Bible. London: Faber & Faber [1962].

Potter, Karl H. Presuppositions of India's Philosophies. New Jersey: Prentice Hall [1963].

Radhakrishnan, Sarvepalli. Indian Philosophy. Muirhead Library Series, London: Allen & Unwin [1923]; 2nd edn. [1929].

________________ and C. A. Moore. A Sourcebook in Indian Philosophy. Princeton: Princeton University Press; Bombay: Oxford University Press [1957].

________________ et. al. (eds.). History of Philosophy: Eastern and Western. Muirhead Library Series, London: Allen & Unwin [1952-1953].

Ranade, Ramchandra D. A Constructive Survey of Upanishadic Philosophy. Poona: Oriental Book Agency [1926].

Sen, Priyanath. The General Principles of Hindu Jurisprudence. Calcutta: University of Calcutta Press [1918].

Sharma, C. A Critical Survey of Indian Philosophy. London: Rider [1960].

Singh, Shivaji. Evolution of the Smṛti Law. Varanasi, India: Bhāratīya Vidyā Prakāṣana [1972].

Smart, Ninian. A Dialogue of Religions. London: S.C.M. [1960].

____________. Doctrine and Argument in Indian Philosophy. London: Allen & Unwin [1964].

Sternbach, Ludwik. Juridical Studies in Ancient Indian Law. Delhi: Motilal Banarsidass [1965, 1967].

____________. Bibliography on Dharma and Artha in Ancient and Medieval India. Wiesbaden: Otto Harrassowitz [1973].

____________. Bibliography of Kauṭilya Arthaśāstra. Hoshiarpur: Vishveshvaranand Institute [1973].

Thomas, E. J. History of Buddhist Thought. London: Kegan Paul, Trench, Trubner; New York: Alfred A. Knopf [1933].

Turner, R. L. "Karma--doctrine of," in Encyclopaedia of Religion and Ethics, VII.

Varadachariar, S. The Hindu Judicial System. Lucknow: University of Lucknow [1946].

Varma, P. V. Studies in Hindu Political Thought and its Metaphysical Foundations. Delhi: Motilal Banarsidass, 3rd edn. [1974].

Weber, Max. "Rebirth," in JRAS [1865].

____________. The Religion of India--the Sociology of Hinduism and Buddhism. Translated and edited by Hans H. Gerth and Don Martindale. Illinois: The Free Press, Glencoe, Illinois [1958].

Westermark, Edward. Early Beliefs and their Social Influence. London: [1932].

Zimmer, Heinrich. Philosophies of India. Joseph Campbell, ed. London: Routledge and Kegan Paul [1951-1952].

Modern Ethical, Juridical and Other Works

Armstrong, K. G. "The Retributivist Hits Back," Mind, Vol. LXX [1961].

Baillie, Donald M. God was in Christ. London: Faber & Faber [1948].

Berkson, Larry Charles. The Concept of Cruel and Unusual Punishment. Lexington, Mass.: D. C. Heath [1975].

Bonhoeffer, D. Letters and Papers from Prison. N.Y.: Macmillan [1972].

Devlin, Patrick. The Enforcement of Morals. British Academy, Maccabean Lecture in Jurisprudence [1959]. London: Oxford University Press [1959 and 1965].

Dublin Review, Crime and Punishment. Special issue No. 471. London: Burns & Oates Ltd. [1956].

Elliott, David W. and John Crossley Wood. A Casebook on Criminal Law. London: Sweet & Maxwell [1969].

Ewing, A. C. The Morality of Punishment. London: Kegan Paul [1929].

Flew, A. G. N. and A. C. McIntyre. New Essays in Philosophical Theology. London: S.C.M. [1955].

Flugal, J. C. Man, Morals and Society. London: Duckworth [1945].

Gerber, Rudolf & Patrick D. McAnany (eds.). Contemporary Punishment: Views, Explanations and Justifications. Notre Dame, Indiana: University of Notre Dame Press [1972].

Goodhart, A. L. English Law and Moral Law. London: Stevens & Sons [1953].

Grunhüt, M. Penal Reform. London: Oxford University Press [1948].

Hart, H. L. A. Punishment and Responsibility. Oxford: Clarendon Press [1968].

____________ and A. M. Honore. Causation in the Law. London: Oxford University Press [1959].

Hawkins, D. J. B. Man and Morals. London: Sheed & Ward [1960].

Huxley, Aldous. Heaven and Hell. London: Penguin Books [1959].

Keys, A. The Biology of Human Starvation. University of Minnesota Press [1950].

Kleinig, John. Punishment and Desert. The Hague: M. Nijhoff [1973].

Knox, T. M. (trans.). Hegel's Philosophy of Right. London: Oxford University Press [1942].

Law Reform Commission of Canada, Fear of Punishment: Deterrence. Ottawa: Government of Canada Ministry of Supply and Services [1976].

Laird, John. On Human Freedom. University of Liverpool Forwood Lectures [1945]. London: Allen & Unwin [1947].

Lewis, H. D. Morals and the New Theology. London: Gollanz [1947].

___________. Morals and Revelation. London: Allen & Unwin [1951].

Lewis, C. S. "The Humanitarian Theory of Punishment," Gerber, Rudolf J. and Patrick D. McAnany (eds.). Contemporary Punishment: Views, Explanations and Justifications. Notre Dame, Indiana: University of Notre Dame Press [1972].

Longford, Lord (Frank Packenham). The Idea of Punishment. London: Geoffrey Chapman [1961].

May, J. B. Crime and its Treatment. London: Longmans [1971].

Maclagan, W. G. The Theological Frontier of Ethics. London: Allen & Unwin [1951].

McCloskey, H. J. "Utilitarian and Retributive Punishment," in Journal of Philosophy, Vol. LXIV [1967].

Moberley, Walter. Responsibility. Riddell Memorial Lecture. London: Oxford University Press [1951].

______________. The Ethics of Punishment. London: Faber & Faber [1968].

Pauley, W. C. de. Punishment: Human and Divine. London: S.P.C.K. [1925].

Playfair, Giles. The Punitive Obsession. London: Gollanz [1971].

Pollock, F. Essays in Jurisprudence and Ethics. London: Macmillan [1882].

Robinson, N. H. G. Faith and Duty. London: Gollanz [1950].

______________. Christ and Conscience. London: Nisbet [1956].

Smith, J. M. "Punishment: A Conceptual Map and a Normative Claim," in Ethics, Vol. LXXV [1964-65].

Stevas, Norman St.-J. Life, Death and the Law. London: Eyre & Spottiswoode [1961].

Temple, William. The Ethics of Penal Action. First Clarke Hall Lecture. London [1934].

______________. The Ethics of Punishment. The John Howard Anniversary Sermon, The Howard League for Penal Reform [1945].

Tennant, F. R. The Concept of Sin. Cambridge: University Press [1912].

Thomas (Aquinas). Summa Theologica. English translation by some Dominican Fathers. London: Burns Oates & Washbourne [1915]; 2nd ed. [1927].

Vidler, A. R. (ed.). Soundings. Cambridge: The University Press [1962].

Wootten, Barbara. Social Science and Social Pathology. London: Allen & Unwin [1954].

Warren, Max. Interpreting the Cross. London: S.C.M. [1960].

GLOSSARY

(Note: the meanings of the Sanskrit words are only those which are applicable to this essay.)

ācāra : custom, particularly religious practice; see also *sadācāra*.

ācārya : spiritual preceptor.

adhikaraṇa : a topic, theme, subject, argument treating a certain subject.

adhyāya : a chapter, section, or large division of a literary work.

adṛṣṭa : imperceptible; hence *adṛṣṭam*, the invisible one, destiny, fate, unforeseen danger or calamity; the Nyāya hypothesis of the stock of merit and demerit accruing from past actions and determinative of one's future lot in terms of reward and punishment, happiness and suffering; in the Vaiśeṣika philosophy, the determinative principle of the creative Will of God (Māheśvara) and of the process of natural evolution.

agamyāgamana : unlawful sexual intercourse between persons of different castes; one of the five deadly sins; see also *balahatyā*, *brahmahatyā*, *gohatyā*, and *strīhatyā*.

agas : sin, fault, offence.

agham : sin, misdeed, fault, crime, impurity, defilement, evil; an accident, calamity.

anugraha : grace, favour, kindness, propitiousness; synonymous with *prasāda*.

anṛta : contrary to Ṛta; falsehood, untruth.

aprārabdhakarma : "unripe karma," i.e. karmas whose fruition will not occur in this life; see also *prārabdhakarma*.

apūrva : potential, potentiality; the Mīmāṃsā theory of virtue and vice as potentialities (*śakti*) generative of future retributions, and comprising the soul's propensity for experiencing the fruition of (ritual) actions.

anupātaka : comparable crime or sin; cf. *upapātaka*.

āpaddharma : "the dharma of distress" propounded by Bhāradvāja and being an act, practice, profession, or procedure, not normally permissible for a caste, but allowable in times of extreme personal distress or social or natural calamity.

āraṇyaka : a "forest" treatise; a class of religious and philosophical writing connected with the *brāhmaṇas*.

artha : aim, motive, objective, purpose, anticipated or desired aim or end, means, wealth or resources, money, prosperity, the attainment of which is regarded as one of the four proper ends of purposeful human existence; see also *puruṣārtha*.

arthaśāstra : polity, politics, the science of government, synonymous with *daṇḍanīti* and *nītiśāstra*; a species of literature concerned with the science of government, etc. as for example, the Kautilīya Arthaśāstra.

āśrama : hermitage, abode of hermits or ascetics; any of the four stages, orders, or periods of the (religious) life of a brāhmin: *brahmacarya*; *gṛhastya*; *vānaprastha*; and *saṃnyāsa*.

asukha : unhappy, sorrowful.

ātman : selfhood, the individual soul, self, essence, nature, personhood; spirit, vital principle, basis of consciousness and activity in human beings; hence *Paramātman*, the Supreme Self or Universal Soul.

avidyā : ignorance; see also *ajñāna*.

Āyurveda : the science of health, long life, medicine.

balahatyā : infanticide, one of the five deadly sins; see also *brahmahatyā*, *strīhatyā*, *gohatyā*, and *agamyāgamana*.

bhāgya : luck, good fortune; cf. *durbhāgya*, bad luck.

bhaktimārga : the way of devotion, one of the three ways of salvation in Hinduism; see also *jñānamārga* and *karmamārga*.

bhāṣya : scholarly exegetical commentary of a *sūtra* or *śāstra* or other authoritative text, as for example, *Vedabhāṣya*.

bheṣaja : a medicine, a purificatory and health-giving substance, a life-enhancing medium; hence *prāyaścitta* as a form of *bheṣaja* in the Carakasaṃhitā and Cakrapāṇi's commentary.

Brahmā : the Creator or progenitor of the worlds and the primary manifestation of the self-existent Lord (according to the Manusmṛti), self-created from ether (according to the Rāmāyaṇa).

brahmacarya : religious studentship, the first stage of life of a brāhmin boy as a student of the Vedas immediately following his investiture by his *ācārya* with the sacred thread; religious study, chastity, sexual continence, celibacy; hence *brahmacāri*, one who lives as a *brahmacārin* and practices *brahmacarya*.

brahmahatyā : slaying of a brāhmin, one of the five deadly sins; see also *strīhatyā*, *balahatyā*, *gohatyā*, and *agamyāgamana*.

Brahman : the Absolute, the Supreme Reality, the Supreme Being regarded as impersonal; according to the Vedāntins, the efficent and material cause of the Universe.

brāhmaṇa : vedic ritual text.

caṇḍāla : untouchable, used especially of those who handle corpses and carcasses.

caritra : custom, usage, common practice; cf. *ācāra*.

daiva : divinely ordained destiny, the inscrutable will of the gods; synonymous with *haṭha* or cosmic, astrological influence, *vidhi* as one's appointed lot, and *diṣṭa* or divine decree.

damam : fine(s), hence *damanam*, punishing, chastising, fining.

daṇḍa : punishment, chastisement, 'the rod,' right or authority to punish.

daṇḍanīti : a synonym of *arthaśāstra* relating to the science of government.

daśāparādha : ten violent acts (Nar. Dhs. 5.2).

devayāna : "the way of the gods," one of two ways to the Hereafter described in the Mahābhārata; see also *pitṛyāna*.

dhāma : that which is ordained by *Dhatṛ* the Ordainer.

dharma : duty, obligation, law, religion, usage, custom, ordinance, statute; religious or moral merit, virtue, righteousness, prescribed or approved conduct; right, justice, equity, propriety, decorum; morality, ethics; essential quality, peculiar or essential characteristic, property or attribute; hence *dharmapatha*, the way of virtue.

dharmapāla : 'protector of the law'--an epithet either of a just king or of punishment or chastisement.

dharmarāj : 'righteous king,' an epithet of Yama.

dharmaśāstra : a regulative code; jurisprudence, text on morals and law.

dharmasmṛti : a species of regulative literature comprising *dharma* in respect of approved custom, morality, and law.

dharmasūtra : a text comprising brief regulations on religious, moral and public conduct.

Dhatṛ : in the Mahābhārata, the divine Ordainer.

dhātu : constituent, essential element, ingredient, secretion of the body, humour, of which there are seven or ten.

divya : ordeal, ordeals, or 'trial by ordeal,' an ancient Indian juridical method of inquiry and deciding of doubtful suits due to insufficient or uncertain evidence.

doṣa : fault, offence, misdeed, blame, fault, defect, blemish, blunder, weakness, error, sin, guilt, offence, crime, harmful quality, morbid condition, affection or affliction, disease, physiological disorder, defect of composition.

duṣṭa : spoiled, damaged, tainted, defiled, corrupted, depraved.

dvija : 'twice-born,' an epithet for initiated members of any of the three higher castes.

enas : sin, offence, fault.

gaṇa : a professional group or gathering such as a guild.

gandharva : a celestial musician; the soul after death prior to its incarnation in a new earthly body.

gohatyā : slaying of a cow, one of the five deadly sins; see also *brahmahatyā*, *strīhatyā*, *balahatyā*, and *agamyāgamana*.

guṇa : quality of material substance; hence *triguṇa*, the three constituent qualities of material substances: *sattva*, *rajas*, and *tamas*.

gṛhasthya : the second or householder stage or period (*āśrama*) in a brāhmin's vocation. See also *brahmacarya*, *vānaprastha*, and *saṃnyāsa*.

hatyā : criminal slaying as in *brahmahatyā*, the slaying of a brāhmin.

jīva : living, existing, an individual with a body inhabited by a soul which imparts to it consciousness, sensation, and motion; *jīvātman*, a person, living being, creature, so possessed of a soul.

jñānamārga : the way of knowledge, one of the three ways of salvation in Hinduism.

Kāla : Time, Fate, also Death; synonymous with *Mṛtyu*.

Kalivarjya : an act hallowed by the Tradition (*smṛti*) but prohibited in this present, degenerate *Kaliyuga* age.

Kaliyuga : the fourth and last age of the present cosmic era, from *kali* meaning strife, dissension, quarrel.

kalmaṣa : sinful, wicked, foul, dirty, stained; sin, fault, offence, wrong, evil act.

kāma : wish, desire, affection, attachment, sensuality, sensual enjoyment considered as one of the four *puruṣārthas*.

kaṇṭakaśodhanam : 'eradication of thorns,' a euphemism in Manu (9.252) and the Kauṭilīya Arthaśāstra (4.1) for the suppression of criminals and formentors of social discord, and/or for criminal law.

karma : act, action, deed, execution, performance, a religious rite, duty; destiny, fate, the inevitable consequences of former deeds, the principle of moral causation; in Vaiśeṣika philosophy, motion--a category of things; in Jain philosophy, contagion adhering to the soul.

karmamārga : 'the way of works,' one of the three ways of salvation in Hinduism. See also *jñānamārga* and *bhaktimārga*.

khaṇḍa : a section or chapter of a literary work. See also *adhyāya*.

kilbiṣa : sin, fault, offence, hurt, injury, guilt; sickness, disease.

kṛpā : pity, compassion, tenderness, graciousness, merciful-kindness.

kṣatriya : a member of the second *varṇa*.

kula : guild or corporation; also race, flock, family, collection.

kulācāra : ethnic and family custom(s).

liṅgaśarīra : also called *sūkṣmaśarīra*, the 'subtle body' which according to the Vedāntins exists in conjunction with the material or gross body (*sthūla-śarīra*) but does not perish at death, migrating instead with the soul (*ātman*) to the next gross body. In the Sāṃkhya philosophy, this is one of three bodies, there being, according to Vijñānabhikṣu, a transitional (*adhiṣṭhāna*) body which supports the subtle body during its passage from one gross body to another.

mahāpātaka : grave sin(s); heinous crime, such as *brahmahatyā*, *surāpānam*, *steya* (theft), and *agamyāgamana* (unlawful sexual-intercourse); any major transgression.

mahāprasthāna : 'the great Departure,' an extreme suicidal penance for grave sin.

mala : moral and spiritual 'impurities,' polluting agents, waste products, noxious substances.

mārga : path, way, means of self-realization in *jñānamārga*, *karmamārga*, and *bhaktimārga*, q.v.

māyā : trick, device, jugglery, enchantment, an illusion, image, unreal form; in the Vedānta philosophy, unreality, the illusion that the manifest forms of the universe are realities distinct from the supreme Reality; in Rāmānuja's teaching the conjuror-like wondrous projection of the natural universe or the creative power of God.

mleccha : a non-Hindu, one not speaking the Sanskrit language, or not conforming to a Hindu institution; a foreigner in general, a barbarian, an outcast, low-born individual (according to Baudhāyana), a wicked or evil person.

mokṣa : release, liberation, salvation, rescue, deliverance, final emancipation from *saṃsāra* q.v.; the last of the four *puruṣārthas* (q.v.) or meaningful ends of human life.

mṛtyu : death, decease; an epithet of Yama, of Brahmā, of Viṣṇu, of Śiva, of Māyā, and of Kāli; synonymous with Kāla q.v.

nāma : individuality, name, contrasting with *rūpa*, that is, the essential reality of anything as distinct from its manifestation, outward appearance, or form.

naraka : hell, the infernal regions, there being 21 reputed hells or regions where sinners experience different kinds of tortures.

nāstika : atheistic or heterodox; an atheist, unbeliever, who denies the authority of the Vedas, future life, and the existence of a divine creator and supreme ruler of the universe; hence *nāstikyam*, atheism, heterodoxy, or heresy.

nibandha : a literary digest, such as a digest of sacred law.

niyama : a restraint, check, restriction, limitation; a rule or precept or regulation couched as a negation; a necessary abstinence or dutiful restraint; in Mīmāṃsā philosophy any rule or precept which specifies as necessary something which in the absence of that rule would be optional; in Yoga philosophy, 'restraint of the mind,' one of the eight steps of yoga-meditation.

nirodha : imprisonment, confinement, physical restraint; also *grāhya*.

niṣkāmakarma : non-self-interested action; egoless dutifulness, the central ethical doctrine of the Bhagavadgītā.

nīti : conduct, behaviour, course of action, propriety; polity, the science of social management, moral science, ethics, moral philosophy.

nyāya : a method, rule, or system; a quality of justice, virtue, equity, righteousness; a lawsuit; a judicial sentence, or a legal judgement.

pāda : the fourth part of a stanza or line, of a chapter, or of a book.

paṇa : a sum in coins or shells, a silver or copper piece equal in value to 80 cowries, used in measuring fines or paying wages.

pañcāyat : a village tribunal comprised of four or more brāhmins learned in the law, there being separate tribunals for each caste in a village.

pāpa : sinful, evil, wicked, vicious; sin, crime, vice, guilt; hence, *pāpaśīla*, prone to evil, evilminded, reprobate.

pariṣad : a religious assembly or synod; a council or public audience.

pārūṣya : abuse, assault, violence in word or deed.

pāśa : fetters, afflictions, particularly divine afflictions, punishments; disease-fetters.

pauruṣa : free will, effort, human action.

piśāca : a species of demon or evil spirit.

pitṛyāna : 'the way of the fathers,' one of two paths to the Hereafter described in the Mahābhārata. See also *devayāna*.

pradiśā : a command, order, instruction, ordinance.

prajñāparādha : 'misuse of intelligence,' a source of sickness and disease according to the Caraka-samhitā.

prakīrṇaka : miscellaneous, scattered about; miscellaneous regulations, a chapter of a literary work containing miscellaneous rules; an equivalent for criminal law, or for the rules of administration of criminal justice.

prapatti : throwing oneself down, submission, the virtue of self-surrender to, or taking refuge in, God.

prārabdhakarma : 'ripe karmas,' past acts ready for fruition in the present lifetime as distinct from *aprārabdhakarma*, q.v.

prasāda : kindness, favour, auspiciousness, graciousness, a serene disposition, an attribute of God's nature synonymous with *anugraha*.

prāyaścitta : penance, atonement, religious expiation of sin.

pūga : a local assembly; cf. *gaṇa* and *śreṇi*.

punarmṛtyu : 'repeated death' mentioned in the Śatapatha-brāhmaṇa (2.3.3.8) as a punishment of the wicked in the Hereafter.

puṇya : holy, good, pure, virtuous, meritorious, pleasing, lovely, auspicious; hence *puṇyam*, moral or religious virtue, merit; the opposite of *pāpa*.

purāṇa : legendary literature containing *smṛti*.

purohita : domestic priest.

puruṣārtha : any of the four principal aims of human life, namely, *kāma*, *artha*, *dharma*, and *mokṣa*.

Put : one of the twenty-one hells listed by Manu; a particular division of the infernal realm to which childless persons are said to be condemned.

putra : son, 'a deliverer from *Put*' (Manu).

rājanīti : science of rulership, polity.

rajas : activity, passion, drive, one of the three constituent qualities (*guṇas*) of material substances said to be predominant in humankind. Cf. *sattva* and *tamas*.

rājaśāsana : a royal decree, a royal ordinance.

rākṣasa : an evil spirit, a demon, a being having a demoniacal nature; hence *rākṣasī*, a female demon.

Ṛta : Order, Right, Eternal Law.

rūpa : form, phenomenological character as distinct from *nāma* q.v.

sabhā : council, hence *rājasabhā*, chief council or royal council.

sadācāra : approved custom, the example of pious brāhmins, hence a source of *dharma*, synonymous with *śiṣṭācāra*.

sadana : a place, abode, or residence, as for example *Yamasya sadana*, Yama's place.

Sādhana : means, method, effecient cause, such as asceticism, penance, yoga, meditation, etc.

sāhasa : an infraction of the law; any violent criminal act (Manu); any heinous and forceful crime (Nārada and Kātyāyana).

śakti : power, ability, capacity, the dynamic genius of a deity or his consort, the potentiality inherent in a cause for its necessary effect. The general Mīmāṃsā theory of potentiality as an imperceptible ontological existent which effects fruitions of acts in accordance with the principle of Karma. See also *apūrva* and *adṛṣṭa*.

samana : an ascetic, *saṃnyāsin*, one who has adopted the fourth *āśrama*.

saṃhitā : a collection of liturgical, or magical, or medical etc., texts.

samiti : a council or gathering.

saṃnyāsa : the fourth or last stage (*āśrama*) of the religious life of a brāhmin in which all natural human ties of family, property, business, etc. are broken for the assumption of a solitary ascetic vocation.

saṃnyāsin : one who renounces temporal concerns or worldly ties; a brāhmin in the fourth order of his religious life.

saṃsāra : rebirth, transmigration, the wheel of rebirth; the opposite of *mukti* (liberation) and *mokṣa* (salvation).

sanstayā : approved custom, synonymous with *sadācāra*.

śapatha : cursing, imprecation; the making of an oath; used in older dharmasmṛtis with reference both to oaths and ordeals, and in later smṛtis solely with reference to ordeals or *divya* q.v.

śarīra : the body or material form of animate and inanimate objects, and hence *sthūla-śarīra*, the gross body as distinct from *liṅga-śarīra*, the subtle body, q.v.

śāsana : teaching, instruction; also a rule, order, command, or directive, a precept, or a written agreement.

śāstra : a science, authoritative treatise on legal, medical, jurisprudential, etc. science; a religious or sacred work, book, or treatise.

śāstrika : related to the śāstras; a pandit or *śāstrin* (fem. *śāstriṇī*), one who has mastered the śāstras.

sattva : being, essence, spirit, vitality; one of the three constituent qualities (*guṇas*) of material substances said to be predominant in heavenly beings. Cf. *rajas* and *tamas*.

śikṣā : learning, study, acquisition of knowledge; teaching, training, instruction.

śiṣṭa : upright, instructed person, one devoted to the principles and rules of upright or approved conduct, one whose life and conduct embody and express *dharma*.

śiṣṭācāra : the conduct of *śiṣṭas* synonymous with *sadācāra*.

śloka : a literary stanza or verse of two lines, each having two groups of eight *pādas*.

smṛti : 'remembered;' tradition as a source of *dharma*; a species of literature serving as the repository and vehicle of tradition, law, morality, hence *dharmasmṛti*, the designation for such literature.

śreṇi : guild, corporation of merchants, traders, or artisans.

śrotriya : proficient or versed in the Veda; a learned brāhmin, one possessing great sacred learning.

śruti : 'hearing,' news, oral communication, the Veda known as *śruti* as distinct from *smṛti* (q.v.); sacred text, divine revelation, vedic knowledge.

sthūlaśarīra : 'the gross body,' the material and perishable body, as distinct from the *sūkṣma-* or *liṅga-śarīra*, q.v.

strīhatyā : slaying of a woman, one of the five deadly sins. See also *brahmahatyā*, *gohatyā*, *bālahatyā*, and *agamyāgamana* q.v.

śūdra : a member of the fourth *varṇa* (q.v.).

sūkṣmaśarīra : 'the subtle body,' synonymous with *liṅga-śarīra*, q.v.

surāpānam : drinking of spiritous liquor, a grave sin, *mahāpātaka*, q.v.

sūtra : a thread, line, or cord; a rule, canon, or decree; any concise rule or short aphoristic statement for memorization; hence a collection or compilation of epigrammatic aphorisms is a *sūtra* or *sūtrapiṭaka*.

tamas : darkness, mental lethargy, illusion, error, ignorance; one of the three constituent qualities (*guṇas*) of material substances said to be predominant in demonic beings. Cf. *sattva* and *rajas*.

tantra : thread, principle, rule, theory, science; systematized framework of procedures, ceremonies, rites or rituals; a principle, doctrine; a religious treatise; a composition of occult and mystical teaching on occult practice, worship of deities, or the development of supernatural or extraordinary powers; a class of texts devoted to 'applied science' (*sādhana*), that is, the instrumentation of theoretical teaching in ritual, medicine, mathematics, astrology, etc.; any scripture of a *tantrika* sect in Hinduism or in Buddhism.

tapas : based on the root '*tap*' meaning 'to be hot,' 'to burn;' applied subjectively to ascetic practices (*tapta*) aimed at 'burning away' karmas; objectively considered means diseases, afflictions, misfortunes which the Deity inflicts on sinners. A general term for retribution when self-inflicted or divinely imposed. Ascetical purificatory practice, the voluntary self-infliction of pain.

upādhyāya : a professional teacher, one who is paid for his services; hence *adhyāpanam*, instruction, teaching, lecturing, one of the six duties of a brāhmin, undertaken for charity, for wages, or in consideration of services rendered.

upaniṣad : a philosophical and/or theological text attached to the *brāhmaṇas* purporting to ascertain the esoteric meaning of the *vedas* with respect to true knowledge (*jñāna*) of the supreme Being, as the one hundred and eight such texts mentioned in the *Muktopaniṣad*.

upapātaka : a minor sin or offence, a transgression for which light penalties or penances may be imposed.

vadha : corporal punishment; also *vadha-daṇḍa*; also *vadha-bhumi*, capital punishment.

vaiśya : a member of the third *varṇa*.

vānaprastha : the anchorite or hermit stage (*āśrama*) in a brāhmin's religious career. See also *brahmacarya*, *gṛhasthya*, and *saṃnyāsa*.

varṇa : colour, hue, complexion; a class of men, tribe or caste, especially with reference to the four principal castes; a race or species, hence *cāturvarṇyam*, the four primary castes.

varṇāśramadharma : the duties or obligations of *dvijas* (q.v.) as prescribed for their castes (*varṇas*) and avocations (*āśrama*).

vidhi : appointed lot, predetermined end, preordained destiny; a rule, ordinance, injunction, precept, sacred command; any religious rite or ceremony; fate, destiny, luck, time.

vidyā : knowledge, science, learning, one of the four or eight sciences or areas of knowledge.

vikara : physical illness, sickness, disease.

vivāda : disputation, contention, argumentation; a lawsuit, litigation; hence *vivādavastu*, the matter in dispute.

vivāsa : banishment, expulsion, exile.

vrata : any act of religious devotion and austerity; penances (*prāyaścitta*) are a form of *vrata*; ordinance, ordained path.

vṛjina : crooked, bent, curved; wicked, sinful; hence *vṛjinam*, a sin.

vyavahāra : judicial procedure or practice, investigation of a case, a legal suit, litigation, administration of justice; a title of legal procedure; hence, *vyavahārāṅgam*, the body of civil and criminal law; and *vyavahārapāda*, any one of the four stages of a legal proceeding leading to the fourth stage, a verdict or decision.

yajñā : a sacrifice, sacrificial rite.

yama : to check, restrain, curb, control, subdue; to grasp, possess, take hold of [for example, the breath], to punish, chastise, bring under restraint; hence to bind, imprison, confine, immobilize; restraint, control, self-control, any major observance such as *taptayama*, ascetical restraint, there being five or ten, comprising the first of the eight branches (*aṅgas*) or means of attaining unification-realization in classical Yoga. As a proper noun, Yama is *Yamarāj*, the Lord of Death, and *Yamayātanā* are the terrible tortures which Yama administers to sinners after death.

Yoga : joining, uniting, union, conjunction; a yoke or yoking; the philosophical system of Patañjali independent of, or as a second division of, the Sāṃkhya philosophy. Hence *yogin*, *yoginī*, a practitioner of yoga, a yoga adept.

yuga : one of the four ages of the present world, cosmos, or present cosmic era, as for example, *Kaliyuga*, the present degenerate age.

INDEX[1]

[1] *Q.v.* after a word indicates that further references are to be found under the main entry.

SR SUPPLEMENTS

1. **FOOTNOTES TO A THEOLOGY**
   The Karl Barth Colloquium of 1972
   Edited and Introduced by Martin Rumscheidt
   1974 / viii + 151 pp. / $4.25 (paper)
2. **MARTIN HEIDEGGER'S PHILOSOPHY OF RELIGION**
   John R. Williams
   1977 / x + 190 pp. / $5.75 (paper)
3. **MYSTICS AND SCHOLARS**
   The Calgary Conference on Mysticism 1976
   Edited by Harold Coward and Terence Penelhum
   1977 / viii + 121 pp. / $5.00 (paper)
4. **GOD'S INTENTION FOR MAN**
   Essays in Christian Anthropology
   William O. Fennell
   1977 / xii + 56 pp. / $2.50 (paper)
5. **"LANGUAGE" IN INDIAN PHILOSOPHY AND RELIGION**
   Edited and Introduced by Harold G. Coward
   1978 / x + 98 pp. / $4.50 (paper)
6. **BEYOND MYSTICISM**
   James R. Horne
   1978 / vi + 158 pp. / $5.75 (paper)
7. **THE RELIGIOUS DIMENSION OF SOCRATES' THOUGHT**
   James Beckman
   1979 / xii + 276 pp. / $6.00 (paper)
8. **NATIVE RELIGIOUS TRADITIONS**
   Edited by Earle H. Waugh and K. Dad Prithipaul
   1979 / xii + 244 pp. / $6.00 (paper)
9. **DEVELOPMENTS IN BUDDHIST THOUGHT**
   Canadian Contributions to Buddhist Studies
   Edited by Roy C. Amore
   1979 / iv + 196 pp. / $6.00 (paper)
10. **THE BODHISATTVA DOCTRINE IN BUDDHISM**
    Edited and Introduced by Leslie S. Kawamura
    1981 / xxii + 272 pp. / $6.00 (paper)
11. **POLITICAL THEOLOGY IN THE CANADIAN CONTEXT**
    Edited by Benjamin G. Smillie
    1982 / 400 pp. estimated / $6.50 (paper)

EDITIONS SR

1. **LA LANGUE DE YA'UDI**
   Description et classement de l'ancien parler de Zencirli dans le cadre des langues sémitiques du nord-ouest
   Paul-Eugène Dion, O.P.
   1974 / viii + 511 p. / $8.00 (broché)
2. **THE CONCEPTION OF PUNISHMENT IN EARLY INDIAN LITERATURE**
   Terence P. Day
   1982 / iv + 328 pp. / $6.00 (paper)

STUDIES IN CHRISTIANITY AND JUDAISM / ETUDES SUR LE CHRISTIANISME ET LE JUDAISME

1. **A STUDY IN ANTI-GNOSTIC POLEMICS: IRENAEUS, HIPPOLYTUS, AND EPIPHANIUS**
   Gérard Vallée
   1981 / xii + 114 pp. / $4.00 (paper)

Also published / Avons aussi publié

RELIGION AND CULTURE IN CANADA / RELIGION ET CULTURE AU CANADA
Edited by / sous la direction de Peter Slater
1977 / viii + 568 pp. / $8.50 (paper)

Available from / en vente chez:

WILFRID LAURIER UNIVERSITY PRESS
Wilfrid Laurier University
Waterloo, Ontario, Canada N2L 3C5

**Published for the Canadian Corporation for Studies in Religion/
Corporation Canadienne des Sciences Religieuses
by Wilfrid Laurier University Press**